"Smart companies have often learned the hard way about how not to sell to women, but for those who have found success, the rewards are phenomenal. The beauty of *The Power of the Purse* comes from Fara Warner's ability to put us in the room as major companies make costly mistakes and a few ultimately find the bright path. Backed with compelling statistics and devoid of polemics, *The Power of the Purse* should be required reading for executives who think they know what makes women tick."

—**Larry Kamer**, North American president of Manning Selvage & Lee, a global PR firm whose clients include some of the world's leading brands, including GM, The Home Depot, JPMorgan, Pfizer, and Philips

"Anyone trying to gain market share in a consumer products business will find *The Power of the Purse* a big "Aha!" delivering insight and inspiration. Fara Warner has recognized and documented an important demographic shift: individuals and family members are choosing to play to their strengths instead of following outdated traditional gender roles. The roles don't change: executive, homemaker, breadwinner, caregiver, athlete, cook, shopper, historian, financial manager, do-it-yourselfer, and so on. What *has* changed, which this book proves using examples that hit home, is that *the roles are evolving to be gender-neutral*. Smart marketing requires challenging, long-standing assumptions about who does the cooking and cleaning, who brings home the bacon, and what motivates them to buy. As this book shows, those who figure that out have a big opportunity to gain market share from those who don't."

—**Donna Horton Novitsky**, venture partner for Mohr, Davidow Ventures, and global entrepreneurial marketing lecturer, Stanford University

"In *The Power of the Purse*, Fara Warner shows how companies like Nike, DeBeers, Kodak, and The Home Depot have become market leaders by finding answers to the age-old question: 'What does a woman want?' Just as Bratz has toppled Barbie, this book topples many of the myths and misconceptions about marketing to women. And with in-depth case studies and a strategy checklist, every marketer can learn something new about their most important customers."

—**Martyn Tipping**, president and director of Branding Services, TippingSprung

THE

POWER

OF THE

PURSE

HOW SMART BUSINESSES ARE
ADAPTING TO THE WORLD'S
MOST IMPORTANT CONSUMERS—
WOMEN

By Fara Warner

Upper Saddle River • New York • London • San Francisco • Toronto • Sydney
Tokyo • Singapore • Hong Kong • Cape Town • Madrid
Paris • Milan • Munich • Amsterdam

Library of Congress Number: 2005926100

Publisher: *Tim Moore*
Acquisitions Editor: *Paula Sinnott*
Editorial Assistant: *Susie Abraham*
Development Editor: *Russ Hall*
Marketing Manager: *John Pierce*
International Marketing Manager: *Tim Galligan*
Cover Designer: *Sandra Schroeder*
Managing Editor: *Gina Kanouse*
Project Editor: *Christy Hackerd*
Copy Editor: *Elise Walter*
Indexer: *Lisa Stumpf*
Compositor: *Fastpages*
Production: *Specialized Composition, Inc.*
Manufacturing Buyer: *Dan Uhrig*

©2006 by Pearson Education, Inc.
Publishing as Prentice Hall
Upper Saddle River, New Jersey 07458

Prentice Hall offers excellent discounts on this book when ordered in quantity for bulk purchases or special sales. For more information, please contact U.S. Corporate and Government Sales at 1-800-382-3419 or corpsales@pearsontechgroup.com. For sales outside the U.S., please contact International Sales at 1-317-581-3793 or international@pearsoned.com.

Printed in the United States of America

Second Printing, October 2005

ISBN: 0-13-185519-0

Pearson Education Ltd.
Pearson Education Australia PTY, Ltd.
Pearson Education Singapore, Pte. Ltd.
Pearson Education North Asia, Ltd.
Pearson Education Canada, Ltd.
Pearson Educatión de Mexico, S.A. de C.V.
Pearson Education—Japan
Pearson Eduction Malaysia, Pte. Ltd.

To my mother and grandmother.

Contents

Foreword

Let's get serious, folks. Let's ask the hard questions, the right questions, the questions worth asking and worth answering. To her credit and to our benefit, Fara Warner is asking a great question—a hard, deep, important question. Warner is asking nothing less than, "What's wrong with so many global companies?" Or, to put it more absolutely, "What's wrong with business today?"

This is the Big Question, and it is a question so big that most business journalists won't touch it with a stick.

Fara Warner whacks it with her stick because that's the only way you can get the attention of this stubborn-as-a-mule question.

Pay! Whack! Attention! Whack! This! Whack! Is! Whack! Important! Whack!

This question is important because this carefully researched and cogently written book, with its case studies of such serious companies as Procter & Gamble, McDonald's, Nike, The Home Depot, and Kodak, offers genuinely powerful insights into the changing role of women. Simply put, women need to be seen for what they are: the vital emerging majority, not the easily dismissed minority.

But if you think that's the only message in this book or even the most important wake up call it has to offer, then you are mistaking the subject of the book for the purpose of the book. The subject of the book is how women are changing the world of business—and the world. The purpose of the book is to change how we see business working—and how it will work from now on.

Warner has charted with great factual accuracy and with absolute intellectual clarity just how complete and total the changing power of women in business really is. If you are a businessperson who insists that business is all about the numbers, consider these numbers:

- Women and money—Women account for more than 50 percent of all stock ownership in the United States. By 2010, women will account for half of the private wealth in the country, or about $14 trillion. By 2020, you can expect that number to reach $22 trillion as wealth continues to shift from men to women.

- Women and consumer and business spending—Women control $7 trillion in consumer and business spending. They are responsible for or buy 94 percent of home furnishings, 91 percent of house purchases, 60 percent of cars and trucks, and 50 percent of business travel.

- Women and work—Women-owned businesses employ more people in the United States than the Fortune 500 companies employ. Today, women-owned businesses account for 33 percent of all firms in the country.

- Women and education—In 2002, women earned 57 percent of the B.A.s awarded in the United States. In graduate programs, women now make up 49 percent of law school and 50 percent of medical school attendees.

- Women and social norms—Sixty percent of adult women in America work outside the home, up from about 30 percent in 1955. In 1955, 80 percent of Americans lived in a traditional nuclear family; in 2003, only 50 percent of Americans lived in that traditional social structure. Thirty percent of married women now out-earn their husbands; on top of that, there are now 46 million American women who are divorced or widowed, or who never married.

- Women and technology—In 2003, women surpassed men as the majority users of the Internet. In 2004, women surpassed men as the primary consumers of electronic equipment, including computers, cameras, and personal digital assistants.

See a pattern here? If you do, you are way ahead of the vast majority of American business*men* who steadfastly refuse to recognize what should be obvious: women are transforming business and society. Women are changing and they are changing everything with them: money, power, sex, family, technology, and ultimately society. It doesn't matter what business you're in—cameras or running shoes, toys or hamburgers—your business is being changed right now, right around you. Ignore, neglect, and disregard this emerging reality—this *fact*—at your own peril. If you think Warner's top-line message doesn't apply to you, chances are you're in deep trouble—if you're not already dead.

The possibility that you or someone you know has simply missed this shift of the social tectonic plates raises a question worth asking: How is it possible not to see this going on around us? As Warner suggests, the biggest obstacle to change is the old movie that too many men have been playing in their heads, a tape loop filmed in black-and-white and dating back to the mid-1950s when men were the breadwinners and women were the homemakers.

The business myths of that era—The Man in the Gray Flannel Suit, The Organization Man—have largely been superceded by a new world of business competition, fast-paced technological change, and border-leaping global competition. But the iconic image of the *Leave It to Beaver* world is apparently hard to shake, apparently much harder to accept than rapidly changing "business realities." The difference between what qualifies as "life" and what constitutes "business" may account for so many businessmen who hold fast to a soft-focus gender world that no longer exists while they vigorously adopt the harsh competitive dynamics of strategic, financial, and technological change.

That juxtaposition—what qualifies as life and what qualifies as business—is Warner's bigger theme and her analysis of it is her great contribution to today's lackluster business conversation. The question at the heart of this book is huge: What's wrong with today's business? And the answer is just as big because to answer the first question, you have to ask a second one: What's the real nature, the actual art, of business today?

First, consider what business today is *not*. Contrary to the teachings of our economics mentors, business is not guided by the "rational man" theory. In fact, much like the old saying about the Holy Roman Empire (that it was neither Holy, nor Roman, nor an Empire), business today is neither predominantly rational nor driven by men.

As Fara Warner's book demonstrates with story after story, business today is fundamentally about the art (and it is an art) of staying as close as possible to the enormous, unpredictable, powerful social and economic developments that have transformed business and society over the last several decades and that will continue to do so for the foreseeable future. This is no easy task, in large part because change is not only what is happening to business—change has become what business is about.

As a consequence, the tools, techniques, and tactics of smart business leaders have to change. Today, business is about biology, technology, and sociology. Companies that understand the way those three factors shape their markets, customers, and products—and companies that stay close to the ground in tracking the way their interactions combine to form whole new sub-categories and spin off completely unanticipated lines of innovation—actually stand a chance of being alive and relevant in the future. Those who either can't see it or don't try might as well pack it in right now.

So here's the Big Answer to the Big Question: Business today requires the questioning mind of a trained social detective, the pattern recognition aptitude of a skilled designer, the field study experience of a biologist, and the human decoding capabilities of an anthropologist. It takes intuition and empathy, the ability to feel what your customers are feeling, to find not just their wallets but also their pulses.

Business is much harder now because the fields of study are much softer, there are more choices and fewer certainties, change is faster and therefore reaction times must be faster, the margin for error is much smaller, the price of failure is much higher, and the requirement for authenticity is absolute.

No wonder so many companies seem mired in the past, re-running old and outdated tapes that bear little relationship to the shape-shifting social norms of today. No wonder so many businessmen would rather retreat to the world of numbers where the answers seem so clear and hard—and so much easier than this impossible-to-get-your-arms-around world of constantly evolving attitudes and rapidly changing sensibilities. No wonder there's so much wrong with business today—the world is changing, and too many companies simply cannot or will not change with it.

So what to do about it? If you read this book, you'll know.

You'll know that to get the right answer, you have to ask the right question. That's what Avon did—it changed its question from, "What do young women want in the way of new beauty products?" to "Where does beauty emanate from now?" The right question always gets you better answers.

You'll know that you can't change your company if you're not listening to the right people—which is why 50 percent of McDonald's focus groups are now women-only. But then, how many businessmen know how to practice active listening in the first place?

You'll know that you can't alter your course unless you study the right map. It took Nike looking at the lessons of biomimicry and the role of lionesses in hunting for their prides for the company to overturn its entire approach to women and sports.

You'll learn that you can't change unless you're ready to accept the inevitability of change. If you want to make it into the 2010s and 2020s, Warner tells us, you've got to leave the 1950s behind.

You might as well embrace the new facts of business life—the old ones are not just outmoded and dull, they simply don't work any more.

Alan M. Webber
Founding Editor, *Fast Company* magazine
Former Editorial Director, *Harvard Business Review*

About the Author

Fara Warner has written about marketing, advertising, and consumer trends for more than fifteen years for the *Wall Street Journal*, the *New York Times*, *Fast Company*, *Brandweek*, and other national publications. Warner joined the *Wall Street Journal* in 1994 from *Brandweek*, where she wrote extensively about the advertising and marketing industries. In 1995, she became a correspondent for the newspaper's Asian edition covering consumer trends, media, and marketing throughout the region from her base in Singapore. In 1998, she came to the *Journal's* Detroit bureau, where she covered e-commerce, marketing, and Ford Motor Co. In 2000, she joined *Fast Company* as a senior writer, where she wrote "Nike's Women's Movement," an extraordinary behind-the-scenes look at how Nike transformed the way it sells to, designs for, and communicates with women. She is currently a contributing writer to *Fast Company*. She holds a master's degree from Columbia University's Graduate School of Journalism. She is the recipient of a Knight-Wallace Fellowship at the University of Michigan for 2005-2006. She lives in Ann Arbor, Michigan.

Introduction

It takes a pretty shocking ad to stop me in my tracks. After 15 years of writing about marketing and advertising for the *Wall Street Journal*, *Fast Company*, and the *New York Times*, I have become mostly immune to marketing's siren song. But as I flipped through the pages of *Vanity Fair*, I did a double take.

"The left hand rocks the cradle. The right hand rules the world."

In those two simple sentences I saw a view of women I had not seen before in advertising. Here was a company—DeBeers diamonds, surprisingly enough—that had the guts to openly talk about what women were still struggling to understand and embrace.

It attacked head-on the misconception held by many marketers—and indeed many women—that women were caught in a struggle to choose between traditional or "left-hand" roles of wife and mother and the more modern or "right-hand" roles that had given women power and independence over the past five decades. The campaign instead brought to light what a growing number of women had been considering for years: those roles didn't have to be mutually exclusive. Indeed, instead of tossing away one role to have the other, more and more women were working on making them peacefully co-exist.

As striking as the copy was the product being pitched in the ads: glittering diamonds in big dramatic settings called "right-hand rings." Certainly, diamonds have always been marketed to women. DeBeers itself promoted the idea of men giving diamonds and women receiving them in its lush, romantic "a diamond is forever" ads. This new campaign, however, promoted the idea of women giving themselves diamonds—a striking acknowledgement that women had reached a level of economic power where they could afford expensive jewels and weren't afraid to show them off.

The ad campaign did more than stop me in my tracks. In just two years, sales of right-hand rings skyrocketed, creating a $4 billion segment that hadn't even existed five years before. The rings are now sold everywhere, from the finest jewelry stores to Wal-Mart. Culture trendsetters such as Madonna and Beyoncé Knowles flash diamond-encrusted rings on their right hands wherever they go. But the trend isn't limited to the "bling-bling" crowd. Katie Couric of *The Today Show* sports a right-hand ring, as do the less well-known ranks of independent economically self-sufficient women who have turned right-hand rings into a multibillion-dollar business.

The story behind how DeBeers uncovered the desire in women to balance the old with the new and struck gold with the approach is just one of the many successes that you'll read about in this book. These stories will make you think differently about the women who walk into your stores, buy your products, or use your services every day.

The stories certainly changed the way I think about women and what they want from companies. I'll be honest—some of the approaches rubbed me the wrong way at first, notably a campaign called Nike Goddess. And I know more than a few women who were at first dismissive of the DeBeers campaign. Some remain unimpressed; others have gone out and bought right-hand rings for themselves. I expect that you, too, will find yourself arguing against the way some of these companies approached women.

But keep an open mind. Many of the ideas in this book are counterintuitive. They go against the conventional wisdom set down by marketing experts and extolled in other books about "marketing to women." Some will run counter to what you think women want; others will ring very true to you as they did me.

Such dichotomies exist because we are entering a brave new world where there are no pat answers, no magic bullets or easy templates for how to reach women—if indeed there ever were. We are on the verge of a major transformation in the way corporations view women consumers and how they then adapt to women's needs and wants in the future.

This transformation is driven by profit. In the U.S. alone, women account for $7 trillion in consumer and business spending and control more than $13 trillion in personal wealth, an amount that will almost double to $20 trillion in the next 15 years. Women make more than 80 percent of all consumer purchases around the world. Reaching these increasingly wealthy women is now and will continue to be a key factor in the success of any company.

But just how do we reach these women? That's where this book comes in. The companies profiled here all have realized the power of the women's market and have been challenged to reach out to their women consumers in new and innovative ways.

Here then is a glimpse of the lessons that several smart, insightful, sometimes courageous companies have learned and then used to boost profits, increase revenues, and often rejuvenate brands that were struggling against tough competitors.

The Home Depot, for example, could have easily taken the traditional route with a "women's marketing" strategy by cleaning up its stores and adding more home décor items. Such strategies had worked very successfully for its competitors. But The Home Depot wasn't content with such an approach. Instead, the company dug beneath those surface changes to get inside the psyche of its consumers to find a new woman called the "do-it-herselfer," the woman who does far more than influence home renovations. She does them herself. The Home Depot also looked at the changing nature of relationships between men and women. Its senior-level executives—yes, they walk the floors of their stores—talked to the couples shopping in its stores and found "power partners," couples who create homes together, share home renovation tasks, and consider each other equal partners.

The Home Depot's big breakthrough wasn't adding more paint colors or even teaching women how to use a circular saw. The breakthrough was being "inclusive" of both genders instead of excluding one gender to reach another. Segregationist strategies had been common practice for companies in the past, strategies that offered women separate, "feminized" products like smaller tools with brightly colored plastic handles (and higher price tags). But such a practice no longer works for many women consumers who see through the charade. The Home Depot instead put women front and center as equals to the men who had always shopped its stores. The Home Depot's "power partner" strategy has helped boost the company's revenues by billions of dollars in the past three years after several years of sluggish growth that threatened to derail the company's 30 years of success.

The story of Procter & Gamble is one of the surprises in this book. Unlike The Home Depot or even DeBeers, the marketer of Tide and Pampers has long known that women were its most important consumers. The company spent years researching and watching women change diapers and do the laundry. But by the turn of the twenty-first century, many women considered P&G's marketing irrelevant at best, if not downright condescending. Taglines such as "Strong enough for a man, but made for a woman" especially struck a discordant chord with younger generations. P&G realized that it needed to take its blinders off when it came to today's women, ripping apart stereotypes and prejudices it had about its consumers. Like DeBeers, it unearthed an interesting duality going on inside women. Traditionally, marketers of household cleaners had pitched their products as time-saving devices for the harried housewife, a favorite stereotype of companies and marketing experts alike. But P&G went deeper, asking women about the emotional quotient of having a clean home. P&G discovered that although women had moved far beyond the home as the center of their lives, they still believed that a clean home was important to caring for their families. That insight led P&G to a break-through way of marketing the Swiffer. Instead of casting it as a time-saver, the Swiffer was marketed as an effective and fun way to get a home really clean. Gone were the images of drudgery or nagging housewives berating their husbands and children for messing up a clean floor. Instead, women danced to the tunes of Devo and looked on as their husbands cleaned up their own mess in the kitchen. The tactics have helped propel Swiffer to $500 million in sales in just five years and have made it one of P&G's most successful new brands ever.

Nike's story is my personal favorite. The transformations I first learned of four years ago formed the basis for this book, and this story resonates with all the themes that are so integral to this book. Nike shifted its thinking about women from a niche market to a majority consumer. It too tore off its blinders about what women wanted from the brand. It dashed long-held stereotypes about what women are capable of. It even redefined and broadened what a "sport" can be. Where Nike once focused primarily on male-dominated competitive games like football and basketball, it now defines female-dominated pursuits such as yoga and dance as sports worthy of its focus. By 2005, those changes had helped pull Nike out of several years of stagnating sales. From 2001 to 2004, its sales surged from $9 billion to $12 billion, a boom driven in part by its new attitude toward women that went far beyond its past attempts.

During its more than 30 years in marketing its brand primarily to men, Nike had taken the occasional detour to reach women. It created often-uplifting advertising about women and sports, including the now famous "if you let me play" campaign that movingly illustrated how sports could forever change women. But even as women applauded its ad campaigns, Nike remained an also-ran in the women's athletic apparel market. It was discouraging, especially for the women executives who often pushed for the marketing efforts. But the failures weren't that big of a concern to Nike because it was still raking in billions of dollars in sales from doing what it had always done so well—selling the Nike brand to boys. But by the turn of the twenty-first century, that strategy was beginning to fail as women—not teenage boys—started driving the big sports and fitness trends in the U.S. and around the world. By the early 2000s, yoga and Pilates had become national obsessions. Women were joining gyms in double the numbers of men. Running—the sport Nike was founded on—was a booming activity for women, myself included.

In the spring of 2001, I stopped off at the Niketown in San Francisco in search of a pair of running shoes. I was in the first few tough weeks of marathon training and in desperate need of a pair of shoes that would see me through the hundreds of miles ahead. I spent the first 15 minutes of my lunch break just trying to find the women's section at Niketown—"Go up several floors and then head to the back," one salesperson told me. I spent the rest of the time trying on running shoes without finding a pair that felt good enough to run a mile in—let alone 26.2 miles. By the time I left the store, I was discouraged and empty-handed. Standing on the street corner outside the store, I watched as a troop of teenage boys—laden with shopping bags—came bursting out of the store's big glass doors.

I was baffled at how I could be empty-handed when they weren't. How was it possible that one of the world's most successful brands could do such a stellar job reaching teenage boys and such a poor job reaching me—a woman who could and would spend a good amount of money on running equipment, a sport that I expected to keep doing for most of my life? Was it because Nike didn't understand me? Could its marketing and design experts not figure out what I wanted in running shoes and shorts? Was I that much more mysterious than a teenage boy? Did Nike simply not see me as a consumer it needed in its stores?

By the time I returned to my office, my frustration had turned into professional curiosity. The reason I had even stepped foot inside Niketown was the suggestion of a company executive who had told me of a new marketing and retail strategy called Nike Goddess that was meant to change women's perceptions of the brand. I saw no indication that Nike was in transformation, so I made a telephone call to Nike headquarters to get the scoop.

During the following six months, I met and interviewed a number of Nike executives who were in the midst of creating a strategy to turn around Nike's women's business. The research would become a *Fast Company* cover story: "Nike's Women's Movement."

The story chronicled the first changes that Nike made to reach women—from redesigning its clothes and shoes to fit women's bodies better to creating women's-only stores. I thought that the cover story would be the end of the Nike story. I expected that, like many companies I had written about in the past, Nike would have considered its work done with women and would move on. But in fact, I was wrong. Instead, those first few steps in the right direction were the beginning of an ever-evolving transformation that continues today at Nike—and one you'll read about in Chapter 6, "Finding the Goddess: Nike's Marathon to Reach Women." Nike's willingness to keep listening to and learning from its women consumers showed me again that real, lasting change was on the horizon when it came to companies understanding and adapting to women, now the world's most important consumers.

As I finished this book, I began reading a novel called *Tending Roses* as a way to unwind. I didn't expect that there would be any relevance to my book in a novel about a granddaughter's final days with her 90-year-old grandmother. But often we find lessons in the most unusual places.

In the middle of the story, the grandmother is attempting to explain to her granddaughter that if she continues to use the same tactics in approaching her husband, she will end up getting the same results. The grandmother has watched as her granddaughter continually gets caught in the same trap of trying to persuade her husband to take care of their child, turn off the computer, and stop thinking about work. None of her tactics work, and her husband keeps doing the same things over and over. Her grandmother tells her that if she keeps taking the same road, she will only get to the same place. If it's not the place she wants to be, she needs to change her course.

The same is true for reaching women consumers. If there is one lesson to be learned as you read these stories it is this: all the companies here have found a different road to reach women. Each is unique to the company, but there are universal lessons throughout. DeBeers combined the past with the present. P&G found a modern take on a traditional role. The Home Depot found insight in the new relationships between men and women. The lessons are as different for Kodak, McDonald's, and Bratz as the companies are. But they all found new ways to reach women when they realized that their old routes weren't getting them where they needed to be. Building new roads is rarely easy, but for the many companies profiled here, the rewards for looking at women differently have gone beyond even their own expectations. Now, it's your turn to experience that kind of success by building your own new road to women consumers using the insights that have helped put these companies on a new path with their most important consumers.

CHAPTER 1

From Minority to Majority

McDonald's Discovers the Woman Inside the Mom

T*o help revive the company's sales and profits, McDonald's shifted its strategy toward women from one of "minority" consumers who served as a conduit to the important children's market to one in which women are the company's majority consumers and the main drivers behind menu and promotion innovations.*

For Bill Lamar, chief marketing officer, McDonald's USA, 2002 was about to go down as one of the worst years in his almost 20-year career with the fast-food giant. On December 17 of that year, McDonald's posted a quarterly loss of $343.8 million, its first-ever decline since the company went public in 1965. Happy Meals, a cash cow for close to 25 years, were in a three-year sales slump. Same-store sales—which tracked the sales in restaurants open more than a year and served as a crucial gauge of how well McDonald's was performing with return customers week after week— had slid every month in 2002.[1] The ad campaign "We love to see you smile" wasn't a huge hit, and sales of new products like McSalad Shakers were so poor they were going to be pulled from the menu.

Something was definitely amiss at the Golden Arches. But just what was wrong? On the surface, McDonald's was doing okay. More than 20 million people were still eating at the company's more than 13,000 restaurants in the U.S. every day, bringing in sales of more than $18.6 billion through November 2002.[2] The hamburger and fries were still America's two favorite foods. Yet throughout McDonald's quiet, wooded headquarters in Oak Brook, Illinois, a suburb just outside Chicago, there was a sense that the company's tried-and-true strategies of expanding overseas, opening new stores, and focusing primarily on men and children in its marketing were failing to work their magic.

In Lamar's corner of the company, there was pressure to find a strategy that would put the company back in the good graces of its consumers—and turn around the embarrassing slide in sales for a company that had turned a profit for nearly 50 years. Marketing certainly wasn't solely responsible for the problems at McDonald's—nor did anyone think that it would be the company's savior. But marketing was one of the first places that new chief executive Jim Cantalupo turned to for help. Cantalupo had been called out of retirement to replace Jack Greenberg just 12 days before the fourth-quarter sales were announced.

Marketing couldn't single-handedly pull the company out of the nose-dive. But it might be able to help in the short term with a new advertising campaign or promotional strategy that would begin to turn around the company's sales and brand image. It had happened before. Over the years, the advertising the department had helped create, with the aid of some of the biggest and best ad agencies, had defined McDonald's to billions of consumers around the world. Many of its jingles had become pop culture icons. People could recite the Big Mac song with its riff of "twoallbeefpattiesspecialsaucelettucecheesepicklesonionsonasesameseedbun" more readily than the Pledge of Allegiance in some cases. McDonald's promotions—especially the Happy Meal toys tied to popular movies and television programs—were legendary for driving customers into the restaurants to try new products and enjoy old favorites.

Lamar needed answers fast to what had put one of the world's best and biggest brands into a sharp downward spiral. He turned to a new senior vice president of marketing recently hired from Procter & Gamble (P&G), Kay Napier, for help. Napier had built her marketing muscles at the company credited with creating today's modern brand marketing tactics. In her last job at P&G, she was vice president of North America pharmaceuticals and led the company's women's "health and vitality product" unit. To her, there was a simple answer to what was wrong with the company she had joined in October 2002. But the problem, she knew instinctively, wouldn't be solved with yet another advertising campaign.

"We simply had stopped being relevant to women," Napier says bluntly.[3]

Colliding with the Power of the Purse

McDonald's had run headlong into the challenge that many companies will face in the coming decades if they haven't already collided with it: the power of the purse. While most companies have come to accept that women are the most powerful force in the world's increasingly consumer-driven economy, many—like McDonald's—still face the challenge of creating successful strategies to reach those women—112 million in the U.S. alone—who have changed dramatically during the past 50 years.[4]

In the U.S., women control far more money than they ever have in history—$7 trillion in consumer and business spending combined, to be exact—a number that exceeds Japan's economy.[5] In an economy so dependent on consumer purchasing—personal consumption accounts for close to 70 percent of all spending in America—women have a vast impact on what keeps America growing and thriving. Women control the vast majority of what America buys, from cars to computers to healthcare to hamburgers. Women are responsible for or buy 94 percent of home furnishings. They influence 91 percent of home sales and buy 51 percent of consumer electronics. They buy 60 percent of cars and trucks. They make up 50 percent of business travelers.[6]

Women are no longer the "minority" market so many companies have considered them for decades. Women are *the* majority market. But that effect doesn't stop with women's immense purchasing power. In fact, women's propensity for shopping is just the beginning.

Women and society are being radically transformed by women's growing economic power and their escalating acquisition of money through work. Today, more than 60 percent of adult women work outside the home, up from about 30 percent in 1955 when Ray Kroc began selling his burgers, fries, and shakes to America's middle-class families.[7] Back then, 80 percent of Americans lived in a traditional nuclear family. By 2003, just 50 percent of Americans lived in such family structures—a shift driven in part by women's ability to pay their own way. According to the 2000 U.S. Census, single people now head 26 percent of American households, with 58 percent headed by women and 42 percent by men.[8] More than one quarter of women age 15 and over have never married; a third of men in that age group are single too.[9] If and when women do marry, they bring with them far more economic power than any generation before them—shifting the balance of power in families as well as in society.

Historically, women's work and the money it brought into the household were often considered vital to a family's economic stability. But women were not considered to be "in control" of those funds or the primary financial caretaker of families. In the 21st century, women are increasingly the primary breadwinners in families. In 30.7 percent of marriages where women work, women now out-earn their husbands, according to new data from the Bureau of Labor Statistics and the 2000 U.S. Census, as noted by *Newsweek* in its 2003 cover story, "She Works. He Doesn't."[10] Women are now the sole providers in more than 800,000 U.S. families. From 1995 through 2010, women are expected to accrue 85 percent of the $12 trillion in personal wealth that will be amassed during those years, according to figures from global publisher Conde Nast.

In 2004, U.S. women earned 80 percent of what men earned, up from 62 percent in 1980, according to new statistics from the U.S. Department of Labor, showing a marked increase from a period of stagnation in the 1990s.[11] When women and men of equal education, abilities, and similar social status are compared—for example, single men and women with college degrees and no children—the pay disparity disappears.[12] Those women make as much as, if not more than, their male counterparts. Forty-one percent of the 3.3 million Americans with incomes exceeding $500,000 are women. While women still lag behind men when it comes to getting to the corner office—only a handful of the Fortune 500 companies have female chief executives—women-owned businesses now employ more people in the U.S. than those Fortune 500 companies employ combined. That makes women a far more powerful force in business than has been recognized traditionally, according to statistics compiled by the National Council for Research on Women.

Education is driving much of this increase in women's economic power as women's education levels outpace men's. According to the National Center for Education Statistics, 37.2 percent of women between the ages of 18 and 24 were in college in 2002 versus 30.7 percent of men. Since 1992, there has been an 11 percent increase in the number of women in college, but in that same 10-year period, the number of men in college has edged up only 3 percent. The NCES projects that by 2012 a million more women than men in that age group will be in college.[13] In 2002, women earned the majority of bachelor's degrees, 57.2 percent, according to the American Council on Education. The Pell Institute for the Study of Opportunity in Higher Education found that while the number of men receiving bachelor's degrees has increased 20 percent in the last 30 years, the number earned by women has increased 117 percent. In graduate programs, women now make up 49 percent of law school attendees and 50 percent of medical school rolls. "On their twenty-first birthday, only about one in four men are in college full-time, compared with one in three women," writes Peter Francese in *American Demographics*.[14] There is literally no end in sight for the continued escalation of women's economic power. Economists and historians predict that women will continue to gain economic power in exponential amounts in the coming decades in the U.S., Europe, and especially throughout the developing world. Many countries are now realizing that one of the quickest and most effective ways to boost their economies is to educate women and give them access to the business world.[15]

Yet, even as women undergo this social and economic revolution, many companies haven't changed the way they think about women. They haven't taken that next important step beyond accepting that women are *the* majority market. Many have heard and even agree with management guru Tom Peters that "women are opportunity No. 1 for the foreseeable future."[16] But many companies still haven't explored how the social, economic, and cultural shifts that brought about women's access to money and power are affecting how those women think about brands, business, products, and services. The reasons for this lack of exploration are obvious. There's only recently been agreement that women are indeed the world's most powerful consumers. While the social and economic trends have been building for decades, they are just now beginning to resonate and radiate into business as they have become entrenched in the mainstream of American society.

Delving deeper into the trends that are profoundly changing women is the next big step that many companies simply haven't been forced to take—yet. But, like McDonald's, they will. As Napier put it so simply: McDonald's had stopped being relevant to women. Why? The women the company targeted through traditional advertising pitched to children, and menu items created in the mid-1950s, had ceased to exist—if they ever had. Women had changed even as McDonald's had stood still. McDonald's continued to talk to women through traditional roles and stereotypes even as those roles and stereotypes had long since stopped making sense to a growing number of women. "The change at McDonald's is driven by seeing women through the complexity of their lives. They are playing multiple roles at the same time. So we began to realize that we needed to see women as more than moms. They wanted to be a woman first and then mom second," says Wendy Cook, vice president McDonald's U.S. menu management. "Women simply didn't like be talked to as a stereotype. They want to be talked to as the women they are today."[17]

So, who are the women of today? That's the question McDonald's and the other companies featured in this book have set out to answer. These companies have taken that next important step to dig deeper into the psyche of their most important consumers. What they are finding is an ever-shifting, ever-evolving group that defies any and all stereotypes. This is no longer the monolithic homogenous "women's market" of recent history where a single advertising campaign or a few tweaks to a car's interior make it acceptable for all women. Today's women's market is vast, varied, and in constant motion. Women require far more than one-off ad campaigns or subtle changes to product—the standard operating procedure for "marketing to women" in the past—to draw them to a brand or product. These companies have learned that female consumers require far more targeted, holistic, and long-term approaches that meet them where they are in their lives today and where they are going in the future—not where marketers think they are based on outdated stereotypes and traditional roles. That kind of deep and broad approach requires that companies view women through a new lens that encompasses all their roles and responsibilities in society—some from the past, some from the present, and some just being formed for the future.

For companies such as McDonald's, The Home Depot, and Nike, the shift has been first to see women as majority consumers and then to rethink those women in new ways, throwing out presumptions about who they think their female customers are. "Mostly moms" was how McDonald's traditionally thought about women. It learned that such stereotypes were far from the truth. The Home Depot had to cast off assumptions about women and home renovations—for example, that they liked painting rooms and buying furniture and appliances. The Home Depot learned that women and men were working together on home renovations and that women often were taking charge of the toughest of the home improvement tasks. Nike had to slough off several stereotypes, such as thinking that women would respond like men to marketing featuring well-known sports stars, in order to finally get at a strategy that rang true with women.

For companies such as Procter & Gamble, DeBeers, and Kodak, digging below the traditional stereotypes has been a matter of combining the past with the present. Even as women have moved deeper and deeper into the workforce, women continue to hold on to traditional roles and responsibilities of the past. "It is very difficult for many women to relinquish the traditional roles. They wanted to be both a terrific breadwinner and a terrific wife," says Randi Minetor, author of *Breadwinner Wives and the Men They Marry.*[18] Women are still often the emotional centers of their family. They cherish family and friends while driving hard up the corporate ladder. They still worry about a clean home and fresh laundry. They still want the engagement ring even as they out-earn their potential husbands in the workplace. This tension between the old and the new, the pull of the past and the push of the present, has created opportunities for companies that have looked beyond the "corporate superwoman" and "soccer mom" stereotypes that have been popular for decades.

Kodak found a place for its digital cameras with women who enjoy being the emotional centers of their households even as they move rapidly into spheres once considered totally male—like technology. DeBeers sought to balance the "power of the right hand to rule the world" with the "left hand that rocks the cradle" to draw a whole new group of purchasers of diamond rings: women. Even companies whose primary consumers have always been women have had to shift their thinking in the face of this struggle between the traditional and the new. P&G found that it needed to delve into just what a clean house—once a sterling example of a woman's achievement—meant to a modern woman. Uncovering the desire for a clean home despite all the changes in women's lives led P&G to create the Swiffer, one of the most successful new brands in its history.

Indeed, companies and industries that thought they knew women well have found themselves facing a future that is still being mapped by a new generation of women. These women continue to evolve the definition of what it means to be a woman in the 21st century. Avon, long a leader in knowing what women wanted, felt the future bearing down on it as it realized what had resonated with women for decades no longer made sense to a new generation of women. Torrid, an upstart division of teen retailer Hot Topic, set the fashion industry on its heels when it rolled out belly tees and racy undergarments for teenage girls in sizes 15 and up. Barbie, the doll that had come to define so many of the stereotypes of beauty and womanhood, has been knocked from her pedestal by a group of dolls called Bratz. The dolls were created by listening to dozens of young girls who were looking for friends to play with, not a blonde stereotype.

For all these companies, the process of digging deeper in terms of women and the social and economic revolutions that are shifting and shaping their world has done more than attract more women to these brands. These strategies have turned around sales slumps, recharged executives, emboldened newcomers, and often drawn as many male consumers to their strategies as they have the target these companies set out to hit: women.

For McDonald's, finding out who women were meant dismantling a notion the company and the fast-food industry had held about women for decades. Since 1955, when Ray Kroc began selling burgers and fries, women consumers had fallen into two broad categories in the fast-food industry. They were either ignored in favor of focusing on men— generally considered the industry's most frequent users and therefore its most important consumers—or they were cast in the role of moms who were simply conduits to their children.

When it came to women, the standard operating procedure for many fast-food companies was to pursue children with a steady and constant diet of marketing. This strategy worked for many years. In the early days of the fast-food industry, a trip to McDonald's was a treat, a once-a-month respite from cooking at home or to celebrate a birthday or a winning soccer game. Happy Meals, introduced in 1979, played into that treat-like atmosphere with toys that captivated children and easy finger foods like fries and Chicken McNuggets. By 2002, Happy Meals made up 20 percent of McDonald's annual sales, about $3.5 billion, according to company reports. The success of the toy giveaway had made McDonald's one of the largest distributors of toys in the world, with tens of millions of items distributed every month. The importance of Happy Meals, however, went beyond their sales. McDonald's surveys showed that receipts that included a Happy Meal were 50 percent higher than those without, indicating that Happy Meals were being bought along with other meals, most likely meals bought by moms.[19]

But Happy Meals' decades-long success story masked big problems, problems exacerbated by the fact that McDonald's was paying scant attention to the women who opened their wallets to buy those Happy Meals. McDonald's marketers could quite accurately predict what toy would tempt toddlers, but they hardly knew the women who brought the toddlers into their restaurants. Yet over the two decades since Happy Meals were introduced, women and moms had changed considerably as America's social and economic fabric shifted dramatically. A trip to McDonald's was no longer a treat by the early 2000s. It was often the easiest way to feed the kids as longer work hours, soccer practices, and ballet classes began to eat up the evenings of many Americans. The drive-up window had become the way America made dinner. The shift from once-in-a-while treat to a weekly, if not daily, occurrence was a boon to fast-food sales. By 2002, McDonald's sales had surged to more than $38 billion globally and $18 billion in the U.S. But the shift also represented a huge problem for the company. McDonald's food—those burgers, fries, and shakes—had been created as treats, not as everyday lunch. By 2002, the food that McDonald's had built an empire on had become one of its biggest liabilities—especially for women.

By the turn of the 21st century, trends in obesity and weight-related illnesses began appearing across a broad swath of the U.S. When

McDonald's went public in the 1960s, Americans weighed 25 pounds less than they did in 2002. Men weighed an average of 191 pounds in 2002, up from 166.3 pounds in 1960. Children ages 6 to 11 had put on 10 pounds, averaging 74 pounds. Women weighed an average of 164.3 pounds in 2002, up from 140.2 in 1960.[20] Weight-related diseases were on the rise, including diabetes and high blood pressure. Bariatric surgeries—where stomachs are reduced to the size of an egg to help grossly obese people lose weight—had become so popular that they were shown in great detail on television morning shows.

As Americans watched their waistlines expand, the statistics that flowed out of the Surgeon General's office and the National Institutes for Health served as a wake-up call. Women, as McDonald's would realize, were the most likely to make changes in their own diets and those of their children—no matter how much their kids asked to be taken to McDonald's for a Happy Meal and the toy.

"Women are a large influencer of how we eat in this country," said Harry Balzer, vice president of market research firm NPD Group in Chicago.[21] In fact, women are often the "early adopters" of nutrition and diet trends. Such influence already was playing out throughout the vast multibillion-dollar food industry. For example, the organic food industry had seen a huge increase in interest and sales as women searched for healthier and better food. The industry grew from a tiny niche in the 1980s to a $10.8 billion industry by 2003, according to the Organic Trade Association's 2004 Manufacturer Study. "While studies show that interest in organic foods cuts across many demographic categories, it's still predominantly women who buy organic foods," said Katherine DiMatteo, executive director of the Organic Trade Association.[22] Women also would be behind the sharp rise in sales at fast-casual restaurants such as sandwich maker Panera Bread, soup seller Zoup!, and a host of Mexican fast-food chains like Baja Fresh and Qdoba that pitched themselves as fresher alternatives to the traditional burger and fries.

Given McDonald's dominance in the food industry—it serves close to 50 million people globally every day—it wasn't long before women's concerns about diet and health began to hit the company's radar with increasing regularity. In a sign that McDonald's was listening, the company ordered its suppliers to stop using antibiotics and growth hormones in many of its meat products. Those moves, however, didn't reflect a real change in the way McDonald's perceived the women customers it had neglected for years. It would take the dismal year of 2002 to force McDonald's to dig deeper to determine what drove modern women when it came to food and health—and to create products that would make sense for both women and McDonald's.

Finding the "Woman Inside the Mom"

In early 2001, a new product category entered McDonald's rigorous menu development pipeline. It was a line of salads designed to take the place of the ill-conceived McSalad Shakers that had been introduced in 2000 to replace side salads it already had on its menu. The "shakers" were designed so that consumers could eat a salad out of a cup. It was the fast-food version of a salad far more than it was a concerted effort to bring healthier food and vegetables to McDonald's menu. Poor design and lack of interest from consumers doomed the product, even though by pulling it McDonald's knew it would be far behind traditional competitors such as Wendy's. Moreover, it would offer nothing to compete with new rivals such as the "fast-casual" food outlets like Panera Bread. They offered more modern takes on "fast" food, such as Asian chicken salads, low-fat chicken noodle soup, and sandwiches made with chipotle mayonnaise and gourmet cheeses.

With the new Premium Salads, McDonald's hoped it was on to a product that would expand the brand's appeal without sacrificing McDonald's core qualities. "It wasn't like our menu in the past didn't appeal to women. Fifty percent of Big Mac sales are to women," Cook points out. "We are at our heart a burger and fries place." But in today's world and with today's women, McDonald's had to be what it was in the past and find a way to link that to the present. "We knew that women loved many of the products on our menu," Cook said. "But there were women who wanted a salad instead of a hamburger and that had become a reason not to go into our restaurants." But the salads had to do more than make the statement that McDonald's was putting more healthy products on the menu. They had to be salads that made sense for McDonald's to sell. With

McSalad Shakers, the innovation was the delivery device. Shaking up a salad in a cup with dressing made it very fast. But the salad wasn't very good, especially because the dressing was not distributed throughout the salad. The salads had to be much more than just fast food. The innovation needed to come from some other place.

In 2002, when the new salads made their way through the company's intense two-year development process, they came to the attention of Napier and her marketing team as McDonald's moved responsibility for menu changes from operations to marketing: a significant move that put menu changes in the hands of consumers instead of executives. "The change meant that the people coming up with the new items were talking to consumers from the very beginning of product development," Cook says. In the past, menu changes were often conceived inside and then vetted through traditional focus groups and then handed off to marketing to sell. For Napier, having input into what went into the salads—not just the marketing of them after they were created—was the key. She needed more than another feel-good ad campaign or a product targeted at women through their children—the old way of reaching women at McDonald's. "It's easy to get caught up in the heritage of being all about children," Napier says. "It's an honorable heritage with Ronald McDonald. But what we needed was a consistent focus on women, not just moms." The salads were exactly the kind of product Napier needed to make McDonald's relevant to women—whether they were moms or not. "When I was given the salads as a project, I felt they would resonate with women," she says. "Mostly what I had seen before from McDonald's was all about family and moms."

The shift from a "mom-centered" focus on women to women as primary consumers was a major step for McDonald's. It was driven by a major change in the way the company conducted its focus groups. Traditionally, the company had used mixed-gender focus groups to bounce ideas off consumers and get their feedback on new menu items. Those focus groups were meant to mirror who McDonald's thought its consumers were: a broad cut of the entire lower- to middle-class population of the U.S. But to test the salads, men were asked to stay home while women in the focus groups lunched inside a semi-truck trailer outfitted to look exactly like a McDonald's restaurant. As the women ate the salads and offered suggestions to marketing and menu executives, chefs redesigned the salads according to the women's feedback.

The women-only focus groups proved eye-opening for the executives who were still debating internally about how to make McDonald's relevant to today's women. Some were still certain that it was moms and children they should be speaking to, especially because Happy Meal sales were still sinking. "Is it women? Is it moms?" said Carol Koepke, senior marketing director–family brand, of the questioning that went on in 2002.[23] With the issues of childhood obesity and the concerns moms had about their children's eating habits, it would have been easy to focus on adding new items to Happy Meals. But that's not what Napier's team heard from their women-only focus groups. "What women told us was that all moms are women, but not all women are moms, so why weren't we trying to reach all women?" she says. "We realized we should be finding the woman inside the mom."

So began the mantra that has come to define McDonald's strategy toward women: finding the "woman inside the mom." Everything that McDonald's did for the women's market over the next two years—and what continues to drive its strategy going forward—flows from that mantra.

First up for redesign was the Premium Salads line, which was already well along in the development cycle. But for everyone working on the salads, from menu management executives such as Cook to Napier in marketing, there was an intense desire to make certain that the salads did more than fill a competitive niche. They had to be more than just another salad a woman could buy from a competitor. "We had to run our game instead of somebody else's, which is what we had been doing," Koepke said, referring to McDonald's strategy under Greenberg of following after competitors' strategies instead of creating its own. The company had gotten into a bruising battle of "value" menus that pitted its $1 burgers against $1 burgers from its competitors. When Cantalupo came back to the company, he overhauled the company's entire strategy. Instead of high-growth targets set by Greenberg and his predecessors that could be attained only by opening thousands of new locations every year, Cantalupo focused attention on same-store sales. Future growth, he said, had to be about having customers come back again and again to their local McDonald's instead of simply opening another location.[24] In his "Plan to Win" strategy, introduced in mid-2003, Cantalupo outlined five strategies that he believed would put McDonald's back on the right track. They were people, products, place, price, and promotions.[25]

Therefore, the salads, one of the first new products introduced under Cantalupo's new strategy, had to chin the bar in a way that few new products ever had to. They had to be the kind of salads that women would want to keep coming back for week after week. For Cook that meant going far further than making certain the ingredients were nutritious. They had to be a treat. "In focus groups, women would tell us that iceberg lettuce just wouldn't do," she says. "Many of them wished they could buy the specialty lettuce from the expensive grocery stores, but they couldn't afford it. So we came up with a mix of 16 different types of lettuce. We put crumbled blue cheese on it, and instead of making our own salad dressing, we decided to offer Paul Newman's dressings." Cook adds that she would never have gotten to that kind of feedback in the traditional "mass developments" that McDonald's had used to create new menu items. "We would have created a list of favorite salad ingredients in America and then thrown them all together in a salad," Cook says. But as the women opened up in the focus groups, they shared little details that made all the difference. "The details help differentiate you, and they send you off in a place where women are going to think, 'Oh, they thought of me; they knew I'd appreciate that.'" She says the women wouldn't have opened up with all those details if they had been in a mixed group with men. Today, McDonald's conducts 50 percent of its focus groups as women-only groups. After women have given their input, however, many of the items are tested with men and mixed groups.

By March 2003, the salads with their radicchio, Boston, and Bibb lettuce, enhanced with ripe grape tomatoes and a choice of several Newman's Own salad dressings, were ready for their debut. Now Napier and her team, including Koepke, had to turn "the woman inside the mom" mantra into an advertising campaign that would resonate with women in ways that even the best McDonald's ads had never done. "Like so many marketers, we marketed to a media target based on the media we were buying," Koepke says. "We'd buy a television spot that was supposed to hit with adults 18 to 49." But that old approach wouldn't cut it with a target that was so disparate, divided, and different as the women of today.

The media-buying team decided to broaden its spending beyond national television—where McDonald's had traditionally spent most of its money.

The team chose to buy heavily in women's magazines, a medium that McDonald's had rarely used. But magazines, far more than television, were key to reaching women. "For many women, those magazines are their treat at the end of the day," Napier says, noting that she often settles down with a stack of magazines in the evening. "It's better than a sleeping pill to relax you." The magazines also were an elegant way of targeting women in the many roles they live through each day while letting McDonald's focus on a specific salad that would appeal to readers of a particular magazine. In an ad placed in *Shape*, a magazine targeted at health-conscious women more likely to be single career women, the salad that got the biggest play was the Caesar with the lowest-calorie dressing option. In *Parenting*, Koepke focused on the experience women have when they come to McDonald's with their children, but with the added benefit of having food that they would actually want to eat. That ad featured the crumbled blue cheese treat salad and ranch dressing. "Moms already had an emotional connection to McDonald's. They remember it fondly from their childhood. But what we lacked was the relevant product that would talk to today's mom," she says. With the salads, the relevance issue Napier had honed in on just six months before was well on its way to being solved. Instead of continuing to talk to women as moms—irrelevant in a world where women were so much more than that—McDonald's had found both a product and a marketing message that would draw women—moms or not—into their restaurants.

"Don't Launch and Leave"

Many companies would have stopped there. The Premium Salads were a success from the first day they hit the restaurants. By 2004, the company was selling more salads than any other restaurant in the country. Overall sales at McDonald's had started to turn a corner by the middle of 2003, and by May that year same-store sales had started to edge up for the first time in two years.[26] But for Napier, Koepke, and Cook, there was a lot of work left to do to make McDonald's truly resonate with women. "We knew from talking to women that once you connect with them, you simply can't walk away," Koepke says. "You simply don't get a second chance with women. We started out with the salads and the focus groups, and those first steps were like baby steps. Now this is the way we do business."

Next on the list of things to do? Overhaul the way women—and the world, for that matter—viewed McDonald's as a purveyor of wholesome, nutritious food. The salads certainly helped. But a menu change wasn't enough to overcome increasing concern and criticism that McDonald's and the majority of the food it sold—the Big Macs, Supersize fries, and 40-ounce sodas—were helping drive the obesity epidemic in America. In 2002, two girls filed suit against McDonald's, claiming that eating at the restaurants had led to their obesity-related health problems. The documentary *Super-Size Me* took direct aim at McDonald's. The filmmaker, Morgan Spurlock, chronicled his experiment with what would happen if he ate every meal for a month at McDonald's and followed the sedentary lifestyle of most Americans. The results were not unexpected, save for some damage to his liver that even his doctors didn't see coming. He gained 20 pounds. He often found that he was tired and cranky before eating and then euphoric afterward. His blood pressure and cholesterol increased. Spurlock dramatized the changes in his body and health in a way that made eating at McDonald's seem like a quick route to the hospital.[27]

Despite the mounting criticism, McDonald's executives weren't going to stop selling the food that had made the company very famous and very rich. There was simply no use in denying that McDonald's was what it was: a burger and fries joint. But could the company change the way people thought about McDonald's food in relationship to their overall diet? Napier's team began asking itself. Could they give consumers tips and advice on how to control their weight and make better choices when they did eat out? Could they do a better job of offering nutritional information so people could at the very least make an informed choice about what they were feeding themselves and their children? Again, the company found itself turning to women as a way to hone in on what McDonald's had to do to make itself relevant in a world where the burger had become a bad thing.

As the salads began to take off, talk inside the marketing group turned to how to create a promotion that would drive more women into the stores to try them. The magazine ads were working well, and good word of mouth was helping drive sales beyond the company's expectations. But a special promotion seemed like the next logical step to get the word out to women who would otherwise rarely consider eating at McDonald's. That was an important next step for the company if its strategy toward women would be a success. On May 5, 2003, Kim Todd, a vice president with Golin Harris, the public relations agency for McDonald's, called a meeting with Michael Donahue, the company's vice president of communications, and a fitness guru named Bob Greene.[28] Greene had made a name for himself as Oprah Winfrey's personal trainer. His books on losing weight and exercising were bestsellers. The pairing of Greene, who espouses not eating after 7:30 p.m. and having dieters sign a weight-loss covenant with themselves, with McDonald's seemed like an odd choice. Why would a fitness expert with such a solid reputation and the incredible imprimatur of Winfrey become a spokesperson for McDonald's—apart from an endorsement fee? Todd said there was something in Greene's message that made him the perfect choice for McDonald's. "His philosophy, I felt, was very much in line with what McDonald's needed to try." He was very much about moderation, and his new book, *Total Body Makeover*, was more about exercising and eating well than it was about dieting. Donahue liked Greene so well that he pulled Lamar into the meeting to introduce him to Greene. Thirty minutes later the endorsement deal was signed. Now came the tough part: creating a promotion that would resonate with the broad swath of women—moms, single women, teenagers, retirees—that McDonald's needed to reach.

Again Napier searched for a way to build rapport with women that was novel for McDonald's but a tried-and-true strategy for marketers who'd been focusing on women for years. She wanted to offer women a free gift that would help drive them to purchase meals at McDonald's in the same way that cosmetics companies used free gifts to drive the purchase of perfume and lipstick. Ironically, the "free gift" idea was what had helped drive Happy Meal sales for so long. But for McDonald's, the idea of creating a promotion around women was a wholly new approach driven by the marketing team's mantra of "finding the woman inside the mom." The final product was the "Go Active!" Happy Meal, the first boxed meal designed for adults, which featured a salad, bottled water, and a free gift of a pedometer.

On September 16, 2003, the meal went into an Indianapolis test market. By the end of the month-long test, salad sales in the Indianapolis area had shot up substantially versus the month prior, even as sales of Premium Salads around the nation dipped slightly. The company went national with the Go Active! promotion, handing out thousands of pedometers in the space of a few months. The pedometers came with a booklet written by Greene outlining a few basic steps to take toward a healthier, balanced lifestyle. The Happy Meal, designed primarily with women in mind, ended up changing perceptions of McDonald's food—even though the company had made only small changes in its overall menu. But by promoting balanced eating along with adding an exercise almost anyone can do—walking—McDonald's found relevance with women—and a growing number of men—without changing its core identity: fast-food joint. For the majority of McDonald's consumers, the advice and the pedometer offered them access to information that may not have been readily available to them. "We feed 47 million people a day around the world," says Dr. Cathy Kapica, global nutrition director for McDonald's.[29] Her position was created in 2003 as a way to coordinate McDonald's efforts at making the creator of the Big Mac relevant in a world where nutrition had shifted profoundly from the 1950s. "For a public health scientist like myself there is no better place to be. We reach a lot of consumers who would never get this kind of information if we didn't provide it. We need to be on top of this trend if not ahead of it."

While the Go Active! meal was the first attempt to change consumers' behaviors about how and what they ate at McDonald's, it wouldn't be the last, as the company continued to overhaul its image based on its insights into women. Kapica has led much of the reform, especially in providing nutrition information, another "product" designed to appeal to women. "The world has changed," Kapica says. "When McDonald's started, nutrition wasn't an issue. It was offering a clean place to eat with safe food made of high-quality ingredients." While none of those demands have gone away, nutrition has crept up the scale of importance, she says. "Today we are busier, but more sedentary. Food is far more widely available. There's also a lot of confusion over what is the best way to eat. One day it's low carbs. The next it's low fat," she says. Add to that the fact that the science of nutrition has changed, she says, and that means McDonald's has to be far more proactive in the nutritional information it provides. Several McDonald's executives, including Kapica, point out that the company has made its nutritional information available for 30 years. But until very recently, the information was difficult to find for even the most nutrition-minded consumer. There was a toll-free number to call for information, and restaurants were supposed to have a chart of nutrition information for the menu hanging on the wall where consumers could see it.

Kapica next decided to focus most of her attention on the easiest way to get nutrition information to people who care, notably women. Tray liners with calorie counts were added, and brochures were printed with nutritional information instead of McDonald's relying on franchisees to display its nutrition charts properly.

But Kapica determined that the best place to put the statistics was online. Women now make up more than 60 percent of Internet users. They also increasingly use the Internet as a place to "manage their lives and the lives of their families," says Kelly Mooney, president and chief experience officer of Resource Interactive. This interactive agency based in Columbus, Ohio, creates Web sites for companies such as Reebok, Hewlett-Packard, and Victoria's Secret.[30] What better place to put nutritional information than the Internet? Kapica concluded. There women can determine ahead of time how many calories are in a typical Big Mac and fries lunch and how to fit a trip to McDonald's into a balanced eating plan. In 2002, McDonald's had already created a section on its Web site called "Bag a McMeal," which allowed users to determine the calorie counts for all its products. Kapica and other executives wanted to go a step further. She wanted even more customization so that consumers concerned about calories, fat, and sodium—many of them women, she believed—could determine ahead of time exactly what they could do to bring down calorie counts. The new Bag a McMeal feature lets a consumer fully customize and compare meals to see what happens if they leave off the mayo (a savings of 100 calories) or pick a small serving of fries over the large (a 300-calorie difference) without giving up McDonald's altogether. In late 2004 and early 2005, McDonald's tested several more nutrition ideas, including offering consumers a tally of calories with their sales receipt.

By mid-2003, McDonald's executives were finally ready to turn their attention to the Happy Meal, the product that had helped tip off the company to the fact that it needed to catch up with women. The Happy Meal hadn't been seriously overhauled since it was launched in 1979. While the focus had been specifically on women for most of 2003, marketing and menu executives knew they needed to take another look at Happy Meals if they were going to remain relevant with women.

But instead of dramatically overhauling Happy Meals, McDonald's chose to add just a few new menu items that would appeal both to moms and children. The insight for the targeted changes to Happy Meals came from listening to women. This time the focus was flipped on McDonald's new mantra from the "woman inside the mom" to the "mom inside the woman." The company already had seen Happy Meal sales increase when salads were added to the menu throughout the company's more than 13,000 U.S. restaurants, Napier says. This highlighted again how important it had been to focus on what moms wanted to eat, not simply on the Happy Meal, which would have been McDonald's traditional approach.

So, did that mean the food inside the Happy Meal wasn't a big issue for moms, given how quickly sales had picked up after salads were introduced? McDonald's let women explain it to them. "When we talked to moms, we didn't get a sense that they were overly concerned about the food inside of a Happy Meal," Napier says. "It was still a treat for children, not something they would be eating every day." Still, there was an underlying feeling among the executives that if they could offer just a few new choices, they would strike the right balance of nutrition and fun that was needed for both moms and children. "You don't want to do something so new that it makes everybody unhappy," says Cook, head of U.S. menu management. McDonald's had already made that mistake during a test of Build Your Own Happy Meal in the mid-1990s. The items offered included apples and bags of carrots. While the choices were certainly healthy, the product never went national. There were too many choices, making it difficult for moms to get their children to settle on the perfect combination. Moreover, products like whole apples didn't make a lot of sense for children, who couldn't eat the whole thing and then had no place to put the core. The key to the Happy Meal's success—beyond the toy—was that it was a quick and fun way for moms to feed their children, devoid of arguments over vegetables and fruit, and it was easy to clean up. So throughout 2003, the company worked on the Happy Meal menu to appeal to mothers without turning off the children. By the summer of 2004, the company was ready to roll with a small set of new products designed to make moms and children happy. Chocolate milk and regular milk in resealable jugs and apple juice were offered as alternatives to sodas. Presliced apples with low-fat caramel dipping sauce provided an alternative to fries. In six months, McDonald's milk sales had doubled, and Apple Dippers were being ordered in an increasing number of Happy Meals.

Going Forward

Two years after stumbling through the worst financial quarter in its history, McDonald's had successfully reversed the decline despite massive tumult in its executive suite that could have easily derailed the company's efforts to shift its focus toward women consumers. Cantalupo, who put in place several of the far-reaching changes that made the women-centric focus a core strategy, died from a heart attack 16 months after taking over as head of McDonald's. He was replaced by Charlie Bell, who was forced to retire in late 2004 after being diagnosed with colorectal cancer. He died unexpectedly in 2005. Despite those executive shifts, the top leadership at McDonald's stuck with the ideas espoused by people throughout the company, including Napier, Cook, Koepke, and Kapica. The payoff for paying attention to women? From May 2003 to May 2004, same-store sales were up for 13 straight months.[31] In one year, McDonald's share price doubled from $12 to $25. By 2005, the company was selling more apples than any other restaurant as Apple Dippers caught on.[32] Since they were launched, McDonald's has sold 300 million salads. People buying salads had total bills of $8 or more, double that of people who opted for a cheeseburger and fries. Surprisingly, men made up 40 percent of the salad purchasers—an added benefit McDonald's hadn't even hoped for when the salad line was launched in 2003. "The targeting of women hasn't stopped men from buying our products," Napier says. "Instead, we sell more products in the end because we did focus on women." Company executives credit the radical rethink about women for helping with the quick turnaround in McDonald's fortunes. "We wouldn't be where we are if it hadn't been for a direct focus on women," Koepke says.

But McDonald's isn't sitting still after learning its lesson the hard way in 2002 of remaining relevant with women. It's taking its women-centric focus around the world. In Japan, one of the company's biggest markets, it has revamped its menu to appeal to young women, a demographic it has rarely served in the past. But with its core consumer group—families with children—dwindling in Japan, McDonald's has had to begin offering food options that appeal beyond burgers and fries. In mid-2003, the company's Japanese unit introduced higher-priced offerings with more gourmet touches, such a ratatouille sauce for hamburgers and a fried green spring roll with red bean sweetener, for single Japanese women.[33] Napier was reassigned to Europe after her success in the U.S. to help bring new ideas to the company's struggling operations across the continent. "Again it was a matter of offering choices to women, giving them a reason to come back in the door," Napier says, adding that in Europe, McDonald's was adding more salads, yogurts, chicken sandwiches, and fruit.

The company also didn't stop thinking about how to keep changing with women consumers in the U.S. In 2005, the focus moved to the restaurants themselves. The company's new leadership team, headed by chief executive officer Jim Skinner, who replaced Bell, remained committed to Cantalupo's strategy of increasing same-store sales instead of growing by opening new stores. To bring people back to the stores week after week, McDonald's turned again to its mantra of "finding the woman inside the mom" for guidance. In mid-2005, the company pushed forward with plans to revamp thousands of restaurants and hundreds of PlayPlaces to make them more comfortable for moms and women. "We heard from women that they would really like a place that was geared toward them, not just their children," Koepke says. When they were designed, PlayPlaces didn't take moms into account. They were designed to fit the needs of children. Parents were forced to sit outside the space on hard plastic chairs while trying to watch over their children in the play area. In the renovated PlayPlaces, McDonald's moved in couches and comfortable chairs and installed wireless Internet access—much more like the "fast-casual" environments of Panera Bread or the look and feel popularized by Starbucks. Koepke says, "We realize that our sterile environments just aren't what women are looking for anymore."

Key Observations

◆ Use women-only focus groups for new products and marketing strategies—even if products will be marketed to all consumers. McDonald's used this strategy to create new salads and revamp nutritional information on its company Web site.

◆ Shift media buying from "monolithic" 18-to-49-year-old adults to targeted media buys focusing on specific roles women play in society.

◆ Overhaul organization to coordinate menu creation and management with marketing strategy.

◆ Make constant adjustments in tactics used for women consumers to create relevant messages for a quickly changing consumer. McDonald's used this strategy to overhaul the interior of its restaurants in 2005.

McDonald's turned around its sales and overhauled its menu for a new century by readjusting its view of women from a minority market to a majority consumer. It rethought a woman's traditional role as mother and revamped it for today's consumers. In the next chapter, we'll address how The Home Depot shifted its focus on women by radically rethinking women's roles inside the home—and in home renovation.

CHAPTER 2

From Property to Partnerships

HOW THE HOME DEPOT DISCOVERED POWER PARTNERS AND DO-IT-HERSELFERS

R*enovated the number two retailer's stores to appeal to women in novel ways to go beyond its competition by focusing on the changing structure of America's families and the shifting roles of women inside the home—and in home renovations.*

On a chilly evening in Marietta, Georgia, in January 2004, with an ice storm snarling traffic, a group of about 40 women gathered at their local home improvement store, The Home Depot, for a "do-it-herselfer" workshop. It was the first in a series of quarterly seminars that would be held nationally during the year on the same day by America's number two retailer to educate women in home improvement projects. First on the evening's program was an hour of talk and hands-on instruction on installing Pergo flooring, a quick way to achieve a "hardwood" floor look without the high price. Then came instructions on Legato tiles, a way to carpet floors that had become popular after they were seen on the hit home improvement television series, *Trading Spaces*. After a quick break for coffee and cookies, the women would hear tips on installing a closet system, including a discussion of the psychology of clutter and an in-depth tour through The Home Depot's cavernous aisles to check out the closet systems the store sold.

As the evening got underway, seminar leaders Kim Temples and Wendy Tijerina asked for volunteers in the audience to take turns using an electric saw to cut through a piece of the tough laminate flooring. Sheila Miller, flanked by her two young daughters, raised her hand. She strapped on a pair of safety goggles and grasped the black rubber handles on the circular saw. Her daughters started cheering. At first, nothing happened as she waited for the saw to do all the work. But with a little guidance from Tijerina on putting her weight behind the saw, she deftly sliced through the tough laminate. Hands shaking, she removed the safety goggles, but she was smiling.

Later she would recount the number of small home-improvement projects she had done after moving into her new home after a divorce. They included sanding and sealing a kitchen countertop. For her, learning how to use the saw was a breakthrough. "Now I'm coming to the bigger tools," she says. "They are my biggest fear, but I'm not paying someone to do something I can do myself."

The group of women gathered around her, congratulating her on tackling the power tool. They traded tips on how to use such a saw to cut crown molding and talked about replacing the plumbing and electric wiring in their houses. Some of the women had similar backgrounds to Miller. They were divorced with children, learning for the first time to take care of home renovation chores. Others were young single women ready to tackle anything in the new homes they'd bought for themselves. Others were married, and a few husbands had tagged along. The husbands took seats at the back and along the sides so as not to get too involved in what was clearly their wives' domain.[1]

The January event, which was attended by close to 40,000 women throughout the country, couldn't have gone better if The Home Depot executives had scripted it themselves. It was exactly what they were hoping for when they set out to overhaul the company's image with women consumers two years earlier. The Home Depot had been burned by competition from its rival Lowe's Companies, which had started targeting women in the late 1990s. So, The Home Depot embarked on a fact-finding mission to determine how best to undertake its own renovation project to do a better job with all consumers. It focused on attracting more women to its stores and making its existing female customers—46 percent of its overall consumer base—feel more at home when they shopped at The Home Depot.[2]

As the executives made their way through an 18-month study of thousands of consumers, they came across some trends that ran counter to what the home improvement industry had traditionally used in its approach to women. They found that the industry was so focused on certain stereotypes about women and home repair—making special tools for women or focusing heavily on paint and décor areas, for example—that it had missed a critical shift in women's roles inside the home.

Many hardware brands had renovated their stores and products based on the traditional roles women played inside the home. Barbara K! Toolboxes, created by commercial contractor Barbara Kavovit, offered lightweight tools with turquoise handles for women who needed to pound a nail in a wall every so often or drill a hole for a curtain rod.[3] Her kits, ergonomically designed for smaller hands, didn't include big tools like the circular saw Miller trained on at The Home Depot. Home decorating stores, such as Michael's, focused heavily on craft projects—often considered a traditional task for women.

The early changes Lowe's made to attract more women focused on cleaning up its stores and widening aisles. It also increased its paint selections and added merchandise to attract women, whom it perceived as primarily interested in paint colors, appliances, and draperies. Certainly these changes were a much-needed and much-applauded shift from the other toolmakers and hardware stores that had all but ignored women despite statistics showing that women made 52 percent of the home improvement decisions by 2001.[4]

But their efforts hadn't factored in the social and economic changes that were rapidly redefining women's roles in the home and home renovations—a redefinition that The Home Depot felt it could use as it remodeled its stores. Its consumer study revealed that women had moved far past being the "influencers" of home renovation and their traditional roles in choosing décor items for those renovations. The company found that many women, whether single, divorced, or married (like the women attending the January "do-it-herselfer" event), were increasingly "power partners" inside the home. This phrase was coined by John Costello, the company's executive vice president for merchandising and marketing. "I think too many companies are locked into a definition of the nuclear family where men's and women's roles are strictly defined," Costello said. He recounted one of his favorite stories of walking through one of the company's stores and overhearing a conversation in which a woman was explaining the electrical system inside their home while the man listened. "The reality is that women are now equal partners, be it in home renovation or anywhere else inside the house. As a retailer that serves these people, we have to understand these new roles for women and how the evolving demographic structure of society is affecting them."[5]

By focusing on these bigger social and economic developments instead of adding better lighting and cleaning up its paint section, The Home Depot created a home improvement store that would seemingly do the impossible: make everyone—from professional contractors to the women who were interested only in paint chips—feel at home in its stores.

The payoff for those efforts has been remarkable. For the fiscal year 2004, the company's sales hit $73.1 billion, an increase of 12.8 percent and a record sales year for a company that hit $50 billion faster than any other company on the Fortune 500. Women accounted for almost 50 percent of the company's total transactions that year. In a sign that repeat customers were coming back, an important indication that the renovations were working, same-store sales were up 5.4 percent, the highest they had been since 1999.[6]

From Property to Partners

Costello's "power partners" have become increasingly evident throughout society and business as women's economic wealth and financial freedom have released them and men from the traditional and often very strict gender roles of the past.

Whether it truly reflected reality or not, the 1950s television show *Leave It to Beaver*, with June Cleaver in the kitchen and Ward hard at work in the office, at the very least outlined the desired form of America's family structure in the 20th century. In 1950, 80 percent of Americans lived in a family that looked a lot like the Cleaver household. That family structure—in which the woman controlled the inside of the home and the man everything outside—had been that way (with variations on the theme, certainly) for centuries. Indeed, household roles have been defined by gender for hundreds, if not thousands, of years. As far back as 15,000 years ago, during the age of hunters and gatherers, anthropologists have determined that roles and responsibilities were often defined by gender in many cultures. Women were foragers, while the men were the hunters. In those early societies, there was a balance of power because women's foraging skills often kept the family or tribe going through winters—her contribution to the family was critical. "Among the early hunter-gatherers, men and women had distinct but complementary tasks and shared important economic and religious duties. Though women never ruled over men, as the term matriarchy implies, they once enjoyed more equal footing," writes Stanford University history professor Estelle B. Freedman in *No Turning Back: The History of Feminism and the Future of Women.*[7]

Still, in general, women controlled the home, cooked the food, and tended the children. By contrast, men worked outside the home, hunting for food and defending the tribe. Through the centuries, those gender-based roles in the family deepened, dividing the sexes even more as societies began to evolve.

Over time, laws and rules were created that placed women in general under the control of their husbands—or another male figure, such as a brother or father. Women were often considered more property than the partners that Costello found shopping at The Home Depot. Even if women worked—a fact of life for a majority of families throughout the centuries—they were limited in their economic power by laws that kept them from controlling that money and using it for their own means. By the 1800s, in much of Western Europe and the U.S.—and indeed globally—the safest, surest, and most socially acceptable route to economic stability for women was through marriage. By the Victorian era, it became socially significant if a man's wife didn't work—it spoke of his ability to provide—and that ideal pervaded throughout much of the next 100 years. "At that time, marriage shifted from one in which women were co-providers to one in which men owned everything and there was the male breadwinner ideal," says Stephanie Coontz, author of the book

Marriage, A History: From Obedience to Intimacy or How Love Conquered Marriage and a professor at Evergreen State College.[8]

This dependence and idealization countered thousands of years of history in which a majority of women had worked on the farms and in the fields, assuming that they didn't live in a privileged economic class, where marriages were more often than not economic arrangements between families.

But these long-held, strictly defined gender roles began to break down in the late nineteenth and early twentieth centuries, particularly in the U.S. and Western Europe. The first major crack in the structure came as the Industrial Revolution moved women out of the home and into factories. Women found themselves faced, ironically, with diametrically opposed choices. On the one hand, women were being both drawn and driven to stay at home—in the traditional gendered roles—by husbands who considered a working wife socially unacceptable. On the other, factories offered a new world of work for women up and down the social and economic spectrum. Still, even when women did work, it was rarely considered a career. Marriage was still the preferred economic contract for women. Even if women continued to work after marriage, the money they earned was not considered their own, but added to the family coffers.

By World War II, the cracks were deepening as women went to work to replace men who had gone to war. Millions of women worked through the war years, many in jobs, such as manufacturing, that would never have been available to them if men had been around to do the work.[9] While the 1950s brought something of a return to the traditional family structure, it was short-lived. Changes in women's economic power finally began to transform America's basic family structure from one of the nuclear family to a national trend that *BusinessWeek* named "Unmarried America" in 2003 following the release of new 2000 Census data.[10] The data revealed that 50 percent of Americans lived in nontraditional family structures where the heads of household weren't married, a major shift from the nuclear family of the 1950s. That shift in the family structure has been driven, in great part, by the economic freedom that women gained as they entered the workforce. Marriage is no longer a woman's only safe bet for economic security. In 1940, 29 percent of women worked outside the home. By 1970, that number had jumped to 46 percent. In 2000, more than 60 percent of women over the age of 16 worked.[11] With that work came both freedom and responsibility that many women had seldom experienced in the traditional family structure. "Marriage has changed more in the past 50 years than it has in the past 5,000 years," says author Coontz. "We have broken with thousands of years of tradition. But we aren't giving everything up. We are taking the best of what prevailed and combining it with the greater ideals of today. It's totally revolutionary."

Over time, barriers that held women back from controlling their own money were also breaking down. In the 1960s, women couldn't open a bank account alone or sign for a home mortgage without a man to cosign for them. Just 20 years later, such restrictions had become unthinkable. By the 21st century, single women had become the second-biggest purchasers of homes. As women's roles in business improved from secretaries to managers to chief executives, women gained even more power and control over their professional lives. Inevitably, that power began to spill into their personal lives as women found it difficult to leave their positions of power at the front door to don the traditional roles inside the home. As dual-income families became the norm instead of the exception throughout the 1980s and 1990s, women were shifting from obedient housewives to equal partners.

These shifts aren't happening only in the liberal segments of society. They can be seen throughout society, including in more traditional groups such as new immigrants and conservative religious groups. For example, data released in 2004 indicated that Hispanic women are choosing to have fewer children as they face the same demands of balancing work and family that Caucasian women have faced for more than two decades. In California—the state with the largest Hispanic population—demographers recalculated downward the future population trends because of sharp drops in birthrates for Hispanic women. In 2003, Latina women had 2.6 children per woman, down from 2.8 in 1997 and 3.4 in 1990.[12]

Black women also are notable for their dramatic rise in money and power, outstripping black men in their ascendancy to the middle class and dramatically reshaping their family structures. Many have simply eschewed the idea of marriage, with 47 percent of black women ages 30 to 34 never married, according to the 2000 Census, compared to 10 percent for white women.[13] In older couples—many of whom formed some of the first dual-income marriages—there has been a shift in power. The Census 2000 statistics showed that there were more than two million couples where the man 55 or older hadn't worked in a year, but his wife did work.[14] These couples accounted for 10.9 percent of couples, up from 1.6 million couples, or 9.6 percent, in 1990. "This is the first generation that has ever had to deal with this, because in the past it was typically one retirement per family," says Phyllis Moen, a sociologist at the University of Minnesota and co-author of the book *The Career Mystique: Cracks in the American Dream.* "Today most couples experience two retirements—his and hers—in a world in which our lives no longer fit traditional molds. In fact, women's lives have never fit the old lock-step model of first years of education, then a lifetime of paid work, 'rewarded' by retirement. We never experienced such orderly arrangements and increasingly men are finding their careers and lives are unpredicatable as well."[15]

Despite initiatives by the Bush administration in 2004 to promote marriage, even traditionally conservative groups are acknowledging that women will continue to take on greater economic roles—either by necessity or choice. Speaking during a September 2004 annual meeting of the Mormon Church's Relief Society—an all-women's group within the conservative religion—a counselor in the Church's First Presidency, Thomas Monson, noted statistics that a majority of women will have to provide for themselves financially at some point in their lives. He urged the women to pursue an education and learn marketable skills so "if needed you are prepared to provide."[16]

Such advice wouldn't come as a surprise to the 30 percent of women who now make more money than their husbands and are increasingly the sole financial support for their families. One of the most surprising statistics to come out of the 2000 Census was the finding that in 30.7 percent of marriages, the woman makes more than her husband—a trend that has been explored in cover stories in *Newsweek* ("She Works. He Doesn't"), *Fortune* ("Trophy Husbands"), and *New York* ("Power Wives"). Demographers have dubbed the group the "Alpha Earner Wife." Even when demographers eliminated couples in which the husband was a retiree or a student to arrive at a more precise accounting of the true "Alpha Earner," the percentage was still 11 percent. The researchers considered this significant because the outperforming wives didn't even show up in the 1990 Census.[17]

There is no sign that this trend will reverse, given women's increasing education levels, as outlined in Chapter 1, "From Minority to Majority: McDonald's Discovers the Woman Inside the Mom." As Peg Tyre and Daniel McGinn wrote in their *Newsweek* cover story, "Regardless, (the Alpha Earner Wife) is a trend we'd better get used to. Like runners passing the baton in a track event, many couples will take turns being the primary breadwinner and the domestic god or goddess as their careers ebb and flow." Indeed, the shifts in family structure and the upsets in gender roles are expected to be even greater in younger generations that have grown up with dual-income parents and single moms. "Younger generations are crafting lives in innovative ways as they respond to larger social and institutional shifts," says Kathleen Gerson. She is a professor of sociology at New York University who in 2005 was researching a book tentatively titled *The Children of the Gender Revolution*. "Women's growing economic autonomy is one factor fueling a desire for personal independence. As new generations of women build an autonomous economic base, their identities are less defined by marriage and children alone."[18]

The Power Partner in the Bedroom

When Pfizer launched its male impotence drug Viagra in 1998, the drug company focused solely on men with a subtle advertising campaign that featured Bob Dole talking about "E.D." The elder statesman never mentioned the words "male impotence." He certainly never discussed sex in the somber ads with medical overtones. Over the years, Pfizer stuck with that game plan even as Viagra took on a far more racy attitude on the street as more and more men used it as sexual stimulant even if they didn't have a medical reason to use it.

In 2004, two new competitors entered the market with plans to radically change the way in which male impotence drugs were marketed. The approach was a direct response to the more powerful role women were taking in the home—and in the bedroom. The two brands—Cialis and Levitra—had conducted research showing that women were taking on more assertive roles in the sexual side of their relationships, just as they had taken more control over home renovation tasks. "When it comes to sexual satisfaction, women are clearly involved. They are part of the decision-making process in couples, so they play an important role for us," Nancy K. Bryan, Bayer Corp.'s vice president of marketing for men's health products, said in June 2003.[19] Bayer, with its partner GSK, at the time was preparing to bring its erectile dysfunction pill, Levitra, to the U.S. after it received FDA approval.

The shift from focusing on men's medical concerns to women's passion is a telling illustration of how the shake-up in the balance of power in couples and families can reshape the marketing for even the most male-focused products. Moreover, both of these companies have shown that exploiting such social shifts can result in substantial increases in market share when used effectively.

Levitra, approved by the FDA in late 2003, was the first to try what might best be referred to as "role reversal" marketing in the male impotence industry. The women-led marketing teams from Bayer and GSK had a tough challenge ahead of them. Their pill worked very much like Viagra, causing an erection quite promptly after the pill was taken. The Levitra team knew it needed to be more than a Viagra wannabe. Levitra needed an edge—a secret weapon—and the team believed women were exactly with whom they needed to be talking. Not only were women becoming more assertive in the bedroom, they also were far more willing to talk to their husbands and partners about impotence as a medical issue—not a relationship problem. In Europe, Levitra used an ad campaign that discussed impotence as a man's problem, not a problem with women not being sexy enough, a traditional belief held by some people. From their European research, Levitra's team knew it would have a better chance of having men seek out a doctor's advice and fill a pre-scription if the message about male impotence were delivered by their wives, girlfriends, and lovers. In fact, men's reticence about discussing the sensitive problem had been a drawback for Viagra, which financial analysts had set a $4 billion sales target by 2002 but hit just under $2 billion that year.[20]

The Levitra team launched its product in the U.S. with a series of racy and risqué ads featuring a sexy brunette in a man's shirt and little else talking about how the drug increases her partner's "desire to do this more often." The ads were a far cry from the stodgy Bob Dole ads that had become the brunt of jokes on late-night talk shows. Although the Levitra ads have been criti-cized as too sexually aggressive, they struck a chord with women, who then talked to the men in their lives. Levitra began taking market share away from Viagra not long after the launch of the ads.

Levitra's ads knocked a hole in the traditional roles that many marketers believed women and men play in the bedroom. But it took another Viagra competitor—Cialis—to take the reversal of roles a step further.

Cialis' creator, Eli Lilly and Co., recognized that women were indeed getting more assertive in the bedroom. But its marketing team believed that women carried with them many traditions of the past—like love and romance—along with the added sexual assertiveness. Levitra's ads cast women as more sexually aggressive—the traditional "male" role in relationships. Cialis advertising focused on couples. While women were still front and center—and still obviously interested in sex—the Cialis ads were as much about romance as they were about men performing better in bed.

The ads, which were teased with 15-second spots during football games leading up to the 2004 Super Bowl, showed a couple holding hands as they soaked in separate bathtubs looking out on a beautiful ocean view. The tagline said simply "Cialis is here. Are you ready?" "The whole strategy is wrapped around communicating to couples—women and men," Lilly's U.S. brand leader for Cialis said at the time.[21] The ads played up a product benefit that Viagra and Levitra couldn't claim. Cialis is effective for up to 36 hours—compared to eight hours or less for Viagra or Levitra, according to company information. With Cialis, women could help choose the moment instead of having it forced upon them because their husbands or partners had taken Viagra a few hours before dinner.

The tactic of marrying romance with women's new sexually aggressive stance has worked well for Cialis. Viagra once held a monopoly on the market. But in 2004, its market share slipped to less than 75 percent. Cialis has snared 13.9 percent of the market, with Levitra at an 11.6 percent share.[22]

Pfizer tried to fight back against the dual blow of female sexual aggression and romance. In its 2004 advertising campaign, Viagra defended its number one position with a whole new approach and tagline, "Get Back the Mischief." In one ad, a man and woman are shopping together. The mood shifts when they shop for lingerie. The voiceover says: "Remember the guy who used to be called the 'Wild Thing?' The guy who wanted to spend the entire honeymoon indoors? Remember the one who couldn't resist a little mischief? Yeah, that guy. He's back." The Viagra "V" then appears above and behind the man's head—giving him the look of a devil. The ads definitely took the medical mood out of Viagra's advertising, but it was a bit too much for the Federal Trade Commission. In November 2004, the regulatory body requested that Pfizer pull the ads from the airwaves for being too suggestive of returning men to sexual function that may not be achieved by taking the pill.[23] Neither Levitra's or Cialis' ads have come under fire from the FTC.

Despite such dramatic shifts in family structure, traditional gender roles have remained firmly entrenched in the minds of many consumers—men and women alike—and definitely in the minds of business executives. "The world many business executives live in isn't the world their customers live in," says marketing professor Neeli Bendapudi at Ohio State University. "Often these people have wives who stay at home. They don't see the shifts in their own lives, so they don't see them in their consumers."[24]

Many marketers still think of the family in the 1950s model, or something akin to it, as The Home Depot's Costello noted. Many still believe in traditional roles driven by gender, despite so many examples to the contrary even within their own families. They still believe that wives don't take out the trash; husbands do. Moms drive minivans; they don't drive sports cars. Women want special floors with security for themselves at hotels; men want gyms and bars. Women still care only about the color of paint and texture of tile in their homes; they don't tear down the walls and install the tile themselves.

But the reality is that the traditional roles are breaking down, becoming more dynamic and unbounded by gender. As Ken Dychtwald, founder of the San Francisco-based market research firm Age Wave, has written, "In the next 25 years, one continuing trend we'll see is a blurring of gender roles and buying patterns. As the generations mature, it will be common for husbands to do the laundry and grocery shopping before preparing a scrumptious dinner while their wives are busy buying the computers and new cars and managing the family's investment portfolio." Maddy Dychtwald, Age Wave's senior vice president, is the author of the book *Cycles: How We Will Live, Work and Buy.* "There is going to be so much choice in the cycles of life we lead that we will no longer pigeonhole people into traditional roles," she says. "Today women especially are realizing we can be more than one person in our lives. We can have a second or third career. We can stay at home with our children and we can go back to work."[25]

As these shifts in family structure and gender roles begin to sink in as permanent—not transitory—changes, companies such as The Home Depot have found it far more fruitful to stop assuming that men and women will continue to follow traditional gender roles. Instead, they have looked at the social and economic reasons for these shifts and have begun focusing on where consumers are going, not where they have been. McDonald's found its way through the maze of marketing to women by throwing out the stereotypes it had of moms to find "the woman inside the mom."

For The Home Depot, finding the "power partners" and "do-it-herselfers" inside women has been the key to success. "Gender roles can be an artificial filter when applied to brands," says Ellen Dracos, the company's vice president of brand marketing. "What's more important than gender is finding ways to be relevant to today's consumers. For instance, making a store easier to navigate isn't something that just appeals to women. It makes sense for all of our customers. It's about gender 'inclusivity' as opposed to gender exclusivity."[26]

Finding Power Partners and Do-It-Herselfers

In 2000, Robert Nardelli left his executive post at General Electric Co. to become The Home Depot's chief executive officer. He took over as the company was struggling to maintain the frantic pace that had catapulted it from little more than a lumberyard in 1979 to the country's number two retailer behind Wal-Mart Stores Inc. After two decades of strong growth driven by opening hundreds of new stores, much like McDonald's growth strategy, the company was in need of a strategic overhaul. While its overall sales were still growing, its comparable store sales were flat or down. The company's stock, once one of the best performers in the Dow Jones Industrial Average, lost more than half of its value in just one year—dropping from a high of more than $52 in 2002 to $20 in January 2003.[27]

By contrast, Lowe's was on a roll. While much smaller than The Home Depot—its sales were $31 billion in 2003 compared to The Home Depot's $65 billion—Lowe's was doing a far better job in the eyes of customers and investors. Its same-store sales had increased 5.6 percent even as The Home Depot's dropped precipitously. One of the key reasons for Lowe's success was an early gamble on women that had begun to pay off by the early 2000s. In the late 1990s, Lowe's took a look at the consumer data stacking up at its headquarters. While conventional wisdom at the time held that home improvement was the sole domain of men, Lowe's research showed that women controlled many of the home improvement decisions—up to 80 percent of them—even if they never set foot inside a lumberyard or paint store. For Lowe's, women were the perfect niche to exploit instead of attacking its far bigger rival on its well-defined turf of "do-it-yourselfer" men and construction professionals.

So when Robert Tillman—a longtime Lowe's employee—was elevated to chief executive in 1996, he decided to exploit the niche that most home improvement and hardware stores had dismissed. "We focused on a customer nobody in the home improvement has focused on. Don't get me wrong, but women are far more discriminating than men," Tillman said at the time.[28]

Such discriminating tastes led Lowe's to overhaul its 800 stores starting in 1999. Out went the dark, dingy look of most hardware stores—including The Home Depot—and in came brighter lighting, cleaner aisles, and lower shelving. Lowe's widened the aisles and knocked off the "end-caps," the pallets at the end of aisles that featured specials or sale items. That got rid of "butt brush," the unwanted contact between customers when they passed each other in narrow aisles that women consumers had told Lowe's they disliked. Though it may have seemed like a small change, the attention to detail showed that Lowe's was sincere about understanding women, not just hoping that a few cosmetic changes, such as a fresh coat of paint, would draw them into its stores. Lowe's also added products it felt would appeal to women. It brought in Christmas ornaments, custom draperies, and high-end cabinetry and bathroom fixtures. By 2003, Lowe's was being hailed in the press and by marketing experts as the home improvement retailer that "got women."

But from its surveys and in-store workshops The Home Depot was finding that women had changed significantly in the five years since Lowe's had overhauled its stores. In early 2002, the results of the consumer survey Nardelli had called for fell into the hands of the company's director of style, innovation, and design, Jason Feldman. Instead of focusing specifically on gender, the study separated the company's customers by how often they shopped in the stores, what they shopped for, and how much they spent. For example, there were the "dabblers," who picked up basic necessities every few months. They made up 25 percent of the consumers but spent very little time or money in the stores. There were the "delegators," about 20 percent of the company's customers, who preferred to have projects done for them and often hired professional services through the home-improvement stores. The "experts"—primarily men—made up about 17 percent, and along with professional contractors were some of the company's most lucrative customers.

The groups were all important consumers to The Home Depot. But there was a category that intrigued Feldman. "Home perfectors" made up just 21 percent of the company's consumers but accounted for close to *50 percent of store sales.* Even more interesting was their gender breakdown. Unlike the mostly male experts, the other group that contributed heavily to store sales, "home perfectors" were evenly divided among genders. Often they were couples who shopped together as they "perfected" their homes year after year. "These people seemed to be on a constant quest to perfect their homes," Feldman says. "The house represented their aspirations. These were people who saw themselves represented by their homes."[29]

These couples also defined what Costello called "power partnerships," men and women who worked together on their home renovations without one or the other taking charge. This sense of equality was underscored by the few gender-specific insights that came out of the survey. "The Home Depot's women shoppers were turned off by pastel colors or anything that remotely pointed out 'women shop here.' If you make it too feminine, our female customers told us, you're messing with the secret sauce of The Home Depot," Feldman says.[30]

Without the consumer input, the retailer would have made a grave mistake by overhauling its stores solely with women in mind. Instead, The Home Depot realized that it needed to create a renovation that worked equally well for men and women. "We couldn't give up on one gender to please another," Costello said. Such insight was critical to its renovation strategy. Companies often have mistakenly believed they needed to cover up or overhaul their brand attributes as they refocus their efforts on the women's market. But as The Home Depot learned from its consumers, such a strategy would have alienated women instead of attracting them to the stores. The retailer had to create store environments that would reflect the company's expertise in home renovation—a strategy that would keep men feeling comfortable in the stores—while implementing specific strategies to make parts of its stores more appealing to women.

"Our Stores Are a Little Schizophrenic"

By the end of 2004, the majority of The Home Depot's 1,850 stores had come to reflect both the subtle and stark changes required to create the balance of such interests. "Our stores are a bit schizophrenic," Feldman says. There's almost a visible dividing line between the new sections designed to appeal to women and the old stores with their stacks of lumber, pallets of insulation, and rows upon rows of nails and screws.

The dual nature is clear in a store that serves as a working laboratory for the company near its suburban Atlanta headquarters. The store is a cleaner, brighter version of its old self—a renovation instead of a total teardown, to use a home construction term. Feldman explained the changes as he guided a tour through the store.

The concrete floors that once looked dingy and dirty had been shined to a high gloss to better reflect the overhead lighting. The lighting itself had received a boost in wattage with new fluorescent bulbs to make the often-oppressive warehouse stores feel airier. The Home Depot's signature orange shelving is still in use, but only in areas where it doesn't conflict with color choices. In the paint, carpet, and tile areas, beige shelving serves as a plain-vanilla backdrop to the kaleidoscope of colors. The shelves throughout are neater and more organized and focused on what the "do-it-herselfer" needs, not a professional. "Women told us time and again that our clutter and chaos was a turnoff and didn't help them achieve what they needed—which was finding the right products quickly," Feldman said. Turn left, however, toward the lumber, siding and other major home repair areas, and The Home Depot's "two stores in one" approach becomes clear. The towering orange shelving makes a comeback, creating canyons down the center of the store with inventory stacked to the ceiling. The "Tool Corral," often the geographic center of the stores, remains untouched—for a reason, Feldman says. "You never mess with a woman's savvy," he said. "Women told us, 'I want to shop where men shop for tools.' Women shop us because they know who we are, and 'This is The Home Depot.'"

That doesn't mean that The Home Depot hasn't sought to appeal to the feminine side of women by bringing in new merchandise or overhauling its marketing to include women in the brand. But even in these areas, the company has remained committed to the concept that stores should be inclusive instead of exclusive. It has expanded its appliances to appeal more to women, adding far more manufacturers and even creating an exclusive General Electric line for the stores called Adora. At the same time, it has expanded its "grilling" section to appeal to men. While it has added far more cabinetry, lighting, and paint choices for women, it's also increased its selection of John Deere mowers and tractors—which appeal not only to men but to a growing number of women. In advertising, the company has taken a notably "gender-neutral" approach with the tagline "You can do it. We can help." The campaign is designed "to appeal to men, women, couples, and home improvement professionals," Costello says.

The focus on being inclusive while paying attention to the specific details that will attract women has been integral to The Home Depot's continued success with both "do-it-herselfers" and the partners in the "home perfectors" category. But another key has been creating far closer connections with consumers, especially women. That has kept the company on top of fast-moving trends, including the shift in women from novices to experts in home repair in just five years. That's where the national workshops have worked to the company's advantage. Indeed, it was through the early women's workshops that the company began to realize that women had moved past home décor.

The impetus for the national workshops had come out of informal "ladies' nights" workshops that focused on home décor and simple projects like faux painting—traditionally considered "women's" projects—that some stores had created in the late 1990s. The workshops were popular enough that when The Home Depot decided to formalize and nationalize the program in 2003, it chose the same home décor projects, assuming that such soft renovation projects remained at the top of women's renovation lists.

"We truly thought they would be primarily on home-decorating tips, like new paint techniques or color trends," says Anna Siefken, the executive in charge of the national workshops. Although the first workshops did draw thousands of women to the stores, Siefken says her team began receiving e-mail and feedback almost immediately that gave her insight into a big shift in the way women thought about home renovations. "These women want to tackle big things," she says of the e-mails she received.

"Many of them were repeat customers, so as they gained confidence doing one project, they wanted to move on to even bigger projects."[31]

The feedback on the workshops revealed that the company couldn't rely on its executives or even store managers to come up with ideas for its workshops. Instead, it turned directly to the consumers, who were turned on by what they saw on home improvement shows on television and, most importantly, by past experiences. At every workshop, the company asks for e-mail addresses from participants. Since May 2003, more than 200,000 women have taken part in the workshops. As the time draws near to set up the curriculum for the national workshop, Siefken sends out a query to the database to find out what's the hottest idea in home renovations. Although Siefken offers suggestions, more often than not the curriculum ends up being driven directly by the women who plan on attending.

But the insight doesn't stop when the workshops ended. The feedback also flows over to Feldman's department, where it helps drive the next store renovation. For example, in 2003, a growing number of women showed interest in learning how to install crown moldings and chair rails. Traditionally, only construction professionals shopped in that section of the store, so it had not been renovated with women in mind. But the workshops changed all that. Feldman had his team design signage and handouts for the section, including more informational books and instructions on how to install the moldings. In the Atlanta prototype, the section featured tidy rows of different types of moldings, rails, and ceiling medallions from the run-of-the-mill to ones that would be at home in a French chateau.

The Home Depot executives also have realized that focusing on women in certain areas of the store has had the added benefit of reaching men in new ways. One unusual shift has been the number of construction professionals—who have been The Home Depot's bread-and-butter customers from the beginning—who have taken to browsing through the mockups of bathrooms and kitchens, Feldman says. In the past, those professionals—a category still dominated by men—wouldn't have ventured beyond the "pro" section that the company had set aside for them several years ago. There, they can receive pallets of paint, lumber, and siding without running into regular customers. But to gain insight into home trends—such as whether brushed nickel is still popular in kitchens or whether shag carpeting is making a comeback—those pros are perusing the other sections of the store for ideas when they build new homes, Feldman says.

The closer focus on consumers—women and men—also has helped smooth the way for The Home Depot's entry into big cities, such as New York and Chicago, where customers have far different needs than their suburban counterparts. Some of what the company learned from women has been adapted into the stores, such as increased use of informational and educational materials, including new "know-how" kiosks. But it also has broadened its offerings by listening specifically to its urban consumers—an offshoot of understanding how important it is to listen to the people who shop its stores. That means larger sections of the store are devoted to home storage and organization products—important to consumers who live in apartments, not large suburban homes.

Key Observations

◆ Use an "inclusive" gender strategy that gives equal weight to the needs of men and women while employing specific tactics that address women's unmet needs in the stores. This strategy was used to focus on "home perfectors."

◆ Renovate only where necessary. This strategy was employed to maintain the look and feel of The Home Depot's "warehouse" stores while updating sections where brighter lighting and softer colors were important.

◆ Use the Internet and e-mail feedback to stay in touch with consumers. This strategy led to the overhaul of "do-it-herselfer" workshops to reflect women's changing needs in home renovation.

◆ Don't deny the core brand attributes of The Home Depot. Instead, find the relevance in those attributes for women.

Charting the sometimes-subtle needs of women consumers as well as the dramatic shifts of women in society helped position The Home Depot beyond its once-traditional core of professionals and "do-it-himselfers." In the next chapter, Procter & Gamble discovers that even as women take on many new roles throughout society, they hold onto traditional roles that continue to fulfill them.

CHAPTER 3

From Drudgery to "Swiffering"

PROCTER & GAMBLE CLEANS HOUSE

*T*o *create the Swiffer, a new brand of cleaning products, Procter & Gamble explored how women perceived their traditional role as homemakers in a modern world—and even learned along the way what women thought about men's roles around the house.*

By 2004, Procter & Gamble Co. (P&G) was heading into its fifth year of sales success with the Swiffer, a plastic mop-like gadget that featured dust-grabbing electrostatic cloths it had launched in August 1999. At the time of Swiffer's introduction, P&G executives expected that the Swiffer would provide the company with a solid new brand it could build over the decades.

What they hadn't expected was what happened. The Swiffer, which eliminated the centuries-old drudgery of the broom and dustpan, had turned into a cultural phenomenon. By 2002, "Swiffering" had entered the country's vernacular. People had taken to saying that they were going to "Swiffer" instead of clean house much the same way they said they were "Googling" when they searched the Internet. By October of that year,

Swiffer had become so much a part of American pop culture that it was satirized on *Saturday Night Live*. By the end of the year, P&G had sold 50 million Swiffers.[1]

By July 2003, one billion Swiffer dry cloths had been sold, and later that year the plastic gadget would receive yet another boost to its pop culture status. The Swiffer appeared on the cover of the November 2003 issue of *Rolling Stone* magazine, clutched in the hands of pop star Jessica Simpson, who had been named "sexiest housewife of the year" by the magazine. P&G didn't even pay for high-profile product placement. The Swiffer was found in the photographer's studio and used as a prop without P&G's knowledge, according to published reports.

By 2004, riding the wave of such popularity, Swiffer had become one of P&G's most successful and fastest-growing brands.[2] Swiffer sales had topped $500 million since it was introduced and had almost single-handedly created the "quick clean" category, which was expected to grow from about $2.1 billion in 2003 to more than $4.2 billion by 2008.[3]

With such success, there was some anxiety among the Swiffer brand team as it prepared for the launch of yet another Swiffer line extension in 2004. Certainly, there had been other line extensions during Swiffer's five years on the market, including the first, Swiffer Max, a bigger version of the original. Then there was the Swiffer WetJet, which eliminated the drudgery of mopping with buckets of dirty water. Next came Swiffer hand dusters that were flexible and strong enough to get between blind slats and soft enough to dust around delicate objects.

But the new product would be the most expensive in a brand lineup that had always pushed to be affordable to the masses. In addition, Swiffer's brand team had an unusual idea on how to advertise the new product. The line extension, called the Swiffer Sweep+Vac, paired the original Swiffer with a small vacuum, pushing the price of the new Swiffer to above $30—at least $10 pricier than the next most expensive WetJet, depending on where consumers bought the product. For the new advertising, P&G and its ad agency the Kaplan Thaler Group decided to feature a man in the leading role instead of putting the Sweep+Vac in the hands of a woman—the traditional housecleaner in the family and the main character in the bulk of Swiffer's ads. "Our culture had taken that step toward being more comfortable seeing a man clean the house," says Linda Kaplan

Thaler, the agency's president. "So there was no reason we shouldn't, although it may have seemed counterintuitive."[4]

In the ad that premiered in September 2004, a man dumps cereal, potato chips, and several other messy items all over the kitchen floor, as his wife and daughter look on aghast. Then, the husband grabs his Swiffer Sweep+Vac, brandishes it in front of his startled wife and daughter, and proceeds to suck every last crumb off the floor. "Swiffer had been primarily about women and for women," says Kristine Decker, Swiffer's brand manager. "But as we talked to consumers about Sweep+Vac, we noticed that it appealed beyond that core. There was this gadget-like appeal for men."[5]

Doing the Gender Flip

The insight was the culmination of a five-year journey by P&G into understanding and then building the Swiffer brand based on two interconnected trends affecting women, men, and society. The first was examining the importance women placed on traditional roles—such as creating a clean home—even as they explored their new roles in society. The second was a trend sociologists, academics, and futurists dubbed "gender flipping," a phrase that refers to the turn and churn of gender roles caused by the breakdown of traditional roles over the past 50 years.

It was this second trend that the new Swiffer ads attacked head-on. Instead of roles being strictly defined by gender, women and men are increasingly somersaulting between the new roles created as women gained more access to education and careers and the traditional roles men and women have held for centuries. Where gender roles once stayed static throughout much of a person's adult life, those roles are now in constant flux. "Where men and women once followed prescribed paths—often defined by gender roles—from school to work and marriage and retirement, they now cycle back and forth between those paths and roles as well," says Age Wave's Maddy Dychtwald.[6]

This gender flipping—or, more precisely, somersaulting, because the roles are in a constant tumbling state—is a relatively new phenomenon that is driven not only by social and economic changes, but also by emotion and psychology, say academics and futurists. In the early days of the women's movement, there was a drive to throw off the traditional roles that had defined women for centuries as they gained more economic and social power. "We knew that we couldn't attain total fulfillment through marriage, so what did all of us feminists do? We said 'we can do anything a man can do,'" says Minnesota University professor Phyllis Moen, coauthor of *Career Mystique*, a title that played off Betty Friedan's work *The Feminine Mystique*. "But then we realized that we had bought into the career mystique that was designed primarily for men with someone else at home who managed the details of daily life. Now neither men nor women believe that work can be completely fulfilling, yet many jobs remain designed around the idea that workers are willing to put everything second to their work obligations. Now we are realizing that there had to be someone at home too."[7]

From the 1960s onward, women struggled first to define themselves in the workplace and then to redefine themselves in the home. That struggle and redefinition also affected men's roles in society and family—and it certainly has affected the way marketers have approached the women's market and portrayed women in their advertising. In the 1970s, a common image in advertising was the driven career woman in her manly suit with big shoulder pads and scarf to mimic men's ties. There were the "You've come a long way, baby" ads from Virginia Slims and the unforgettable Enjoli ad with its "Bring home the bacon, but never ever let him forget he's a man" song. In the 1980s and 1990s, those images were added to the "supermom" iconography of the woman who could "have it all." "Supermoms" struggled to balance a career, a minivan, children, and a husband who didn't help around the house.

But in the 21st century, women (and men) and the roles they play are not so easy to stereotype. "We have had these two role models of June Cleaver and Gloria Steinem. There was the one road in life that said women didn't work and the other road that said women did work," says New York University professor Mary Quigley, author of *Going Back to Work: A Survival Guide for Comeback Moms* with coauthor Loretta Kaufman. "There was no middle road. But now we are creating new roles, inventing these ideas as we go along. We are a new kind of woman."[8]

Professor Quigley saw this trend of moving in and out of the workforce playing out in her own life as well as the lives of the more than 1,000 women she surveyed for her book. It was a follow-up to her earlier book *And What Do You Do? When Women Choose to Stay at Home,* published in 2000. Professor Quigley's "new kind of woman"—where women mix and match the roles and responsibilities of the past and present—is evident throughout society today.

It's no longer easy—if it ever was—to pigeonhole women as a monolithic group that acts and thinks alike. The stereotypes of the past are too simplistic and shallow to truly reflect the myriad of choices and responsibilities open to men and women in the 21st century. Today, women are as likely to choose to stay home with their children as they are to pursue high-powered careers. In 1994, 19.8 percent of married mothers with children under 15 had stayed at home during the past year to care for their children, according to statistics from the U.S. Census Bureau and the Bureau of Labor Statistics. By 2002, that percentage had increased to 22.4 percent.[9] But, as Professor Quigley found in her research, many stay-at-home moms have definite plans to return to the world of work after their children reach school age or go to college—a trend that she used as the impetus for her second book on "comeback moms." "I live in classic suburbia in Nassau County on Long Island, and there's maybe one woman on my block that hasn't gone back to work," she says. "I think there is a new attitude among women about work that they can move in and out of the workforce."

Others are choosing to create new lives and new jobs for themselves outside the traditional corporate world. For instance, women-owned businesses, some inspired by the needs women discovered when they became mothers, are now the fastest-growing segment of the small-business sector. From 1987 to 1992, the number of women-owned firms increased by 43 percent, almost double the rate of growth of all firms during that time period, according to the Small Business Administration. Women-owned businesses account for one-third of all firms in the U.S.

More and more women also are choosing "singlehood"—a growing trend among women both in the U.S. and in countries such as Japan. In 2001, 50 percent of Japanese women aged 30 were still unmarried, compared to 37 percent in the United States.[10] It's not just younger generations who are choosing singlehood over marriage. There also has been a significant increase in the number of people over 55 seeking divorce or separation—double the number in 1990, says the U.S. Census—with women often doing the asking. In a survey by the American Association for Retired Persons, 66 percent of the women surveyed said they asked for the divorce, compared with 41 percent of men. Moreover, the study noted that men more often than women were caught off-guard by the divorce.[11] Single women—either divorced, never married, or widowed—now account for 46 million women in the U.S. They are an increasingly powerful force in the economy, politics, and society.[12]

None of these trends—more women choosing to stay at home with their children, or "singlehood"—mark returns to either the traditionalism of the 1950s or the radical feminism of the 1960s. Instead, these shifts and others are simply more signs that the 21st century really is a brave new world. Many different types of family structures will exist, as opposed to one structure being idealized, as the nuclear family with a working father and stay-at-home mom has been for decades.

Indeed, there are just as many statistics and as much anecdotal evidence that men are gaining satisfaction from staying at home and taking on women's traditional roles while their wives pursue high-powered careers. *Fortune*'s cover story "Trophy Husbands" in October 2002 pointed to a small but growing trend of men staying at home as their wives take on more and more powerful positions in the workplace. "The household arrangements these couples have created are simultaneously radical and conservative," *Fortune*'s Betsy Morris wrote. "Yes, the men and women have traded places. But they have divided their labor quite traditionally. There is a back-to-the-future quality to their domestic relations, a reversion to notions of work and home right out of the 1950s. Except for one big difference: the 21st century organization man could very easily be a woman. And the corporate wife could be a husband."

Although that article focused on women with six-figure salaries and major corporate titles, more couples are rethinking who stays home with the children. Increasingly, it makes more economic sense for the man to stay home, not the woman, as women's salaries continue to rise, as noted in Chapter 1, "From Minority to Majority: McDonald's Discovers the Woman Inside the Mom." In 2002, 189,000 children had stay-at-home dads, according to the Current Population Survey. That's miniscule compared to 11 million with stay-at-home moms.[13] But it's a trend that's likely to keep growing as women's education and income continue to out-pace men's in the next generations. But no matter if it's dad or mom stay-ing at home, by 2004, the number of stay-at-home parents was at its high-est level since the Bureau of Labor Statistics began tracking the phenome-non in 1994.[14]

A major reason for the rise in stay-at-home parents of both genders is the growing realization by many couples that dual-income lifestyles are tak-ing their toll on family life. The idea of balancing everything isn't working for many people. "Instead of trying to balance all of our commitments and passions at any one time, let's acknowledge that anything important, *and anything done well, demands our full investment,*" wrote *Fast Company* deputy editor Keith Hammonds in a cover story debunking the myth of balance. "At some times, it may be a demanding child or an unhappy spouse, and the office will suffer. At others, it may be winning the McWhorter account, and child and spouse will have to fend for themselves. Only over time can we really balance a portfolio of diverse experiences."[15]

As this realization continues to seep into Americans' psyches, gender somersaulting will become even more mainstream as men and women find themselves moving back into the workforce, swapping traditional gender roles several times during their lives, choosing to focus on family then career then family and then possibly career again, instead of opting for the traditional stay-at-home moms and working fathers of the past or the jug-gling of career and family life that has defined the past 20 years. Children and work aren't the only responsibilities forcing these gender somersaults. More people are finding it necessary to take time off work or leave the workforce altogether to take care of elderly parents. The majority of adults in the U.S. who receive long-term care at home—78 percent—get all their care from unpaid family and friends. A majority of those caregivers are women, with estimates stating that women spend 50 percent more time providing care than male caregivers.[16]

This somersaulting between new and old roles already has brought some interesting shifts for both genders—far beyond the "supermoms" of the 1990s. Stay-at-home dads have begun to create their own communi-ties to help them with the new world of being a full-time parent—much the same way that women created mothers' groups. Another trend, "met-rosexuality," referring to heterosexual men who buy typically feminine products such as manicures and spa treatments, hit the mainstream in 2002. This term flew under the radar for close to a decade in big cities such as New York and London. While primarily a marketing ploy driven by companies to expand their consumer base, metrosexuality points to deeper changes brought about by the gender somersault. As women have moved more deeply into traditionally male roles—running companies, overseeing investments for their families—men have moved into traditionally female roles—caregivers to elderly parents, consumers of manicures, and so on.

Yet even when men and women operate in their traditional roles, there are major shifts in how they view those roles—as P&G would find as it began talking to consumers about the Swiffer. As Professor Quigley says, today's stay-at-home moms are far different from the women who stayed at home decades ago. "There are two major changes in what women are expected to do at home," she says. "They have far more authority and responsibility in the home today than ever before. It's a myth that your brain turns to mush when you stay at home. These women are in control of the household finances like never before. As they realize that raising children isn't taking up 100 percent of their time, they take over paying the mortgage, dealing with contractors, and making financial investments. They have become the main decision makers for what comes into their households. They aren't just influencing what happens. They are making all the decisions," Professor Quigley says. They are the "power partners" that Costello found shopping The Home Depot stores. But she points out that even as women take on these so-called "male" roles, they also retain their traditional roles. "We heard from woman after woman as we researched our books that one of the reasons they liked being at home was being the emotional center of the family."

The pairing of new roles driven by women's push into the workforce with the traditional female roles in the home often has been buried over the past several decades as women sloughed off the traditional roles they considered oppressive—like housework. But many women still strive to retain their traditional roles, such as Professor Quigley's "emotional center," even as they take on the new roles afforded to them by the social and economic strides women have made during the past 50 years.

Such tension in women, coupled with the constantly shifting and reforming roles of men and women, requires a far more nuanced approach from business than ever before—as Procter & Gamble found when it began working on an all-new brand and category of cleaning products in the late 1990s.

From Drudgery to "Swiffering"

No company has been more affected by the shift in gender roles and responsibilities than P&G. The company had marketed brands, such as Pampers and Tide, to women in the same traditional ways through the same medium—national television—for decades. But by the time Swiffer was ready to be launched, it had become increasingly clear that the success of the company's 10 $1 billion-plus brands and its newest innovations, such as Swiffer, depended less on its traditional strengths of distribution and brand management and more on understanding its quickly changing consumers. Their success, as P&G would discover, would be more dependent on tapping into the changes its consumers were experiencing today and creating products and marketing that would appeal to this new world of shifting gender roles.

Even before Swiffer, the company realized that what had worked in the past with women simply wasn't getting the job done today. P&G's overhaul of two well-known ad campaigns was evidence of how much of a shift women had made over the decades. For years, the company had used the tagline "Strong enough for a man, but made for a woman" to pitch its Secret line of deodorants. The tagline worked for earlier generations of women, who liked the idea that a deodorant for them would work as well as the ones made for men. P&G believed that women wanted the "guy's deodorant," but wrapped in a pretty package. By the late 1990s, such beliefs had become long outdated, and the tagline had grown tired and more than a bit condescending to a new generation of women, who saw the whole approach as an anachronism. Today, Secret's tagline is simply "Strong enough for a woman."

P&G also made a major shift in its marketing strategy for Herbal Essences shampoo. The product had been defined by its sharp, herbal scent, and the advertising focused on that attribute, a traditional practice of P&G's advertising. But by the time the brand was given to the Kaplan Thaler Group for a new ad campaign, such attributes just weren't cutting it anymore. The ad agency decided to go with an ad campaign that played off much the same shift in the way women perceived their sexuality as the one that was used by the male impotence drugs Cialis and Levitra. In the Herbal Essences ads, a woman goes through an orgasmic experience washing her hair. Gone is any discussion of the product's smell or efficacy, replaced by a titillating, but hardly shocking, expression of sexuality that wouldn't have passed muster with the women of an earlier generation.

But the overhaul in advertising for Secret and Herbal Essences was primarily in the marketing pitch. The company hadn't radically overhauled the products, and neither of them was a new brand. With Swiffer, P&G was starting from scratch to create an all-new product and an all-new brand for the home, an environment that had changed dramatically during the past 50 years.

For centuries, the home was the center of a woman's world. Keeping that home clean was often tied to a woman's perceived success as a wife and mother. But as more women began entering the workforce, the home as a woman's sole domain began to break down and reform. The home was no longer the center of a woman's world. It was just one of several centers that needed taking care of. Many companies jumped at the opportunity to help working women with the task of keeping house. Timesaving products became all the rage—from the first electric washing machines to today's Roomba robotic vacuums. They helped the stereotypical stressed-out mother/career woman who had lost all interest in having a clean, tidy home define her.

As P&G created the Swiffer and its advertising, the company began delving into women's issues with housework. By doing so, company executives uncovered something interesting about women and what they thought about housework. Underneath all the research about stressed-out women who had no time or even inclination to clean, P&G discovered that many women still took pride in a clean home. Indeed, creating a clean, comfortable home was still something that defined a woman—no matter how far up the corporate ladder she had climbed. The home, especially a clean home, was still an important part of that traditional role of being the emotional center of their family. What these women wanted—if they weren't wealthy enough to hire a housecleaner—was to be liberated from setting aside an entire day for cleaning that often included getting down on hands and knees to scrub floors. For them, housework was still drudgery, and it was made even more onerous because it was squeezed between everything else that needed to be taken care of around the home. What they wanted were tools that would help them clean when they wanted to clean and tools that worked better than old standbys, such as a broom and dustpan. "That clean end-state, as we call it, was really desired, but there was simply less time to get there in today's world," Decker says, flanked by the Swiffer line extensions in a conference room at P&G's headquarters in Cincinnati. "We asked women what was frustrating about the task today. What we found was that the desire for a clean house hasn't changed for women. What's frustrating was finding the products that would actually get you to that end-state. There was a lot of frustration that the old broom and dustpan weren't really great solutions. You were just pushing dirt up and around. That insight opened a huge category for us."

That insight would become the driving force behind Swiffer and the creation of the "quick-clean" category. The new category, a new brand, and a new product would require P&G to change many things—from the way it created products to how quickly it rolled out line extensions. This new consumer demand from women—a product that was easy to use but effectively cleaned a house—would force a company known for test marketing products for years to move faster and be far more innovative than ever before. It also required a new approach to advertising and promotion that would stretch the company's once-traditional marketing teams. Yet by acutely understanding what women are keeping (and discarding) from the past as they somersault into new roles, P&G has been able to stay the course with Swiffer through five years of line extensions and evolving ad campaigns to create a $500 million brand. It found a way through the landmines of gender somersaulting by helping women strike a balance between the past and present.

P&G also discovered new opportunities—such as the Swiffer Sweep+Vac and its crumb-conquering man in the ad campaigns—by marrying the traditions of the past with the constantly shifting roles of the present and future. P&G's insight into the importance of a clean home to women—despite how far women have moved from the days of scrubbing floors on hands and knees—gave it the crucial edge over the past "time-saving" innovations that looked at women's lives too simplistically.

Using Innovation to Get to the "End-State"

When Swiffer appeared on store shelves in 1999, it was the first outward sign of a major change inside P&G. The company was known for its ability to nurse along big brands to billions of dollars in sales. The stolid midwestern company was known far less for its innovation. When Swiffer was introduced, it had been more than 15 years since the company had created a new product line. The company's new CEO, Durk Jager, was intent on ramping up the company's innovation quotient.[17] Swiffer was one of the first products created under several of Jager's programs designed to spark innovation. Corporate New Ventures, which brought together disparate groups inside the company to create new brands or products, gave Swiffer its electrostatic cloths that attracted dust and hair like a magnet. They had been created by collaboration between the company's paper division and its cleaning-agent scientists.[18] For later line extensions, Swiffer would use another innovation driver promoted by Jager—licensing outside inventions—to create the Swiffer Duster and the Swiffer Sweep+Vac. The duster line extension resembles a feather duster that uses an electrostatic cloth created by a Japanese company. The Sweep+Vac used vacuums made by Dirt Devil's parent company.

Swiffer, however, had to be more than a sterling symbol of internal innovation. Swiffer had to perform for customers. "It's not so easy to create a product that really gets to that end-state, to that gold standard that comes from getting down on your hands and knees and putting some elbow grease into it," Decker says. "We had to have a solution that got you there or was even better, or it wasn't worth doing. It couldn't be that 'Calgon, take me away' idea, where you are trying to relax while you still know the house is a mess." If Swiffer only helped women do housework faster, but not better, than the old broom and dustpan method, it wouldn't really achieve what consumers requested of the Swiffer team. Timesaving devices were fine, they said, but too often they found that in saving time they gave up too much in terms of real cleaning. For many companies, the tried-and-true approach was to find ways to make women's lives easier or help them calm down. Marketing experts talked a great deal about how busy women were and how they craved timesaving devices.

But very few companies had gone deeper to understand that even as women moved into new roles in society—from heads of companies to heads of households—they still found meaning in (and, in fact, craved) some of the traditions and trappings of their old roles. "There are things you hear on the surface, and then you have to dig deeper with consumers to look at what's below the surface," Decker says. "For us it was listening to women talk about what they learned from their mothers and grandmothers. There's a lot to be captured in there. Women felt like they were doing a good job, being good moms, if they scrubbed their floors. You won't feel okay just giving up on that, because it means that you aren't investing something in your family. I think many things get de-prioritized in the busy lives we lead, but the home is pretty stable, at least from what I've experienced and heard from women. Home is a haven, whether it's creating a nice place for yourself and your friends or for your family. We can relax on some things, but home is still pretty important."

Home as haven certainly was a growing trend as Swiffer was making its entrance. *Home Comforts: The Art and Science of Keeping House*, an 800-page "bible" on how to keep and care for a home, became a surprise best-seller in 2002.[19] Caldrea, a line of expensive soap and detergents with scents like lavender pine and citrus mint ylang ylang, had taken their place alongside old standbys such as Tide and Comet. Caldrea sells its wares at retail, but also through a Web site where the company pitches itself as "the spirit of keeping home." Target stores had launched a private-label version of home and laundry cleaning products called Method that were far more than cheap versions of existing cleaners. In fact, they were highly concentrated versions of laundry detergent and dishwashing liquid in packaging that was more artful and decorative than longstanding brands. The rise of home-improvement shows such as *Trading Spaces* and *Clean Sweep* also supported the belief that people could feel far more comfortable in their homes if they'd just renovate them and clean them up a bit.

It was clear to Decker and the rest of the Swiffer team that the product had to effectively get women to that "end-state," a clean home, or it wouldn't be a successful product. "The burden of proof lies with us to show that we can clean just as effectively as the old ways," Decker said. On the product side, P&G's engineers created a swiveling head that could move in any direction and be pushed into tight spaces, such as behind a toilet. The company's scientists also pushed to make the electrostatic cloths as clingy as possible—to the point that they could pick up pollen and pet dander—dirt that even a wet mopping might not get up off the floor. The cloths are bright white, so they show off the dirt they pick up. "There has to be evidence in the sheet. You have to be able to look at it and know it performed," Decker says. She adds that in consumer discussions the team found that women would use the Swiffer even after they used a broom and dustpan just to see how much the Swiffer picked up. "They'd say, 'Wow! I didn't know there was that much left on the floor,'" she says. She added that the company had to design a product in which consumers didn't give up anything, from ease of use to the desired "end-state" to easy disposability. After each launch of a line extension, Decker says the company goes back to consumers to uncover new ideas. "You have to listen after launch," she says.

When P&G's product developers were certain the product would perform, the marketers moved forward with the advertising campaign. The advertising would be the first opportunity that P&G had to explain to women that housework would be different with a Swiffer. But they also needed to change how women thought about housework. The marketing team knew it had to go beyond the hackneyed "timesaver" tools that were driven by the image of the overworked, stressed-out moms that had become so acceptable in popular culture. Women had to view the Swiffer as more than a simple replacement for the broom and dustpan. What if P&G could actually make housework look fun even as it showed off how well the Swiffer worked? So when P&G launched Swiffer in late 1999, there was no hint of drudgery, no stressed-out mothers, or even a discussion of how much time it would save. Instead, the first ad featured soldiers cleaning up their barracks, making the point loud and clear that the Swiffer could stand up to the spit-and-polish reputation of the armed services. In just three months, Swiffer grabbed 25 percent of the mop and broom market.[20]

That was just the beginning of successive waves of Swiffer products designed to clean everything better and a constantly evolving advertising campaign bent on shifting housecleaning from drudgery to "Swiffering." P&G knew it couldn't stand still with Swiffer. Competitors were starting to come out with their copycat products. Moreover, Swiffer had caught the attention of the company's new CEO, A.G. Lafley, who had taken over in June 2000. Jager was asked to resign after just 17 months on the job when earnings stagnated and the company posted significant market share drops in big brands like Bounty paper towels. Although Lafley was determined to focus on the company's top 10 global brands, which accounted for nearly half of the company's $40 billion in revenues, he was in search of the next $1 billion brand. "In addition to driving today's billion-dollar brands, we need to create the billion-dollar brands of the future," he said a month after his promotion to the chief executive suite.[21]

He also was a huge proponent of listening to consumers. One of his favorite clichés, still heard around P&G's hallways on a daily basis, is "The consumer is boss." Indeed, the biggest driver of continued innovation on the Swiffer brand was P&G's ongoing insight into Decker's consumers and their desired "end-state." "Women kept telling us that they didn't have time to carve out a section of the weekend to clean. They wanted cleaning to fit into their everyday lives," Decker says. "If we could figure out how to do that, while giving them a great experience and maybe make it a little fun in the process, we would have tackled this task head-on." It was one thing to do a simple dust of the floor with the Swiffer, but that still left dusting furniture, mopping floors, and vacuuming. In quick succession, P&G launched several more products to take on each of those tasks. None were revolutionary, but all of them dug a little deeper into the consumer psyche. "The quick-clean category was revolutionary. It didn't exist before the late 1990s," Decker says. "But now was the time to dig deeper into the subtle insights of what a consumer wants. The challenge is for us to listen for those opportunities and be agile enough to address them. Sometimes the challenge is knowing that something isn't going to be revolutionary. We don't have to invent something new, but we can find ways to really help consumers. Sometimes people are at a breaking point, but they aren't aching for something revolutionary."

Such was the inspiration for the Swiffer WetJet, the first major line extension for the brand. Launched in May 2001, P&G dubbed the device the "bucketless mop." It paired Swiffer's swiveling head with cleaning solutions and super-absorbent Swiffer pads—technology adapted from the company's feminine products business. The WetJet went several steps toward ending the quest for a better way to mop that didn't involve lugging around a bucket of dirty water and a slimy-headed mop. Consumers simply popped premixed cleaners—including one designed specifically for wood floors as they became more and more popular—into the device and started "Swiffering." "The WetJet was really an understanding of where women were at today," Decker said. P&G knew that mopping was such a burdensome task that most people left the chore to a day when they had time to do all the floors in the house. While mopping was frustrating to a busy mother, it was still a task she was willing to do, because it was still important to her traditional side. To the Swiffer team, there was deep insight in this idea of traditional needs linked to the new needs of busy moms. If they could figure out a way to make mopping easier and faster, women may actually do it more often—meaning P&G would sell more WetJet materials—and help women keep their houses clean without giving up an entire day to the duty. "I 'WetJet' every night instead of being frustrated all week with a dirty floor and then hoping I have enough time on Saturday to clean," Decker says.

Even as Swiffer was changing how often and even the way in which women did housework, it also pushed forward with the idea of changing how women thought about housework. By the time WetJet hit the market, the Swiffer brand already had picked up steam as a pop culture item— something unheard of for a P&G brand. No one had ever said they were going to "Tide" to mean they were doing laundry. But "Swiffering" had entered the slang lexicon almost immediately. Word had gone around P&G headquarters that Swiffer was receiving unsolicited endorsements from the likes of Rosie Perez and Ellen DeGeneres—celebrities few would have thought knew about Swiffer, let alone cleaned their own floors. Through those endorsements, Swiffer was getting a reputation for actually being fun to use, an attribute the Swiffer brand team had been hoping for when it launched its "barracks" ads. As *Business 2.0* writer Nancy Einhart wrote in March 2003, "to thousands of neat freaks, though, (the Swiffer) has become an object of near-fanatical devotion. Type 'I love Swiffer' into Google and you'll understand."

While P&G had very little to do with those early endorsements, Decker decided that the team could capitalize on the Swiffer's cult status. Such endorsements were a new marketing idea for P&G, which had traditionally spent heavily on national television, a holdover from when it helped to create the modern soap opera. But Decker believed it would be far more effective to focus on pop culture, fashion magazines, and movies—the places most women turned to for information about what was hot or not. "We couldn't keep doing what we were doing and stay true to the spirit of the brand," she says. "We'd revolutionized a category, so why not revolutionize how we connected with our customers? There was this cool underground thing happening with Swiffer, so why not go with it? There's a lot of risk in that, but we had permission to do something different from consumers because they loved this brand." That led to a string of endorsements from celebrities, link-ups with *Trading Spaces* favorite designers, such as Genevieve Gorder, who had a new show, *Town Haul,* in 2005, and a tie-in with the movie *Maid in Manhattan,* starring Jennifer Lopez. P&G also moved into direct-response television ads, launching the WetJet on the QVC home-shopping network and using customer testimonials in a string of ads.

Such pop status helped the company and ad agency Kaplan Thaler Group, hired in 2002, move forward on an ad campaign that went even further than the previous Swiffer work. The new ads, which began in early 2003, broke ground in the housecleaning category and broke ground for P&G, which had never been known for its advertising creativity. The ads featured a housewife dancing to the Devo song "Whip It" as she "Swiffered" her floors. But there was another twist in some versions of the ads that spoke far more to women than the '80s throwback music. The woman who was cleaning the house was a guest, not the woman of the house, leaving the impression that "Swiffering" was so much fun that women would do it even when they didn't have to. P&G had successfully moved housework from the drudgery of the traditional housewife to a core tool for today's women, who somersaulted between the roles of the past and present. Housework, or "Swiffering," had become just another part of the day instead of a day-long chore. The advertising was yet another effective use of the company's insight into women. It didn't stick with the tried-and-true permutations of the past, in which women groaned about having just cleaned the floor when their husbands, children, or pets tracked mud on the clean white linoleum. It didn't show Stepford wife scenarios with women presiding over perfect houses. It stayed away from timesaver pitches. Instead P&G made housework, or "Swiffering," fun.

Even as sales of Swiffer and its various line extensions swiftly rose past the $500 million mark in 2003, P&G wasn't ready to stop experimenting. It had one more line extension to come that would neatly close the loop on the gender somersault that P&G had followed as it promoted Swiffer as a tool that served both the traditional and the modern sides of women. In September 2004, P&G launched the Sweep+Vac, an ungainly looking gadget that paired an original Swiffer with a small vacuum mounted on the handle. The product innovation was in the vacuum, which P&G bought from the maker of Dirt Devil vacuums. The added oomph of the vacuum means consumers "really can throw the dustpan and broom out the door," Decker says, because the vacuum action eliminates the "dustpan line," the never-disappearing line of dust and dirt that's always left over after sweeping. The extension solved a need many consumers in focus groups said the Swiffer never effectively managed—picking up bigger pieces of dirt, not just the dust that Swiffer's electrostatically charged cloths did such a good job on. By turning on the vacuum, the housecleaner—male or female—could simply suck up that line and those pesky bigger particles, while the original Swiffer cloth picks up dust and tiny particles as always.

While the product innovations on Sweep+Vac again met consumer needs, P&G knew it needed to take yet another step with its advertising campaign. This time it would tackle head-on yet another aspect of gender somersaulting—men stepping into roles once dominated by women. In the advertising to introduce the Sweep+Vac, men were finally brought into the kitchen, giving Swiffer a whole new world of consumers to explore. "We heard from women that their husbands and kids loved Swiffers," Decker says. "We weren't just helping her out, but we were also helping the family out."

The insight that husbands and children would actually be interested in housework if it were fun may not seem like a huge leap in consumer insight. But it helped take P&G further into the exploration of gender somersaulting. Decker pointed out that often women hold on to certain tasks inside the home—either from a belief that no one could do it better or from the need to retain control of the home. As men moved into the world of housework, either as stay-at-home dads or as they became more equal partners in housework, P&G's Swiffer made housecleaning a no-brainer. "Swiffering" was something that a woman could actually feel comfortable leaving in the hands of men or children. "The good thing about Swiffer is that you can do it right regardless of whether you're a man or a child, so housework can become a shared task," Decker says. By showing a man, especially a man deliberately making a mess and then cleaning it up, P&G had come full circle to the present and possibly even the future. As women move back and forth between their traditional and modern roles, they may find themselves willingly (or not) giving up some of the tasks they have held on to, especially if they know someone else can step into that traditional role effectively.

The only way, Decker says, that P&G will continue to uncover these small bits of wisdom is by staying in touch with consumers at all levels of the business. "You can't allow your biases to play a part in the creation of the products and advertising you create for them," she says. "You can't go into a focus group and expect to hear confirmation of your idea, or you shouldn't expect to hear what your problems are either." Those are revolutionary ideas inside a company that for decades created products from the inside out with little input from consumers until they showed up in traditional focus groups or lived in one of the company's famously "middle-class" test cities like Provo, Utah. Yet as women have become more powerful as well as radically changed consumers, P&G has found it must create products from the outside in, listening to consumers—especially women—as they move through their quickly changing lives. "What you can do is put the consumer in the middle and then listen to them from all different perspectives," Decker says. "That's the only way we'll keep anticipating our consumers, because we do know one thing: tomorrow's world won't look anything like today's world."

Key Observations

◆ Use in-depth conversations with women to arrive at the "truth" about how they feel about their traditional roles in the home. This strategy was used to shift housecleaning from drudgery to "Swiffering."

◆ Use that "truth" to create products that are not only fast, but also effective, and that bridge the divide between women's traditional and modern roles.

◆ Create advertising that breaks from the tradition of housecleaning as drudgery by making cleaning house fun—even for men.

◆ Continue to address women's evolving needs through new products that attack each area of housecleaning.

P&G found a way to incorporate important traditions from the past to create a cleaning product that made sense for the women of today. In the next chapter, two industries explore the deep feelings women have about marriage and money and how those emotions are changing the way women perceive the industries' products and services.

CHAPTER 4

Diamonds and Dollars

HOW TWO INDUSTRIES SHATTERED THE MYTH OF THE WHITE KNIGHT

*A*s women struggled to balance the *traditions of the past with their new roles in society, two industries created advertising, products, and services that tackled the balancing act head-on with a mixture of humor and insight.*

For more than a decade, the Diamond Trading Co.—the marketing arm of the DeBeers Group—used a single advertising campaign that linked diamonds with love and devotion to sell billions of dollars of the glittering jewels. By 2004, the ads had evolved into tiny, yet poignant, films that offered a romantic view of love and marriage.

For example, in an ad created for its three-stone anniversary rings that debuted in November 2004, a mid-30s couple plays around a fountain outside a museum. He says he would marry her all over, right now, with all the people on the steps as witnesses. She laughs, thinking nothing of it until she looks over to see her mother standing up and her father putting down a newspaper. Other friends and family stand up to witness him bending down on one knee and slipping a three-stone ring on her finger.

A young woman looks on longingly as they kiss. In a second ad, a couple celebrates their wedding anniversary in Venice. In the middle of San Marco Square, he begins to yell, "I love this woman!", scaring pigeons and embarrassing her. To calm her down, he pulls out a three-stone ring and slips it on her finger. She says several times in a sultry, husky voice, "I love this man."[1]

All the ads throughout the years followed two primary rules. First, men gave diamonds; women received them. Second, the ads drove home the traditions of love, romance, and marriage with such a compelling force that they drowned out the real world, a world grappling with revolutions in love and marriage. In the real world, at least 40 percent of marriages ended in divorce; more people were cohabiting, living together without marriage and the requisite rings; and more people, especially women, were choosing to stay single as they gained more and more economic power. As author and professor Laura Kipnis wrote in an op-ed piece in *The New York Times* in January 2004: "The increasing economic self-sufficiency of women has certainly been a factor in declining marriage rates. There is nothing like a checking account to decrease someone's willingness to be pushed into marriage or stay in a bad one." [2]

The 2000 U.S. Census supported such opinions, highlighting the significant leaps women had made in education and employment in the preceding decade. Those leaps—the sharp rise in salaries after a period of stagnation in the 1980s and higher college graduation rates—also had links to shifts in marital trends the Census tracked. The Census supported what many sociologists and futurists had been discussing for years: marriage was in a state of flux. The Census's own researchers wrote: "A reflection of the changing life styles is mirrored in the Census 2000's enumeration of 5.5 million couples who were living together but who were not married, up from 3.2 million in 1990."[3] In a Current Population Report issued by the U.S. Census in February 2002, another statistic stuck out as a sign that marriage trends were shifting dramatically. The report found that almost a quarter of women, 23.6 percent, aged 15 (the age at which the Census begins tracking marriage rates for men and women, which served to skew the statistic) and older had never been married.[4]

By 2002, such real-world issues had become topics of conversation among executives at JWT, formerly known as J. Walter Thompson. This advertising agency operated the marketing council and served as DeBeers' ad agency in the U.S. and other parts of the world. It had created the romantic traditional ads for the Diamond Trading Company.[5] "We were hearing from women that they loved our products and they loved to wear diamonds, but they didn't feel that we were talking to them," says Claudia Rose, a strategic planner for the DeBeers account, from her elegantly decorated office in midtown Manhattan.[6] "They felt excluded from the product because of the messages of love. They would tell us, 'We feel empowered and entitled today, and while those messages of love may be beautiful, they aren't necessarily for me right now.'"

As concern mounted in 2002 over the effect these trends could have on the $29 billion diamond industry, Rose and a team of men and women from backgrounds as diverse as ring design and ad copywriting took that consumer insight and created not only a new advertising campaign, but a whole new category of diamond rings expressly for those empowered women to buy for themselves—instead of having men buy them. In the summer of 2003, ads for "right-hand" rings appeared in the pages of *Vogue* and *Vanity Fair*. They were designed to appeal to women in their mid-30s to early 50s who made upwards of $100,000 a year.[7] They featured sexy, striking women, many sporting muscles and leather jackets, their right hands glowing with a diamond light. The copy of one ad reads: "Your left hand declares your commitment. Your right hand is a declaration of independence. Your left hand lives for love. Your right hand lives for the moment. Your left hand wants to be held. Your right hand wants to be held high. Women of the world, raise your right hand."

The balancing act so deftly captured in the ads' copy spotlighted the tension and struggle that exist inside women as they continue to balance the traditions of the past with the realities of the present. Indeed, so compelling was this balancing act as a trend affecting women that other industries, notably the financial industry, were beginning to underscore the struggle to balance the old and the new in women's roles in their advertising and marketing.

Citigroup's newly created Women and Company unit launched an ad campaign that cut through the clutter of financial advertising by taking a humorous approach to financial planning for women. The ads poked fun at the traditional ideal of a woman holding out for a rich man as a way to take care of her financial future. Women and Company also chose an unlikely place to air its financial ads. Instead of buying space in the business section of newspapers, Women and Company bought space amidst the *New York Times'* wedding announcements. An ad that appeared in the newspaper on October 3, 2003, featured a layout that mimicked the real wedding announcements on the same page—down to the photo of the smiling couple. The photo featured Joanna Mills and Rex Rover. But Rex wasn't a bridegroom. He wasn't even a man. He was Joanna's golden retriever. The tongue-in-cheek nature of the photograph was continued in the ad's copy: "Joanna Mills was not married this week and doesn't have any plans to do so in the immediate future." Read further, and the pointed reference to women's traditional views of marriage and financial stability becomes even clearer. "Realizing that she'd be happy to marry a normal guy, much less a rich one, she decided that it might be time to review her current investment strategy."

Something Old, Something New

These companies in the diamond and financial industries had stepped directly into the nexus of the turmoil women are experiencing as they try to balance the past with the present. Even as women have gained historic levels of financial freedom and social power in the past 50 years, they still struggle to balance the traditions of the past with a present that offers them more choices, but also many more responsibilities.

The strategies of DeBeers, Women and Company, and several other financial firms shed light on a deep and difficult transition women are going through. It extends far beyond balancing the desire for the traditions of wifehood, like a clean house, with a high-powered life outside the home, as Procter & Gamble focused on with the creation of the Swiffer. This balancing act goes to the heart of how much women are willing to give up for their economic freedom and how much of the past they want to hold on to.

"Many of us have been brought up with the fairy tale of the white knight saving the princess," says Susan M. Cooper, executive vice president and branch manager of AXA Advisors LLC, the broker/dealer and investor advisor for AXA Financial Inc. AXA Financial began targeting women consumers more aggressively in 2004. "We still think that someone is going to come along who will save us. But we are finding that, in reality, we are truly responsible for our financial futures. Women are coming of age when it comes to money. We are recognizing that this new future holds both great opportunity and great responsibility."[8]

The experiences of DeBeers, AXA Financial, and Citigroup offer stark illustrations of how companies are adapting to the changes that have taken place in women's social and economic status and the emotional challenges that confront women because of those changes. Many industries will have to understand and explore these transformations in the coming decades as the social and economic trends sparked in the 1950s and 1960s continue to reshape the landscape of women's lives and thus the landscape of society.

As noted in other chapters, these changes have been significant. Sixty years ago, only 8 percent of Americans lived alone. Fifty years ago, 80 percent of Americans lived in the traditional "nuclear" family. Sixty years ago, 29 percent of adult women worked. Today, 60 percent of women are in the workforce and a growing number of them are choosing to stay single and live alone. Those changes in women's economic and social status certainly have provided them with many choices and opportunities that once were off-limits, both economically and socially. Yet the traditions of and ties to the roles that once defined women rigidly as wives and mothers remain with the women of today.

It's the pull of these traditions coupled with the new realities of women's lives that DeBeers, Women and Company, and other companies were beginning to tap into with far greater frequency by 2003. These companies had learned that it is no longer enough to know that women are their most important consumers with lots of money to spend. It's no longer enough to know that women influence 80 percent of buying decisions, an acknowledgment that often passed for understanding the women's market in the past 20 years. The future requires a deeper understanding of how the trends in women's social and economic status will continue to transform women and the world around them for decades to come. Such understanding can lead to some radical departures from the conventional wisdom on how to attract women to a brand or product—as the diamond and financial industries have found.

"Our industry was absolutely missing the boat," says David Bennett, founder of WomensWallStreet.com, an Internet financial portal. "There's been this huge disconnect between knowing that women are an economic powerhouse in this industry and what women needed from the industry. It's not enough to look at the macro issues. You have to look at the micro issues that affect that specific group of people. Women are outliving men. There's a massive transition of wealth from men to women, so what do they want from us now?"[9]

Balancing the Left Hand with the Right Hand

Nowhere has the struggle to straddle the past and the future of women's roles been more marked than in the marketing of diamonds. Since DeBeers pioneered the marketing of diamonds for engagement and wedding rings in the early 20th century, the sparkling jewels have become the quintessential symbol of love and devotion. The giving of a diamond—especially in the form of an engagement ring—brings with it all the centuries-old traditions of courtship. "It hearkens back to those days when a guy would show up with his two goats and mules and the father would say, 'You look fairly successful; you can marry my daughter,'" says Fred Cuellar, president of Diamond Cutters International, who has written several books on diamonds and courtship.[10]

The focus on tradition has been a consistent and valuable source of sales for the diamond industry for decades. So as JWT's team began working on the "right-hand" rings in 2002, it faced a very tricky situation. How could it create products and marketing that would connect with women who might never marry without turning off women who wanted that engagement ring after years of being wooed by the company's ad campaign?

Indeed, those women may be one and the same: women who don't receive a marriage proposal but still hold out hope that the fairy tale in the DeBeers' ads will come true for them one day. Certainly, while the statistics on the falling rates in marriage were compelling, other data suggested that marriage remained an essential part of American life. Indeed, in the same report that noted the unmarried status of women (somewhat skewed because of the young age at which the Census began counting unmarried women), the researchers estimated that, for the foreseeable future, 90 percent of Americans will marry sometime during their lives. How could the DeBeers team balance those seemingly competing trends of marriage and singlehood?

Rose went back to some research that she had conducted in 1999 when she was part of the Intuition Group, a unit created by JWT to conduct research on marketing to women more effectively. One of its most successful campaigns was for Clairol Nice and Easy hair color, in which the team bucked conventional wisdom that said women didn't want anyone to know they colored their hair.[11] The Intuition Group made coloring hair fun and silly in an advertising campaign featuring Julia Louis-Dreyfus, who played Elaine on *Seinfeld*, running around New York coloring women's hair on buses and street corners. "We spent a lot of time looking at how women's power was changing them and the culture as they acquired more and more income," Rose says. "When I came to this new assignment, my head was full of this research."

But for the sticky "balancing act" she faced on the diamond campaign, Rose needed to dig even deeper under the surface of how women's growing income and spending power were affecting their feelings about love and marriage. In research for the new "right-hand" rings, the team asked questions about how this new economic power played out in connection with the traditions of the past. "We talked to women about this dual idea of the diamond purchase. On the one hand you had what we called 'self purchase,' where women treated themselves to diamonds. Then you had the 'gifts of love,'" Rose says. "What we found was fascinating. It wasn't an 'either/or' situation. Women would say 'I wear a diamond to honor myself, but I also adore it when my boyfriend or husband gives me one.' They are both equally important." Rose dug a bit deeper. "We asked if they had to choose between one, which one would they give up? The answer was fascinating. Most of them said they wouldn't want to make that choice," she says.

Using that duality to drive the team's strategy, the group moved forward with ideas for a new diamond ring. Unlike past efforts to market diamonds directly to women—usually in the form of diamond stud earrings or subtle necklaces—the team decided to take a risk and focus on the hands. "It was the last bastion of diamond traditionalism," Rose says. "A ring really means something to women." Although there had been a grow-ing trend of women buying jewelry for themselves, very rarely did they buy rings for themselves. "By the late 1990s, I had many women coming in say-ing I'm not going to wait for a man to buy me some jewelry," Cuellar says. But rarely did a woman ask him to design a diamond ring for herself—no matter what hand she would wear it on. "There is still this amazing respect for 'the diamond ring,'" he says.

But a subtle shift had been happening inside women, Rose says. Women increasingly didn't have a problem with the idea of buying jewelry for them-selves, and they didn't even have a problem considering a diamond, she says. So the leap to a ring didn't seem so risky, as risky as it may have been a decade prior. Women, Rose says, seemed ready to break the taboo of putting a ring on their own finger. "Women would often say they wear the one they bought for themselves to honor what they've done. 'It's about me,'" she says. "It was patronizing to keep telling women that somebody has to buy the diamond for you." But she says women in the research groups were adamant about one thing: the rings could not in any way resemble engagement rings. In 2002, DeBeers put out the word to jewelry designers that it was looking for new designs—but they had to be dramatic, unusual, and nothing like engagement rings or even the "cocktail" rings of the past. Of the more than 300 designs that were submitted, 16 were chosen to appear on the compa-ny's Web site for other designers to replicate or use as inspiration. The final designs featured rings packed with diamonds, instead of the traditional diamond solitaire found in engagement rings. The rings also ran vertically along the finger, taking up a lot of space so that they were very noticeable. That was in direct contrast to engagement rings, which tend to run hori-zontally along the finger.

With the designs determined, the team still faced the challenge of cre-ating an advertising campaign that would strike the right balance between the past and present. Rose knew even the most elegantly designed rings would fail if they weren't marketed to both sides of a woman. "Buying dia-mond jewelry does have emotional significance for women," Rose says. "For some women, buying it means that they are acknowledging that no one else will buy jewelry for them. For others, it may mean that they'll look too assertive to their partners. It might say to their partners, 'What are you for?' No matter what, it can be complicated and scary." Instead of dismissing the emotional significance, Rose and her team told the copywriters and creative director on the account that the campaign needed to talk to a woman's desire for tradition as well as the world in which she lived today. The result was the ad campaign "Women of the World: Raise Your Right Hand." The ads, which continued to appear in magazines throughout 2005, balance the traditions encapsulated by the "left hand" with the new world embodied by the "right hand." The tagline for the ads summed up the balance: "The left hand rocks the cradle; the right hand rules the world." In fact, all the women featured in the ads also are wearing wedding bands. "We had to be as inclusive as we could be," Rose says. "As we talked to the copywriters and advertising directors, we said we need to reflect this idea that the rings don't signal anything about your marital status. They are about you and your taste. It says to the world who you are no matter what your personal situation may be." The campaign and the rings appear to have struck just the right chord with women. By November 2003, right-hand rings started showing up on the hands of Madonna and Beyonce Knowles. By 2004, right-hand rings were on sale at exclusive jewelers, as well as Wal-Mart. In 2005, the Diamond Trading Company estimated that the 15 percent rise in diamond sales during the first half of 2004 had been driven in great part by the 11 percent increase in women buying jewelry—notably right-hand rings—for themselves. It estimated that right-hand rings had become a $4 billion market.[12] JWT continued to evolve the campaign in 2005 as sales rose. The new ads featured slightly softer-looking women, but still with the balance between the past and the present deftly illustrated in the copy. One reads: "Your left hand says 'I love you.' Your right hands says 'I love me, too.'"

Shattering the Myth of the White Knight

Even as the diamond industry was giving women the sense that they could have their "white knights" on bended knee and their "empowerment" rings on their right hand, several companies in the financial industry were moving quickly to shatter the myth of the white knight with a mix of humor, education, and an unabashedly feminine approach in their advertising.

The approaches taken by three financial firms were in direct contrast to how the financial industry had traditionally approached its consumers—male or female. Historically, financial services firms used solemn data-laden ads or pitched investing as a competitive sport with lots of stats and "winner and loser" stocks. When a few companies began focusing on women more than 20 years ago—in response to the growing number of women consumers needing the industry's services—many simply added women to their ads and stuck with their serious tones and somber advice. So when Women and Company launched its humorous ad campaign, it was noteworthy. The campaign broke from the traditions of the industry, marking a major shift from decades-long beliefs about how financial firms should approach women. The campaign indicated that at least some in the financial industry were beginning to take note of shifts in a consumer group that will be its most important in the coming decades.

"While women control slightly more than half the wealth now, it will be a tsunami over the next 15 to 20 years," says Martha Barletta. She is the founder of marketing consultancy TrendSight and author of the book *Marketing to Women: How to Understand, Reach, and Increase Your Share of the World's Largest Market Segment.*[13] By 2000, women made up 51 percent of all stock ownership. By 2010, women will account for half of the private wealth in America—about $14 trillion dollars. That number will climb to $22 trillion by 2020 as the U.S. continues to undergo a major shift of wealth from men to women as more women make more money than their male peers, according to the Business Women's Network.[14] Women now control or influence 67 percent of household investment decisions. Forty-three percent of Americans with $500,000 or more in investable assets are women. Women control 48 percent of estates worth more than $5 million.[15] Women's philanthropy has also been on the rise. The American Association of Fundraising Counsel Trust for Philanthropy estimated that women's charitable giving had increased by more than $15 billion in 1996. Moreover, women control the vast majority of philanthropic projects because they often live longer than men and are given control of those projects after their husbands' deaths.

With the statistics piling up, it became impossible for the financial industry to ignore the influence women consumers were increasingly having on their industry. But even though many financial firms recognized the importance of the women's market, they continued to make the same mistake as many other industries and businesses when it came to the women's market. The industry still approached the women's market as a minority market instead of a majority market that earns its own money and deserves more attention. "Men feel as if they have control over their wealth because they earn it, so they express their opinions about what they want. Why wouldn't that be the same for women?" asks Vanessa Freytag, founder of W-Insight, a women's marketing research firm and a former bank executive who created some of the first women's marketing programs inside banks such as Ameritrust. "But still, companies don't realize how big this opportunity is, and moreover, they aren't armed with the knowledge of both the demographics or the psychographics of women today, so they simply don't forward."[16]

Instead of taking the time to understand where women were coming from and, even more importantly, where they were going, the industry's "marketing to women" approaches often were as simplistic as adding women to their existing ads and treating them just like the men who had made up the industry's core consumers. Indeed, many actively shied away from showing any of the obvious gender approaches that Women and Company took in 2003, claiming that women's needs were no different from men's, assuming that the mere acquisition of wealth somehow brought with it the knowledge of how to manage it.

Women may indeed have the same financial needs as men, but, as Women and Company and AXA Financial found, they bring with them very different thinking about money based on the different history they have with money and wealth. These financial firms found that many women still carried with them fears and concerns about money that came from a past and even a present in which women were too often left out of the financial dealings of their households. Women's approach to money often wasn't the product of their gender, but the product of not making enough money to understand the importance of managing it. "I think a lot of women's investment patterns in the past were based not so much on gender differences as income differences," says Martha Priddy Patterson, a director with Deloitte's Human Capital Advisory Services. "Unfortunately, for all too long, those who earn less and have less to save are females."[17]

Women's incomes still lag men's incomes, especially when the women are single and heads of households. According to the Federal Reserve's 2001 Survey of Consumer Finances, the median income earned by female heads-of-household was $20,000, compared with $39,000 for all American households. Those women also had fewer assets, with a median net worth of $27,850 compared with $86,100 for all households.[18] The wage gap persists despite the gains made by women. In 2003, on average, women earned almost $10,000 less than men, $30,724 versus $40,668. However, that is an increase of 15 percent since 1980, when women made $22,279 to a man's $37,033.[19]

These income disparities have meant that many women simply didn't have the money to invest. It wasn't that women were incapable of understanding finances because of some innate gender difference. They had never been educated in how to save, invest, and plan for their own financial futures, because it hadn't been an option or a need in the past. Moreover, as AXA Financial found, many women carried with them a "minority" mind-set, believing they didn't have sufficient knowledge or understanding of their finances or the financial world to make smart choices about investing. Yet it was clear to many of these women that as they gained more economic power they needed to shift away from such thinking. But first they needed help shaking off those traditional notions—and that's where financial companies could be of help.

By exploring and understanding the shifting psychographics of women as they move through the emotional and psychological changes that come with making their own money and acquiring more wealth, firms such as Women and Company, AXA Financial, and WomensWallStreet.com realized that it doesn't hurt to talk to women through their gender—considered patronizing by many businesses and industries after past attempts backfired—as long as the conversation resonates with where women are today. But just as important, as WomensWallStreet.com in particular has found, is that the conversation must change as women change. Over time, it learned women would become more comfortable and confident with finances and the language of the financial industry.

While there are a number of examples of financial companies that made their way through these upheavals, these three companies offer some ideas—sometimes edgy and out-there lessons that are still being tested for their success—on how to navigate through such changeable times. Each company's efforts illustrate the profound shift going on as women become the majority, not just an underserved minority, in the financial industry and how that shift will require far more thought, rigor, and attention than what the industry had previously believed it needed to commit to what it still considered a minority market.

When a Majority Still Acts Like a Minority

Despite the massive acquisition of wealth by women in the past three decades, many still lack basic knowledge about finance and banking. While tough to admit, it's understandable. Just 30 years ago, it was difficult for a woman to open a checking account or qualify for a mortgage without a man's help. Over the years, those roadblocks have been removed, and women have done a lot of growing up about money. They've learned to balance checkbooks, apply for loans, and invest in the stock market. But many women—even among younger generations who have never known a world where women didn't earn and control their own money—still have fears, worries, and behaviors that keep them from actively managing their finances. The irony is that even as women become more economically powerful than at any other time in history, many remain naive and unknowledgeable about how to effectively manage their money.

For many financial firms, this juxtaposition has posed major problems. They have grappled with how to approach what is fast becoming a majority market that still acts like a minority—meaning that the consumers still don't think of themselves as powerful or knowledgeable—without being offensive or patronizing. It was just that tug-of-war that Citigroup and AXA Financial faced as they separately began sketching out strategies to market financial services to women in the early part of this decade. Both companies faced the same questions, but they ended up approaching them with very different strategies. The questions included: How could they help women get over their fear of money without falling back on the old "we'll take care of you" approach that drove the industry during the 1980s and 1990s? How could they do more than adopt the safe position that many of their competitors had chosen, which was treating women no differently than men? Simply put, how could they use gender as a turn-on for women, instead of a turn-off, as women became the industry's most powerful consumers?

For Citigroup, answers to those questions began coming in as soon as it hired Lisa Caputo, a woman with little financial industry expertise, to run Women and Company. Caputo had been the press secretary to Hillary Clinton, and her knowledge of the problems of women and money were more personal than professional. When she left government service, Caputo had big debts from the Whitewater investigation and virtually no assets. Already in her mid-30s, she had no financial plan for how to get back on her feet, she has said in numerous press reports when Women and Company was launched in 2002.[20] That personal experience helped mold her ideas about what women would want from a financial services firm. But she knew the unit couldn't depend solely on her own instincts about how best to help women. Instead, she asked women to tell her how they felt about money.

Before opening for business, Women and Company surveyed 1,200 women across the country to gain insight that helped the unit recognize several important nuances about women and finances today. First, they learned that women do differ from men when it comes to investing, because they face different roles and events in their lives. For instance, they leave work an average of 11 years to raise children, which means they will likely have fewer funds for retirement, including smaller Social Security benefits, even if they do return to work, as many women must or want to do. They still often make less money than men, even if they continue to work through pregnancies and raising children. Yet many women face longer retirements than men because women generally live longer than men—on average, seven years longer. Such issues do put different financial pressures on women than men. To Women and Company, those issues translated into a belief that women required different approaches. "They didn't want the same financial services for men wrapped in pink," Caputo says. "They wanted something custom-tailored to their needs. Women are so busy taking responsibility for everyone else that when it comes to issues for their own personal finances, they tend to have it take a backseat in terms of caring for everyone else."[21]

The unit offers products that would never have been part of a financial company's offerings when men were the core consumer, but this doesn't make them any less valuable to the company's new core consumers—women. The products include a survivor support line, which helps women create financial plans after their spouses or partners die, child care listings, and an online nanny referral service. Critics have downplayed such offerings as tangential to investment products and far too feminine. But such perks pay tribute to the specific needs women bring with them as they move into new industries as power consumers. Moreover, these perks may end up being useful to quite a few more men in the future, just as The Home Depot found as it used some of its wisdom from the women's workshops to build programs for male (and female) urban customers who knew next to nothing about home repair. Men who focus primarily on careers may not need information about child care or nannies or the help of a financial adviser in planning for life after the death of a spouse. But as more men opt for nontraditional lives, such as staying at home with their children and relinquishing the "breadwinner" role, they too may find such tools useful.

Those same questions about gender—how much to play it up or tone it down—faced AXA Financial as it began exploring strategies to reach women in 2003. "It used to be that we didn't want our gender to separate us," Cooper says. It was part of the need to shed the traditions that had so narrowly defined women, she says. "But now we do believe that women have different needs and, more importantly, it's okay to talk about those needs instead of acting as if women had the same needs as men do. Women often will do double duty as a caregiver to both parents and children. We may be single and on our own for a big part of our lives. We may leave the workforce. We do play these roles, so we need to speak to women through these roles. We want to talk to women about the choices they are going to make as they take on these roles."

Unlike Women and Company, which operates as a separate unit inside Citigroup, AXA Financial took a company-wide approach to build the understanding inside and outside the company that women consumers were a huge, untapped market with distinct needs and wants. Dianne Smyth, a 15-year veteran with the company and one of its top-producing sales associates, was put in charge of the women's markets program. Her first order of business, unlike Citigroup, wasn't talking to consumers. It was talking to people inside her corporation. She felt it was necessary to build knowledge inside the company about the growing importance of the women's market. "We needed to develop leadership inside the company so that we would already have a female-friendly culture when we did start talking to consumers," she says.[22] Women and Company solved that problem by creating a stand-alone unit focused on women. Smyth felt she needed to have champions inside the business first. She wanted a small team that truly wanted to work with women clients, she says, instead of demanding that the entire sales force focus on the market. "Not everyone wants to work in the women's market," she said. "I wanted to make certain I had people who wanted to pursue this opportunity. They would be more successful because of that interest, and that would then draw other people to the idea." Such an internal interest was critical to making the next step of the strategy work. Smyth, working with branch manager Cooper and sales associates in the market, took a relatively inexpensive, low-key approach, creating a series of conferences designed to attack women's fears and concerns about money and investing. They were run by financial professionals truly interested in helping women—no matter their financial situation.

"We don't want more women to end up like the 60-year-old woman who stood up at one of our seminars to tell her story," Cooper said. "She had been in this loving relationship with her husband, but when he died 12 years before, she had no idea what was going on with his business. She lost the business because of debts. Now she's working in retail and is worried that she won't be able to retire." Smyth and Cooper say it's sometimes hard to believe that such things still happen, but they will continue if women don't receive an education in personal finance. They say even in younger women they still see a lot of the past playing a part in how they view money and its role in their lives. "We still see this struggle to depend less on themselves and depend more on the fairy tale of the white knight," Cooper says. "We teach them that money and love may not have any connection. We discuss the two fairy tales we have so often believed in. First is the fairy tale that a man will give you the life you've always wanted to live, and second, that if he does that, then it means he loves you."

While some in the financial industry maintain that such a feminized approach is unnecessary, Smyth and Cooper believe that addressing these issues head-on helps set a tone of comfort and confidence with women. But it doesn't mean that they offer women different products than they do men; they simply package them differently. "We do believe that you speak to women differently about finances and money," Cooper says. "But when we look at the products we have to offer them, I don't necessarily think in gender. I think more like a doctor looking for a specific prescription. We can pull different products and services off the shelf for each woman's specific needs."

Women and Company has taken a different approach to how it packages its financial products. It offers women access to its products through a fee-based system, instead of the traditional "asset" model, in which brokers take a percentage of the customer's assets as their fee. For $125 a year, users have access to all the Women and Company services, from nanny referral to financial advice from Salomon Smith Barney brokers to tax advice from accountants from Ernst & Young. Women and Company doesn't even require members to have a Citigroup account, a traditional practice for most financial firms, which require significant assets be placed with them before customers get personal attention from a financial adviser. The unit's more open system is an important difference given that many women don't yet have the salaries or savings that will get them the kind of attention they may need. A 2003 survey by the National Association of Investors Corp. revealed major differences between men and women when it came to investing. But again, the differences weren't driven by innate gender differences. They were driven by income differences. Women on average invested $20,100, and men invested $86,700, according to the survey. When it came to mutual fund investing, the differences were even greater. Women had just $35,200 invested in mutual funds, whereas men had $133,000.[23]

Such low levels of savings and salaries led Women and Company to take an even more pointed approach in a follow-up campaign to its "weddings" ads. In September and October 2004, it hired dozens of young women, dressed in trench coats dyed to match Women and Company's trademark green, to hand out 60,000 red coin purses in New York. Inside was a nickel, or sometimes a dollar, and a note: "Yes, we're giving money away, which is what you're doing each day that you don't plan for your financial future."

This understanding of the nuances—the fears and hopes that women continue to have about money—has helped set Women and Company and AXA Financial apart from both traditional and nontraditional players in the financial industry. The more "gendered" approaches have their critics.

But both companies say their decisions are based on listening to what real women consumers told them was missing from how the financial community spoke to women. So far, the approach seems to be working. AXA Financial says it hosted hundreds of women at its conferences in 2004 and is planning yet another slate of them for 2005. Women and Company doesn't release statistics on how many accounts it has signed up, and it declined to discuss the company strategy beyond what has been written about the unit in the press or can be found on the unit's Web site. But in a sign that the strategies are working, competitors and other firms involved in the financial industry are following these companies' examples. The April 2005 issue of *Money* revealed an $8.5 million redesign created to appeal to a much broader market than its traditional "get-rich investment guide aimed largely at men."[24] Merrill Lynch has created a Women's Business Development unit. American Express now offers seminars called "Strong Women, Powerful Financial Strategy." Other financial firms are broadening their product and marketing strategies to appeal to more than just the high-net-worth women many of them have focused on in the past. For example, KeyBank has launched a Key4Women program to help women who want to start their own businesses. According to the company's marketing, it offers access to capital, education, and networking. These companies, like AXA and Women and Company, are finally noticing that women—no matter their financial situation—are far more involved in decisions about money than ever before, but bring with them specific and often different needs than men.

Indeed, such gendered approaches may have to change, says AXA's Smyth, as women continue to change. "Our hope is that we'll be so successful that this women's initiative will go away because we won't need to talk about these issues anymore because women will be very adept at handling their finances," she says. That shift is likely to happen as more women take control of their finances and become comfortable with their position of economic power. But even as women gain more confidence with money and finances, that doesn't mean they won't want their financial tools packaged in ways that speak specifically to them.

WomensWallStreet.com, a financial information Web site, found that it needed to both shift with women and remain in touch with their feminine sides on a relatively quick timeline. When WomensWallStreet.com was launched in 2003, it made no apologies for playing up the feminine and talking to women about the issues they cared about—whether it was shopping for shoes or hedge funds. "We definitely set out to have a feminine, pretty site," says Pam Little, the site's editor. "Women don't wear men's suits, so why would we want to use a Web site designed for them? We are different human beings. We do have different emotions about money. You don't have to change your product just because women enter your industry, but you can think about changing the way you talk about that product to women."[25]

The advertising-supported Web site was the brainchild of Bennett, who was a financial adviser for wealthy clients for 13 years. "I found that no matter their education levels, the women were often in the dark about many of the financial matters in their relationships," he says. "The primary barrier holding these women back? Knowledge." Bennett set out to create products and services that would give women the knowledge they needed wrapped in a package that was enjoyable and interesting. The strategy started with the Bennett's choice of a medium—the Internet. Early in its inception, the Internet was considered a male-dominated medium, but by the beginning of the 2000s, the Internet had become more than a place for tech geeks to hang out. It had morphed into a mainstream medium that was drawing huge numbers of women to thousands of Web sites every day. Today, the Internet's early domination by men has been reversed. Women now account for 60 percent of Internet users.[26]

Moreover, women use the Internet to manage their lives—from tracking their children's school activities via the Web to paying bills online. Bennett focused on how women used the Internet to help him create the Web site's content and look. "I knew from my research that men went to lots of sites; they liked to hunt around on the Internet," Bennett said. "But women went to fewer sites and spent more time on those sites that they liked. So logically, I knew it was in our best interest to create a site that had quality content that was useful, but in an entertaining, noncondescending way. Historically, financial information has been a dry and dusty subject. But we can mold it into something more entertaining. We're talking about a subject that is so important that we need to find ways to make women want to read about it." WomensWallStreet.com opted for humor, naming its columns "Stox in the City," after the HBO series *Sex and the City*; "Ask

Jane Dough"; and "Can These Finances Be Saved?", a take-off on the old magazine advice column "Can This Marriage Be Saved?". "The humor was very deliberate," Little says. "We took a look at other women's financial sites, and they weren't ones that we would frequent. I'd rather be surrounded by something that makes me feel comfortable, something that's beautiful. So much of our purchasing, especially as women, is visual. Why shouldn't a Web site for women, even if it's about finances, be visually interesting?"

For Bennett and Little, that meant creating a site that was engaging in both content and looks, a balance they agree isn't easy to attain. The daily e-mail newsletter "Daily Cents" feeds readers lot of financial information in easily digestible nuggets, in much the same way that women receive information from popular shopping and trend sites, such as Daily Candy, a site and newsletter that thousands of women depend on to find out about hot trends. "But in our case, it's not about how to spend money, but about how to save money," Little said. Little also has been willing to stretch financial site boundaries by featuring articles that appear at first to have little to do with investing—but may simply be interesting or important to their core consumers. A series called "Terror in the Skies," about one woman's harrowing plane flight, has drawn tens of thousands of visitors to the site, Little says. "No, it's not information about your 401(k), but it's absolutely about the economy and about money, because terrorism is about the economy and money."

While such features have drawn women to the site (and an increasing number of men as well, says Bennett), the site's financial content has kept them coming back with information about how to buy a home, finance a car, and set up a retirement account. By 2004, the Web site was attracting thousands of visitors a month. Increasingly, they were asking for a lot more information. "The women logging on today are far different than they were when they first logged on a few months or a year ago," Bennett says. By the middle of 2004, Bennett said he knew it was time to consider what the next iteration of WomensWallStreet.com would look like as the feedback from women users began to roll in. For example, they wanted more intermediate and advanced financial advice and a place to keep track of their investments, he says. "Based on that insight, we knew we needed to keep changing our content and functionality," Bennett says. "We found that our users were dropping off as they became intermediate investors. Women became more interested in SEC filings and more in-depth coverage of companies."

So in the first quarter of 2005, WomensWallStreet.com rolled out its redesign to meet the needs of those more intermediate investors, including shifting from the pink tones of its early site to an elegant brown and gray color scheme. New articles explored advanced investing issues, such as the benefits of short selling. It teamed up with *Investor's Business Daily*, an influential hard-core financial publication, to provide even more information on intricate financial products. The revised site allowed members to store their investment information on the site, something the early iteration didn't allow.

But in making the changes, WomensWallStreet.com didn't back away from new users or existing users who weren't ready to move on to more intense investing. It kept popular columns such as "Jargon Busters" and "Stox in the City," and it maintained much of the fun and whimsy that made the earlier site more approachable than other financial Web sites. In late January 2005, as Valentine's Day approached and the season for wedding engagements got off the ground, WomensWallStreet.com stepped into the world of diamonds. It ran a fun, but enlightening, survey about engagement rings that, much like the "right-hand" ring campaign, went straight to the heart—and the power of the purse.

The survey asked a range of questions, from whether women bought their own engagement rings—if so, click the button by "Yeah, I paid for the whole thing, and I'm proud of it"—to the traditional response of "No, I expect my man to shell out for the ring." As with so much in women's lives, the responses still reflected the struggle between the past and the present, but the present seemed to have a bit of an edge. Seventy-six percent of women said it was okay for the woman to chip in on the ring if she made more money than her prospective mate. The answer shifted a bit when the question was whether it was okay for a woman to chip in on the ring if she made less money. Only 61 percent thought that was okay.

Key Observations

◆ Explore and understand women's struggle to balance their traditional roles with new roles. DeBeers used this tactic to create advertising for its right-hand rings that didn't preclude a woman from believing she could have the best of both worlds.

◆ Address women through their gender by using humor and insight. WomensWallStreet.com and Women and Company employed humor to address critical issues that women face when it comes to their finances without appearing condescending or patronizing.

◆ Advertising is never enough. Each of these companies backed up its advertising with products and services that specifically addressed women's desires to balance the past with the present.

◆ Continually update products and services to adapt to the changing needs of women as they advance in their skill and knowledge of the industry.

The melding of the past with the present helped both the diamond and the financial industries adapt to women consumers. In the next chapter, Kodak goes back to the founding of the company to create a strategy focusing on an important traditional role for women while introducing them to a technology of the future.

CHAPTER 5

Who's Behind the Viewfinder?

HOW KODAK EMBRACED MEMORY MAKERS

K*odak went all the way back to its original mission from the 19th century to create digital cameras and photo printers to help women—once the photography industry's primary mainstream consumers—regain their traditional role as the family's social historian without neglecting the technological innovation that drove the digital camera industry.*

In 2001, Eastman Kodak Co. had to face the harsh truth. The best-known brand name in photography had become an also-ran in the digital camera industry that it had pioneered in the mid-1990s. Competitors Sony, Olympus, Canon, and Nikon had taken over as America's best-selling digital camera brands, with Sony sitting at the top of the heap. Kodak, meanwhile, often came in last in the market-share battle. All the companies were engaged in a megapixels-and-storage-space battle with marketing and product plans based primarily on attracting consumers with how much technology the competitors could pack into ever-smaller, lighter cameras.

For Kodak, the battle was becoming grindingly difficult as the new digital technology also began to eat into its traditional film and film-developing businesses, which had once been the company's main profit drivers. The company needed something to pull it out of this rut or face a future in which the Kodak brand would become a bit player in the mass-market photography industry. Its founder, George Eastman, had helped create the industry more than 100 years before when he introduced the first $1 Brownie camera.

Searching for ideas to turn around the digital camera sales slump, Pierre Schaeffer, a marketing executive in the company's digital camera unit, began digging into the company archives for inspiration. He thought some history might help him as he prepared a marketing campaign for the company's newest camera. Internally, the camera was being called the "Dock and Go" because it included a docking device that allowed users to transfer photos from their cameras to computers more easily than with previous technology.

He found inspiration, he says, in a few words uttered by Eastman that had became the company's brand promise: "You press the button; we do the rest." "I know people have a hard time believing me when I say this was nothing more than going back to the genes of the company," Schaeffer says. "But I realized how remarkably similar our challenges were to his at the turn of the last century. We were going through a similar technology trans-formation. George took the chemistry out of photography and made it into a mass-marketed product."[1]

Schaeffer believed Kodak had to take a similar leap to make digital technology less challenging for consumers—but with a twist. Kodak need-ed to give back photography to the very consumers who had helped make the brand a household name for the better part of a century: women. "Women had been autonomous in photography for decades," Schaeffer explains. "They had always been at the center of photography in a family, whether it was taking the photos, pushing for photos to be taken, having the film developed, or putting photos into albums."

With the introduction of digital cameras, much of that autonomy had been lost as camera makers set their sites on male consumers, the con-sumers they believed were the core target because of their "early adopter" status in technology. Each new generation of cameras was a further marvel of high-tech wizardry, even though the industry was maturing and becoming part of the mainstream as prices dropped and more people tried out the cameras. But instead of the industry creating technology that was easier to use, most of the companies focused on innovations that made the cameras more complex. Instead of moving toward women and the mass market, many companies were moving away from them.

Kodak's digital team knew that it could always take the safe road and keep battling against competitors with bigger megapixels and smaller cameras—touting the pixel strength of the "Dock and Go" camera over its ease of use, for instance. Or the company could take a big leap of faith based on Schaeffer's gut instinct that women really were hungry for a digital camera that put them back in the position of "chief memory officer," as he had begun referring to them.

The choice was obvious to Schaeffer. It was just a matter of time before women became a force in the industry—just as they had become important consumers in many technology categories, such as the Internet and personal computers. Digital cameras would be no exception to the rule, Schaeffer and his team believed, especially if companies like Kodak designed their products with women's needs and wants in mind. But the company also couldn't give up any of the technological advances that would keep the industry healthy—and increasingly lure more tech-savvy women to digital cameras. The outcome of that decision would be the creation of the EasyShare line, a new name for the "Dock and Go" and a new direction for the company.

It would take Kodak more than four years and corporate upheaval in the organization to have those convictions confirmed and its strategy stamped with a seal of approval as other companies began following its mass-market example. Even as it was reinventing itself in the digital camera business, Kodak would go through a tough reorganization spearheaded by chief executive Daniel Carp, who retired in 2005. He began a program to cut the company's workforce by one-quarter by 2006, down from a high of 64,000 when he took over in 2000. He also made some significant restructuring changes to focus Kodak on the digital world, including dropping the company's historically high profit margins because of price pressures in the digital camera industry.[2] Such upheaval made staying true to a breakthrough strategy difficult at times, Schaeffer says, including many "internal and external discussions and some pretty tense meetings" about whether Kodak was on the right track with its women-focused strategy.

But by late 2004 and early 2005, three achievements validated Kodak's radical departure from its competition. In the fourth quarter of 2004, the company posted a 40 percent surge in digital sales and services. The next milestone came in January 2005 at the annual conference of the consumer electronics industry. Kodak's latest iteration of the camera it launched in 2001, the EasyShare One, was named the show's "Next Big Thing," an honor that had been bestowed on wireless routers and flat-screen televisions in the past. The camera incorporated wireless technology to move photographs from the camera to computers and printers without the need to connect it via wires or cables to a computer. The swiveling viewfinder, or LCD screen, doubled as an archiving interface where users could keep track of photographs in online albums or tag them to be e-mailed.

Then, in February 2005, Kodak achieved what even Schaeffer hadn't dared to hope for in 2001. Kodak became the best-selling digital camera marketer for the first time in the company's decade-long digital history. Kodak surpassed Sony, nabbing 21.9 percent market share, according to market research firm IDC, which tracks shipments of products, not actual sales.[3] "In 2001, a lot of competitors were having a field day," Schaeffer says. "We weren't, and that forced us to rethink what Kodak wanted to be as we grew up in the digital world. We decided that ease of use and a mainstream market—meaning a focus on women—was where we needed to be."

Technology in Transformation

Kodak's decision to step away from the technology pack came against a backdrop of major shifts in the technology industry driven by a massive influx of women consumers. Conventional wisdom had held for decades that women were wholly uninterested in technology. Such "wisdom" meant that most technology products were created and marketed solely with male consumers in mind. By the start of the 21st century, such thinking was breaking under the weight of statistics that showed women were fast becoming technology's primary consumers.

In 2003, the Pew Internet & American Life Project estimated that women had become the majority users of the Internet—considered a male-dominated technology throughout much of the 1990s. The Pew research revealed that women had reached parity with men that year, with 65 percent of men and 61 percent of women in the U.S. online. The researchers noted that because women outnumbered men in the total U.S. population, women were in fact the Internet's majority users.[4] Even before the release of those numbers, there were signs that women were overtaking men in certain areas of the Net. During the 2001 Christmas holiday shopping season, the Pew Internet project noted that women had surpassed men in shopping online during the holiday season—a shift that occurred in just one year.[5] In 2000, men were still the primary online shoppers. In the intervening 12 months, the online shopping population tilted toward women. In December 2001, 31 percent of female Internet users bought gifts online this holiday season, compared to 22 percent of men, wrote the Pew researchers.

Then in 2004, the Consumer Electronics Association noted that women had finally surpassed men as the primary consumers of electronic equipment. They spent about $55 billion of the $96 billion spent on technology products, such as computers, cameras, and personal digital assistants, in 2003. The association took the extra step of noting that women were buying these products for themselves—not as gifts for the men in their lives. Other studies revealed that even when women weren't the primary buyers of the products, they were significant influencers of purchases—75 percent according to one survey—of such high-tech goods as DVDs, flat-screen televisions, and complex stereo systems.[6]

But there was more to the technology shifts than women becoming the primary consumers of the Internet and electronics. Women—notably women under 30—were being transformed by their access to and increased comfort with technology. Older generations of women often considered technology a part of their work lives or as too difficult and confusing. This was a traditional stereotype but one that may have been true in some cases given that most technology had been designed for early adopters in office settings who were already comfortable with technology. But as technology such as the Internet and cell phones became a part of everyday life, younger women were as likely as men their age to try out new technology—even if it wasn't designed with them in mind.

At the 2005 Consumer Electronics Show, where Kodak took home honors for its new camera, the industry association noted in its recent "Five Consumers to Watch" study that 30 percent of women surveyed considered themselves "early adopters" of technology. A March 2004 study by Harris Interactive and Alloy Inc., a media and marketing company focused on the youth market, offered even more evidence that women were rapidly gaining ground as technology experts.[7]

The study revealed that widely held perceptions that college women lagged behind their male counterparts when it came to technology were wrong. Instead, the study showed that men and women actually shared far more similarities than differences, challenging long-held assumptions that women were slow to adopt technology. The study found that college-age women spent 2.7 hours a week playing computer games online versus men, who spent 2.9 hours online. Women also were equally likely to own a portable video game system and use instant messaging daily. The vast majority of those surveyed—both men and women—had computers and televisions and were increasingly consumers of the broadband technology that was making Internet surfing faster and downloading of games, movies, and music easier.

That lack of gender disparity has shown up most strikingly in some of the newest Internet technologies, including instant messaging and Web logs. Instant messaging, which allows users to correspond via the Internet in real time, had quickly become the communication tool of choice for Generation Y women, ages 18 to 27, according to the Pew Internet Project's report on instant messaging, issued in September 2004. Citing statistics from ComScore, an Internet research firm, the researchers noted that women spent far more time using instant messaging than men—433 minutes versus 366 minutes.[8]

Web logs (blogs), personal online diaries, also were attracting women's attention. While men under 30 were creating the majority of blogs, more women were reading them. Pew researchers found that blog readership had risen 58 percent from 2004 to 2005 and that there was "a greater-than-average growth in blog readership among women."[9]

Gaming Becomes a Girl Thing

In November 2004, the hosts of National Public Radio's *All Things Considered* read from listeners' comments with some embarrassment. In response to a story about the launch of *Halo 2*, the second generation of a popular video game most often played on video game consoles, such as Microsoft's Xbox, a young listener had taken issue with what she considered the sexist comments of the story's author. The reporter had said in the report, "If you're looking for your husbands or sons, you might look in the room with the Xbox." The listener, a 24-year-old female gamer, suggested that the host tell their male listeners, "If you're looking for your wives and daughters, you'll find them in the room with the Xbox."

The NPR journalist could have been forgiven for not realizing that gaming—an ever-expanding $26 billion category that by 2005 encompassed everything from Microsoft's Xboxes to online computer games involving hundreds of players to games played via cell phone—was increasingly dominated by women. In just a few short years, women had gone from being virtually nonexistent as "gamers" to a majority consumer.

In contrast to the industry's macho image of violent fantasy games and scantily clad female characters, women made up 60 percent of online gamers in 2003. Many of them were women over 40, according to a survey conducted by AOL.[10] Mobile gaming, played through a cell phone handset, also had become a primarily feminine pursuit, according to the Yankee Group, a research firm that estimated that women made up 58 percent of mobile gamers in 2004.[11] Women also had moved into the still-male-dominated world of video games played on consoles, as evidenced by the NPR listener's comments. The Entertainment Software Association estimated in 2004 that women comprised one-third of video gamers who played sometimes-violent games on expensive console systems.[12]

How the sprawling gaming industry responded to the sudden demographic shift offers a snapshot of the challenge of dealing with the rapid influx of women consumers. While no one company had proven it could meet the new challenge, many were beginning to make changes as they were forced to rethink who the industry's core consumers really were beginning in 2004.

One major challenge to the industry was the shift in its belief that one size fits all when it comes to the women's market—a strategy the industry had often employed, even with its core men's market. Historically, many game makers had followed a tried-and-true strategy of creating either sports-inspired games or violent fantasy series, because those two products were sure-fire ways to lure their well-defined traditional consumer—the young male. But such a narrow focus has backfired when it comes to women as some companies have realized that the differences between women can often be as wide as those between men and women.

As statistics on women gamers began trickling in during the early 2000s, many game makers took their cues from traditional female stereotypes—instead of listening to the consumers' wants or needs—and created what became known in the industry as "pink" games. The manufacturers focused on fashion and shopping with games like *Barbie Fashion Designer* and *Sony's Magical Mystery Mall*, believing that its primary female consumers would be young girls. Most hadn't even considered older women as a possible audience for electronic games save for Electronic Arts, whose *The Sims* series had been a perennial favorite of women.

Over time, more companies offered more sophisticated versions of "pink" games that took the industry a few steps further toward the reality of what women wanted from the industry. Some sports products were based on female athletes, such as soccer star Mia Hamm.[13] In 1998, game designer Megan Gaiser created a series of games based on the Nancy Drew mystery books. When she was unable to persuade a major video game company to publish the series, she went ahead and published it through her company, Her Interactive. According to the company, it sold 1.8 million units from 2000 to 2004. Gaiser says that most games were created from what "boys like to play in their backyards. Where does that leave girls?"[14]

But as the industry was soon to discover, the "backyard" of young girls had become far more similar to the world in which young boys played. The industry found that young women were just as likely to play violent, action-packed games on their Sony Playstations as their male counterparts. For instance, action games like *Lara Croft: Tomb Raider* and *EverQuest*, in which characters battle each other and often die, had become popular with women under 30 by the early 2000s. While conventional wisdom had held that women were turned off by the violence in video games, the stereotype didn't hold water among young women. Jennifer Baumgardner, coauthor of *Manifesta: Young Women, Feminism, and the Future*, says that video games with women engaged in combat could actually be empowering, "challenging the images of women as passive targets of violence."[15] Indeed, a quick review of women gaming sites, such as gamegirl.com and womengamer.com, showed that the hard-core women gamers who frequented these sites were as interested in the newest releases of top games, such as *Halo* and *Final Fantasy*, as their fellow male gamers.

Yet even as women expressed their desire for stronger, more aggressive female characters, they were also making their specific desires known to the industry. *Lara Croft* (which became a movie series featuring actress Angelina Jolie) appealed to many women gamers because of its strong lead female character. But what didn't appeal to women were the character's proportions. Lara Croft sported a gravity-defying bust, wasp waist, and curvy hips—more in keeping with the pinup fantasies of young boys than the proportions of real women. As more women began playing the game—and expressing their dislike for her outsized proportions—the game's manufacturer, Eidos PLC, decided to bring her physical proportions more in tune with reality.[16]

Along with toning down the sex-kitten looks of video game characters, the influx of women gamers also forced a small, but growing, number of game makers to improve their storylines and create more interaction between the characters, taking a cue from *The Sims*. The game requires players to create virtual worlds and to people them with characters and political and social systems. Women, as well as a good number of men, have long been drawn to the game's intricacy and well-developed storylines. More male-dominated games, such as Microsoft's *Halo* and Square Enix's *Final Fantasy*, took some of those issues into account as they created new generations of the games.

These new rules created by and for women consumers aided two of the newest gaming venues—online and mobile phones—as they began navigating their way through the early stages of what is expected to be a booming women-driven industry. Unlike the video game industry, which focused on creating a few blockbusters every year, online and mobile gaming media aren't so constrained. They can offer thousands of games targeted at different segments of the women's market, which means they can easily target specific niches, instead of viewing women as a monolithic market. Mobile telephone service providers like BellSouth don't even need a majority of consumers to make a mobile game worth putting up on its site for users to download. "We try to get content that's going to be attractive to at least 4 percent of the user base," Tim Hill, Bell South's director of portal services, told the trade publication *Telephony*. "We want to offer content that gets us to all the little niches."[17]

Such a specialty focus is also driving Internet gaming sites. They can offer access to online versions of *Halo 2* for younger women, while a click away, older women gamers can be playing bingo. At Pogo.com, a site created by *The Sims* maker Electronic Arts, users can choose from dozens of games, including canasta, mahjong, and checkers. The company claimed 500,000 subscribers in 2004 and estimated that 75 percent of the members are women, with an average age of 35.[18] Online games also are satisfying the one need most women gamers can agree on when it comes making games for women: social interaction through the Internet. Community and interaction with others was one of the main reasons women had become such avid users of e-mail, which gave them entrée in the Internet, in such a short time. To focus more on this community aspect of gaming, more Web sites were beginning to host "massive multiplayer online games," or MMOGs, beginning in 2005. The MMOGs allowed women to become one or more characters in a game that could be played by hundreds or thousands of people around the world.

By the early 2000s, these transformations—the growing number of women buying technology products and the shift in how younger generations of women perceived and used technology—began forcing more companies to rethink how they designed products and who they designed them for. But early attempts toward the women's market were often more window dressing than truly addressing the specific needs or wants of women consumers.

In 2003, Gateway Computers lobbied to have a bubble-gum pink version of its laptop featured in the movie *Legally Blonde 2*, even though it had no plans to sell such a product.[19] Makers of personal digital assistants such as Palm and Sony offered color versions of their products, including one covered in Swarovski crystals. They offered diet and fitness software for women users because the manufacturers believed such products would appeal to their female consumers. Digital camera brands also marketed their cameras to women through more traditional routes. Olympus' Stylus Verve line, which comes in colors like silvery blue and bright orange, was a sponsor of the 2005 Fashion Week in New York.[20]

While these attempts were somewhat simplistic when it came to their understanding of the women's market, they revealed two things. One, at least companies were aware that women were increasingly important consumers of their products. Second, they revealed that companies were still attempting to reach women consumers through pretty packaging and traditional female stereotypes. They spotlighted the fact that many companies were still far away from making the kind of big changes required to truly adapt their businesses to women consumers. "Women as equals in the world of business is a recent phenomenon," says Kathy Gornik. She's a former chairwoman of the Consumer Electronics Association and chief executive of Thiel Audio, which makes high-end stereo speakers. "There's a lot of inertia when things are done in a particular way. You're talking about having to change the entire orientation and culture of a company."[21]

Finding the Woman Behind the Viewfinder

Such a culture change was exactly what Schaeffer and his colleagues at Kodak were proposing when they decided to break from the competition in 2001. While Kodak's rivals were upping the ante on megapixels, Kodak switched gears on the company's consumer strategy, beginning with the "Dock and Go."

The camera—designed in 2000 with the aid of anthropologists and social scientists who tracked how people used cameras—was designed primarily to make it far easier for users to download photos into their computers. At the time, downloading photos required cables, special software, and a few hours of configuring computers to get the camera to talk to the computer. Most consumers considered the difficulty of downloading photos a necessary evil of digital technology.[22]

But Kodak saw this as a far more serious problem—for both consumers and its own business strategy. While Sony and Olympus were content to sell cameras to make their profits, Kodak's revenues and a significant share of its profits were built on *printing* photos. It sold its photo processing and Kodak photo-quality paper to thousands of retailers around the country. It had spent millions of dollars on ad campaigns to persuade consumers that Kodak paper and film processing were integral to making superior prints.

Such revenues were under duress as digital photography took off. Kodak found that while digital camera owners were taking far more pictures than they had in the past, they were printing far fewer photographs. The reason was obvious to Kodak designers. It was simply too difficult to print photos from a digital camera. The communication between the cameras and computers had yet to reach the "plug and play" stage, where a device could be plugged into a computer and be recognized easily by the operating system. By 2001, Schaeffer believed that "not getting prints simply wasn't okay anymore" for consumers or the company. He said studies showed that the digital cameras purchased by men often went unused because the women who took the photos and organized them were frustrated over the difficulty of printing photos. "Women shouldn't have to beg somebody else to download photographs or show them how to use the camera," Schaeffer says.

The "Dock and Go" solved the problem of downloading photos by eliminating the cumbersome wires and sometimes difficult-to-use software. Users need only "dock" the camera in the device, much like the docks for personal digital assistants that had made "syncing" devices a common activity for both men and women. Then users would press a button to download images to their computer, where they could be printed or e-mailed. The docking device became such an integral part of Kodak's product strategy that three months after the first dockable cameras went on sale, Kodak decided to make its entire camera lineup "dockable." "We were betting on the fact that while women were not a big voice in this market, they were soon going to be," Schaeffer says.

Schaeffer was happy with how "Dock and Go" attacked the downloading problem. It was exactly the kind of mass-market camera he needed to address women's frustrations. He was less impressed with the internal name. "Dock and Go" didn't communicate the kind of message he knew he needed to get across to women. "We knew that men were very interested in the capturing of the photo with digital technology," he says. "But women, who really were going to be the economic force in this industry at some point soon, they were interested in sharing."

Certainly there was strong evidence that women were taking even more seriously their role as the memory makers of their families. Scrapbooking, in which women gathered photos, keepsakes, and other memorabilia to create elaborate albums, had become a multimillion-dollar industry by the early 2000s. Companies such as Creative Memories sold everything for scrapbooking, from albums to archival paper, at monthly meetings that attracted thousands of women around the country. Given how important the "sharing" aspect was for women when it came to photos, Schaeffer wanted his team and its integrated advertising and marketing agency, Eleven Inc., to brainstorm some new ideas. They could go with a more fanciful name, such as Canon used with its Elph brand, or they could go with one that was in the middle—descriptive but still more benefit-driven than "Dock and Go," says Jordan Warren, Eleven's president and chief executive officer. The one name that kept making sense was EasyShare. It said everything about the camera without being too gender-specific. But it still had the emotional element of "sharing."[23]

But a name and a product were just the first steps that Kodak would take to transform its digital camera business into the women-focused force it would become four years later. The Kodak team still needed to rip up its conventional advertising and marketing to persuade women to even consider its digital camera. It also had re-educate retailers who were used to selling digital cameras on technical differences. They needed to understand what the new women consumers would want to know when they came into their stores.

With Eleven Inc.'s help, the Kodak marketing team began tossing around ideas for marketing that would appeal to women. The team knew it needed to strike a balance between the camera's technology aspects and the emotional attributes that were so important to reaching women. "We knew many couples shopped for cameras together," Schaeffer says. "We needed to make sure that men knew we were still delivering the technical fundamentals while signaling strongly to women that this camera was for them. The little edge we would have with women in this equation was going to be the tie-breaker."

Kodak's gender balancing act was not unlike The Home Depot's when it was faced with the task of creating stores that would continue to appeal to men while attracting more women. Kodak had to make certain that its marketing strategy made the point that its technology was simple, but it wasn't stupid. There still needed to be some technical aspects so that men and the increasing numbers of tech-savvy younger women would be drawn to the cameras. As the Kodak executives and Eleven's creative team discussed their options, it became clear that focusing too much on the technical aspects wouldn't get the brand anywhere with the women they wanted to reach. Kodak's task, while akin to The Home Depot's, was far tougher and required more radical actions. That retailer already was the number one home improvement store, and women already made up close to 50 percent of its consumers. Kodak needed something striking as it tried to climb out of its last-place position and draw women—at the time a minority in the digital camera industry—to its brand.

By surveying the traditional digital camera advertising, it became clear to the marketing team that every manufacturer, including Kodak, had been following the traditional methods of camera advertising. Over the years, it had become common practice for cameras—both traditional and digital—to be shown from the front in advertising. Next to the photos were often long lists of technical specs. Digital camera ads sometimes showed a photograph, usually of a woman or a beautiful sunset of striking colors. The woman appealed to men, and the sunset was meant to imply that the camera's technology would aid the photographer in achieving similar great shots.

Kodak needed to do something far different from the traditional. The marketing agency Eleven suggested a radical idea—at least, radical for the camera industry. Why not show the back of the camera? While there wasn't much to look at on the back of a traditional camera, the same wasn't true of digital cameras. Digital cameras' large viewfinders offered the perfect frame for an idea the agency's executives had in mind. The first ad mockup Eleven created for Kodak featured a smiling blond boy shown through the EasyShare viewfinder. "The viewfinder was the glue between the technology of the camera and the emotion of taking photos," says Michael Borosky, Eleven's vice president and creative director.[24] What was compelling for Kodak was that the sole shot of the young boy spoke directly to women without screaming out that Kodak had created a camera especially for them. "We could just as easily have put a sports car in the viewfinder, and the ads would have appealed to men," Borosky says.

Using the viewfinder and its images allowed Kodak to target women specifically without playing off the stereotypes that could have easily turned off women. "I don't like to think of women through stereotypes," Schaeffer says. "Instead, we had to find out what drove our core audience when they were shopping for cameras. For years, people in technology had been saying women weren't interested in our industry because they were afraid of technology. What was far more accurate was to say that women were pragmatic. They are more result-driven, and in photography for women, the end result was the emotional element of taking photos and sharing photos."

Therefore, the EasyShare advertising—including packaging, brochures, and the look of the products online—had to almost shout that the products had been designed to address those needs, wants, and especially frustrations women had with digital cameras. "The Day One insight remained the same throughout the years," Schaeffer says. "How do we put women back in the driver's seat of the category? My idea was that we needed to be an advocate for women."

A Printer You Don't Have to Watch

The next step in Kodak's shift toward women came the next year, when it introduced a printer dock. The dock made it even simpler to print photos than the earlier EasyShare, because it took away the step of downloading photos to a computer to print them. The dock did all the work. It was an important step forward in the company's product strategy to continue addressing the frustrations that women—and most likely men—had with printing photos from a digital camera. Historically, most consumers simply dropped off their film at a processing center at their local supermarket or drugstore. "You never dealt with the infrastructure of developing," Borosky says. "Now suddenly you aren't just the photographer; you're the developer as well. You also become the technician making decisions about how best to print the photo." That kind of control was great for early adopters, who had the time and interest to figure out the intricacies of photo-developing software after they had mastered downloading photos. But for most people—men and women alike—a "chain of pain," as Schaeffer called it, kept people from doing anything with the photos they had stored on their digital cameras.

Kodak needed to create a printing system that again gave women the kind of autonomy they had with the old "drop off your film" system. "What was going to be the equivalent of dropping off the film at the local photo store?" Schaeffer says. The acid test for the printer's design team was to create a device that would print quickly and effectively—without the user having to watch it at all times. "We noticed that most people stood by their inkjet printers to make certain they worked," he says. A photo printer that needed to be watched was a far cry from dropping off film at a local drugstore. "Once you dropped off your film, you went back to your life," Schaeffer says. Kodak had to create a printer that was more technologically advanced than the ones on the market. That a technology product designed for women would be more advanced—not less advanced—was something of a radical idea in the high-tech world. Conventional wisdom had generally held that men were more discerning in innovation and advances than women when it came to high-tech gadgets. But Kodak wasn't so concerned with whether tech advances should be driven by male or female consumers. Instead, the printing dock's innovations were necessary primarily so that the company could remain true to its objective of returning women to their roles as the memory makers of their families. "If we didn't pass the test of letting women hit the button on the printer and then getting back to their life, then we had failed. This simply is about approaching products from a different point of view," Schaeffer says.

The printer—after it had passed all those tests—also struck at the heart of one of Kodak's key business strategies. While its competitors made their money from selling cameras, Kodak needed to keep making money by selling its photo papers and processing services. By adding a printer to its lineup, Kodak built in demand for its photo-quality papers, already well known among consumers from its long-standing advertising campaigns, all while offering a solution that was faster and more effective than most people were used to.

Now Kodak needed to make certain that women really understood that it had finally addressed one of their biggest frustrations. As it prepared to launch the printer dock, Kodak turned to its agency of record, Ogilvy & Mather, to create a series of ads that were a natural extension of Eleven's "viewfinder" idea. One of the ads spoke volumes about how fast the printer was. But more importantly, it wove in the notion of how photography was really more about emotion than technology. In the ad, a mother and her two sons are shown moving into an empty apartment. She asks them to begin unpacking while she goes to buy dinner. Instead of opening boxes, they take a Kodak EasyShare camera and start shooting photos. They print them using the Kodak printer dock. When their mother returns, she finds no boxes unpacked, but a dozen photos are taped to the fridge. Her response: "This really is home."

Kodak continued the theme of emotion with an even more pointed attack on the difficulty of printing digital photos with another set of ads the following year. The "Where are my photos?" campaign featured several people—men, women, and children—asking that question. The answer in the ads was printing at home—with Kodak paper using the company's printer dock—or printing at a growing number of Kodak's self-serve kiosks. The ads—and the focus on Kodak's photo paper business— brought full circle the company's strategy of providing cameras and printers that gave women control and gave Kodak back its important revenue stream from printing.

The Last Links in the "Chain of Pain"

But Kodak wasn't finished with its strategy of addressing the frustrations women faced in the digital camera industry—and making money and growing market share when it solved those frustrations. One more link in Schaeffer's "chain of pain" needed to be addressed: retailers. While Kodak had control over how it designed the cameras and printers and how it advertised them to women, it had virtually no control over how those cameras were sold at retailers, such as Best Buy and Circuit City. This lack of control was a major problem, because Kodak's research showed that salespeople at most electronics stores were not trained to deal with women consumers—no matter their technical expertise. "We knew that all of our efforts could be derailed if we couldn't do something to change the way women were treated in consumer electronics stores," Schaeffer says.

For their part, retailers were skeptical early on that Kodak was on the right track with its new strategy. Their store surveys in 2001 weren't showing a major surge in the number of women coming in to buy electronics. Therefore, they could see little reason to retrain salespeople to deal with consumers who didn't frequent their stores. "In our first discussions with them about EasyShare, they were polite, but skeptical. They would listen to us, but I had the impression that they thought we were a brand that was circling the drain," Schaeffer says.

Kodak needed to do something radical that would show retailers that women were an important consumer group, even if digital camera makers and electronic retailers continued to marginalize their power. In a subtle, but important, twist on mystery shopping, Kodak decided to take hidden cameras into stores around the country and watch what happened as consumers shopped. The company quietly and often secretly followed the consumers into the stores to get the most truthful version of what was happening to shoppers. Instead of using trained mystery shoppers or executives from Kodak, they wanted real-world anecdotes that showed retailers just what was happening at their stores. "We needed to show retailers that they were missing opportunities to sell products because of the way salespeople approached women consumers in their stores," Schaeffer says. The hidden videos were eye-openers for many retailers, who watched as their employees made their sales pitch—usually in what Schaeffer called a "battle of one-upmanship." "Salespeople—usually a man in his 20s—were used to other men coming into the stores who had documented everything about the product they wanted to buy," he says. "It became a technology contest in which the male consumer was more interested in knowing if the salesperson knew as much about the product as he did in buying the product."

For many women, such competition was off-putting, Schaeffer says. Women expected that a salesperson should know about the product and explain the features—a big supposition given the turnover of salespeople at the stores and the dizzying array of products that salespeople needed to learn. The hidden videos revealed that many women left the stores disappointed and without having purchased a camera. "We asked retailers if they could really afford to have a person walk out of their stores without buying something, especially during the critical holiday shopping seasons that accounted for a majority of a store's sales," Schaeffer says.

Some retailers took the videos to heart, he says, while others remained skeptical. It took retailers several years after Kodak's mystery shopping to take the kind of actions they needed to make their stores more woman-friendly—a change often driven by the retailers finally acknowledging that women really were the economic drivers of the technology they were selling. For example, in 2003, Best Buy began an initiative to better target its customers, including the "soccer mom" consumer, whom it dubbed Jill. New prototype stores called Eq-Life (a combination of equilibrium and life) featured sage green walls and items like vitamins and MP3 music players that supposedly helped create that balanced lifestyle.[25]

Kodak, however, couldn't wait for its retailers to catch up to its perceptions about women. As a hedge against stores and salespeople who didn't or wouldn't address the findings of Kodak's hidden videos, the company had the marketing agency Eleven create point-of-purchase materials that would address the questions women—and even salespeople—had about the cameras. "While we focused on materials that would help consumers find the camera they needed, we also realized that we could help salespeople," Borosky says. "Salespeople are just as overwhelmed as consumers. They have three to four cameras to learn every month, so there is no way for them to keep up."

Again, Eleven decided to take a different approach with its in-store brochures—making certain that the emotional elements that worked so well in the "viewfinder" strategy and the "Where's my photo?" advertising campaigns resonated even at the store level. The brochures offered straightforward information about the cameras as well as explaining the intricacies of megapixels and storage. Eleven also changed the size and shape of the brochures, moving away from one-page fliers to booklets that could easily be tucked into a pocket or a purse as shoppers browsed the stores. That way, even if a shopper left the store without a camera, he or she didn't leave empty-handed.

By 2004, Kodak's sales were beginning to move up as women realized that there was a digital camera on the market that took their needs into consideration. But even as Kodak succinctly addressed women's needs, it was beginning to experience the kind of shift affecting other technology companies—the emergence of a tech-savvy female consumer. Indeed, technology companies like Kodak were facing the same challenges of companies such as The Home Depot, Nike, and WomensWallStreet.com. Just as the companies began to find stable ground with women consumers, those women advanced rapidly as they became comfortable with renovating homes, running marathons, and trading stocks online.

For Kodak, the shift of women from tech-novice to tech-literate presented the company with yet another challenge as it began work on the next generation of EasyShare cameras in 2003. How far could it take the technology in its cameras without adding any frustrations to the women consumers who had been turned on by EasyShare's ease of use? EasyShare One answered that question with a lineup of technology advances that appeared, at first glance, to appeal to men. The new camera, which went on sale in June 2005, came with a three-inch liquid crystal display viewfinder that was twice the size of the industry standard. The camera stored up to 1,500 photos with its 256 megabytes of RAM and came with 4 megapixels, which had become the standard in the industry. The viewfinder also doubled as a touch screen—much like the display of a personal digital assistant—that allowed users to organize, crop, and e-mail photos directly from the camera via an optional wireless system.

All that technology packed into a device that could be operated with one hand made it appear to be a shift from Kodak's women-focused strategy. But the target market was squarely on women, with research showing a 60–40 split between women and men as the camera's purchasers. In fact, Schaeffer explains, the technology was driven by the needs of women consumers. "We've been focusing from the beginning on reducing the time between the first emotional high of taking the photograph and the moment you do something with it," Schaeffer says. "EasyShare One is still rooted in sharing."

Key Observations

◆ Use the company's original mission statement as a foundation for making Kodak's cameras and technology relevant to women.

◆ Create easier-to-use products without forsaking technology. This strategy was employed to create next generations of EasyShare that were more technologically advanced as women became more tech-savvy.

◆ Use an advertising campaign to support the product's differences, not one that highlights that the product is "for women."

◆ Expose retailers to the realities of what happens to consumers in their stores to help overcome that final stumbling block to women buying technology such as digital cameras.

For Kodak, two seemingly opposing trends—women's drive into technology and women's traditional roles as memory makers—collided to create a long-term strategy that helped turn it from an also-ran into the leader in digital camera sales. In the next chapter, Nike handles a similar collision as women consumers invade the sports industry.

CHAPTER 6

Finding the Goddess

NIKE'S MARATHON TO
REACH WOMEN

T*o attract more women to the famous-
ly macho brand, Nike broadened its description of "sport" to include everything
from yoga to dance. It also worked to rid itself of gender stereotypes about men,
women, and fitness to redesign clothing and shoes and the way it sold them.*

In April 2002, on a typically cloudy day in Beaverton, Oregon, a group of
Nike executives gathered in a meeting room in the Tiger Woods Building
to take part in a two-day conference designed to help them rethink gender.

Several questions were up for discussion. Was what they believed
about gender driven by true biological differences? Or were they looking
at gender through societal norms? Could observing other creatures—animals, fungi, and flora—help them discover what differences were truly
biological and which were social—and therefore likely to change over
time? Most important for the Nike executives, was there a way to drive the
answers to those questions back into products that were truly relevant to
women's biological needs versus focusing on stereotypes that did nothing
more than turn women off buying the Nike brand?

It was a gender-bending conference for the Nike executives, who were often more comfortable contemplating what would be the next hot sport for teen boys than whether gender traits were driven more by society or biology—or some complex recipe of both. Given that the company was deep into yet another attempt to tap the increasingly important women's market—building on several previous attempts—Nike's leadership was determined to give its employees whatever tools were necessary to determine what women wanted from the famous testosterone-driven company.[1] If that meant sequestering them with a biologist to talk about sex and gender for two days, so be it.

Nike had asked biologist Dr. Dayna Baumeister to take the executives through a series of workshops she had designed for Nike to take off the blinders many people have about gender differences. Her specialty was the relatively new area of science called biomimicry, which looks to other species for answers to problems in the human world. Nike already had used the concept to create an innovative shoe based on the cloven hooves of animals such as mountain goats, which they use to gain more traction. The new shoe mimicked the split hoof by separating the big toe from the other four to create balance and flexibility. The "pads" on the sole were designed with a softer core surrounded by a more rigid rim, thereby allowing the shoe (or hoof) to better grip rocks.

To start the morning session, Dr. Baumeister asked each person in the room to pick an animal or insect that exuded feminine gender traits. Overwhelmingly, the group of men and women picked cats, butterflies, and swans—creatures often described as feminine because of their beauty, elegance, and grace. But as Dr. Baumeister would reiterate throughout the seminar, those perceived "feminine" traits may have little to do with true biological differences. Instead, they may be driven more by social mores than biology. In other species, where societal values of what is feminine or masculine don't color the picture as they do in humans, gender traits break down far differently—often based on biological needs. In other species, traits such as strength, competitiveness, and aggression, often considered "masculine" among humans, can be as common in females as they are in males, Dr. Baumeister explained.[2]

She demonstrated this idea by explaining the role of lionesses in a pride. There's no doubt that a lioness exudes what many people would consider feminine traits, such as beauty and grace. But she is hardly delicate or feminine in the human sense. In fact, she's a killer. Biologists know that female lions are the primary hunters for the pride—not the males, who rarely take part in the actual kill. In lions, the female is aggressive and powerful because she needs to be. The lion pride would likely die out if the lioness didn't hunt.

In humans, Dr. Baumeister said, beliefs about gender are often as driven by society as they are by true biological differences—and that means they can change quite quickly. Males are still considered the stronger and more competitive because for thousands of years they have often been the hunters, or killers, for the tribe. Females were the gatherers, the nurturers, primarily because of their biological role in carrying and then caring for children, although new evidence suggests that women did hunt for small game, primarily using lures and traps. Over thousands of years, and particularly in the past several hundred years, those roles—certainly determined by biology—have been hardened by societal ideas that link strength with men and weakness with women in areas far beyond just physical differences.

But what happens as women become the "hunters"—or what today is often called the "primary breadwinner"? What was happening to women as they became stronger and more agile from sports and fitness training—activities that had for several hundred years been considered "unfeminine"? Would the hard and fast rules the executives had about gender become increasingly unimportant and would new roles take shape?

"The insights from the conference have been a wake-up call for me," said footwear business director Seana Hannah during a break in the conference. "To hear women at Nike saying 'feminine' meant delicate and dainty was incredible," she said. "Most women at Nike would cringe at the idea that we define gender in such a way." Yet that is often what had happened at Nike as it tried to market its products to women over the decades. Despite advertising that often highlighted women's athletic and social achievements, Nike's women's products often did little to address women's true biological differences. Instead, they too often played up the "social" gender traits that Dr. Baumeister was forcing the Nike executives to rethink. "We have to get beyond the flowing lines and passive colors we've always thought worked for women," Hannah said. "Biomimicry has taught me that you can design shoes and clothes that look both feminine and tough."

Such insight, along with several reorganizations, management changes, and constant reevaluations of how the company approaches women, has helped Nike come through what has been one of the most challenging transformations for any company adapting to women consumers. Although Nike's early focus was on running—a personal and often noncompetitive sport—as it matured, the company increasingly focused on the world of male competitive sports with the occasional detours to attract women to the brand. Despite those detours, sports at Nike were still defined as men had traditionally defined them, as highly competitive games that were marketed through the use of sports superheroes like Michael Jordan and Tiger Woods.

By the time Dr. Baumeister took the executives on their gender-bending exercises, the company was realizing that not only was such a narrow definition of sport holding the company back from adapting to women, it was holding back the whole company. After tripling its sales from $3 billion to $9.5 billion from 1994 to 1998, the company's sales flat-lined after Michael Jordan retired. Nike struggled to find replacements for Jordan, who had been a major lynchpin in its success in the 1990s. But none of the heroes it hired in basketball, soccer, or even golf as spokespeople had the kind of power with consumers as Jordan.

In 2001, the company began brainstorming for new ideas beyond its traditional strategies that would pump up sales, which were still hovering around the $9 billion mark. One of the ideas that came out of the brainstorming was a retail and marketing project called Nike Goddess. Designed primarily as a way to rethink how Nike sold its products to women, "Goddess" wasn't meant to radically overhaul the company. But it certainly brought change at the company that helped drive up sales to $12.5 billion by the end of 2004. It did so by focusing the company's efforts on women in far different ways than it had in the past. Instead of focusing on ad and marketing campaigns, Nike overhauled how it sold products to women and how it designed apparel and shoes for women. Then, in January 2005, the "Goddess" project sparked another evolution at Nike. It reorganized a majority of its women's operations to reflect a significant shift in how Nike viewed "sports" in relation to women. Instead of the traditional organization chart of team sports like football and basketball or around footwear and apparel, as the company had been defined for several years, the new organization was built around "fitness sports" as defined by women, such as yoga and dance. These trends had helped the company achieve much of the $3 billion in growth it had experienced during the past three years.[3]

"It's a completely different model for how we do business, how we create products, and even how we talk to women," says Darcy Winslow, a long-time Nike executive who worked on the "Goddess" project and had been chosen to lead the new organization as general manager of global women's fitness. "Our progress toward women has always been stop and start, but each time we have learned something new, and that's how we keep making progress."

If You Let Me Play: Redefining Women and Sports

Nike's halting progress with women has often mirrored the parallel transformation of women in sports. In 1972, the year Nike was incorporated as a public company, the Educational Amendment Act was signed into law to address inequalities in funding and access for women at federally financed educational institutions. One section of the act, Title IX, required the institutions to give equal funding to women's sports programs, forcing many universities and colleges to create women's sports teams where none had existed before. But Title IX did more for women than give them access to sports or teach them the rules of tennis and basketball. During the more than 30 years it has been in effect, Title IX has left an enduring and indelible mark on women and their bodies. It has also served to create an ever-expanding consumer group for the makers of anything related to sports.

As Colette Dowling writes in her book *The Frailty Myth: Women Approaching Physical Equality*, Title IX changed forever how women viewed their physical selves—in particular, their power and strength compared to the women who came before them and their relationships to men. As Dowling writes, "[My daughter Rachel] has a sense of her body's power that eludes most women of my generation. For us, the greatest physical boldness had been walking down the middle of a city street if we got caught in a dicey neighborhood at night. We had swallowed whole the half-baked syllogism of our generation and that of many generations of females before us: Men have strength, agility, and endurance; women don't; and therefore women need men for protection."[4]

During the 30 years following Title IX, girls who grew up playing sports in high school and college would begin to break down those and many other myths about women's physical abilities. They also would become the majority consumers of everything sports- and fitness-related, from footwear to athletic equipment. But, as Nike had found, the world of women and sports was hobbled by many long-held beliefs about gender, women, their bodies, and physical strength that would keep many in the sports industry from realizing the full potential of this growing consumer market.

In 1972, only one out of every 27 women participated in a varsity sport. By 2002, almost one out of every two women was playing a sport in school.[5] But the change wasn't just on the tennis courts or the running tracks of educational institutions. As those young women graduated, they took with them their interest in sports and fitness. By 2002, women held the majority of gym memberships. In 2003, the Outdoor Industry Association estimated that 67.6 million women routinely "played" outside, making up 47 percent of the market in recreation, such as kayaking, cross-country skiing, and trail running.[6] Twice as many women train for marathons as men. In 1972, two women ran the New York City marathon, considered one of the premier marathons. In 2003, 11,715 women ran in the marathon, making up one-third of the participants.[7] The majority of new sports and fitness trends that turned into multimillion-dollar businesses have been driven by women, including yoga, Pilates, and spinning, a class where participants ride stationary bikes at an accelerated speed, often to music.

Throughout the years, virtually every sport that was considered truly "men's only" has grown in popularity with women emboldened by their growing strength and expertise in physical activity. By 2002, Board-Trac, a research firm that tracks action sports, noted that between 16 and 22 percent of the country's 2.4 million surfers were female, with the percentage of women surfing doubling in the prior three years.[8] Fly-fishing has seen significant increases in women participants as well. The Outdoor Industry

Association estimated that fly-fishing among women enthusiasts, a term denoting more than just recreational participation, had increased 400 percent in 2003.⁹ Traditional male team sports, such as baseball, basketball, and soccer, also experienced a female invasion in the 1990s with the creation of the WNBA professional basketball teams and the WUSA (Women's United Soccer Association), which was formed after the U.S. women's team won the 1999 World Cup Soccer Championship. Such participation meant huge growth for the makers of sports apparel. By 2003, Packaged Facts estimated that the market for women's athletic apparel was $25 billion and would grow by 50 percent—to $38 billion—by 2005.¹⁰

Such an enthusiastic and fast-growing consumer market should have spelled immediate success for big sports companies such as Nike, women's sports teams, and any other organization savvy enough to see the potential in the women's sports and fitness market. But the long-term results have been less than what even many women would have expected when Title IX became law more than 30 years ago. Both women and the sports industries have struggled to understand how women—so long kept separate from the world of sports, fitness, and physical power—would relate to sports and how that relationship would change as women gained prowess and expertise in sports and fitness. Just as The Home Depot and WomensWallStreet.com discovered that more knowledge made women want to do more in home improvement and financial investing, the more women played sports, the more they changed—both physically and in their attitude toward physical fitness.

When Nike and Title IX came along in the early 1970s, many long-held beliefs about women and physical strength still persisted. For example, women couldn't or wouldn't run marathons for fear of causing major internal damage. Such beliefs were drawn from the notion that physical exertion could harm a woman's ability to bear children. Others were driven by what Dowling refers to as "learned weakness." Males simply had more innate biological differences that made them stronger and better at sports. Females didn't have those same innate abilities; they were biologically weaker.

But as girls became more active in sports, "differences" once considered truly biological began to break down. "Studies from the 1950s found boys to have a greater ability to 'move with an integrated body pattern' during throwing, catching, and kicking," Dowling writes. As she points out, researchers now know that this ability is *taught*; it's not a part of the genetic code. "In the 1990s, [researchers] finally figured out that…it was really a question of girls just not being taught good form."[11]

By the start of the 21st century, many of the myths about women and physical fitness had been broken. More women had learned the art and science of sport. They were taking on greater and greater challenges. Women such as marathoner Paula Radcliff had proven that women could run a marathon as fast as the top male runners. In 2005, Ellen MacArthur sailed around the world alone faster than anyone else—in 71 days—to shatter several world records in a sport that had been dominated by men.[12] Still, stereotypes about women—what they wanted from sports, sports equipment, and apparel—have persisted.

Some of the stereotypes, like the one that women would hero-worship sports stars just like men, come from the belief that women are similar to men in their relationship to sports. Compelling examples of this "women will be like men" stereotype have blunted the promise of women in sports, such as the rise and fall of the women's soccer league. In June 2003, the eight-team league shut down just days before the Women's World Cup Soccer championship started in Los Angeles. In just three years, the league's management had blown through $40 million in sponsorship money and squandered what had seemed to be the overwhelming popularity of women's soccer after the U.S. team won the World Cup in 1999.[13]

Such a failure would have seemed impossible if viewed on the day the U.S. team won the World Cup Soccer championship game against China, with Brandi Chastain clinching the game with a perfectly landed penalty shot. She stunned many and inspired millions of fans when, in a moment of pure bliss, she ripped off her soccer jersey to reveal her black sports bra. The photo made the cover of most news and sports magazines. It seemed like the perfect time to pull together a professional team, including World Cup heroes Chastain and Mia Hamm. The league's founder was John Hendricks, president of the Discovery Channel, who had been a big fan of women's soccer since watching the gold-medal game in the 1996 Olympics, when the U.S. women's team took home the gold. By 2000, he had persuaded companies such as Maytag and McDonald's to put in $40 million of sponsorship money. He even kicked in $2.5 million of his own money. The money was divvied up among eight teams and was expected to last five years. But after just two seasons of play, the league had huge debts, sinking attendance at games, and miniscule ratings for its televised games.[14]

The reasons the league failed were complex, but some of them struck at the heart of the problems many companies—including Nike—have experienced in reaching women through sports. First, the soccer league expected that women, like men, would flock to watch the soccer games both in person and on television. The league failed to realize that there was no basis for such a belief—other than believing that women would act like men when it came to watching sports. That belief was built in part on Hendricks' personal beliefs, not on any considered insight into women. "I just knew that the missing ingredient then was television," Hendricks said in an interview with online magazine *SoccerNova*. "I believed that if television could be added, it would be overwhelming."

Instead, it was underwhelming. The league's ratings never topped one million viewers, and often the biggest fans of women's soccer were men—not the women who sponsors like McDonald's and Maytag had hoped to reach when they contributed millions of dollars to sponsor the league.[15] Moreover, the league ended up picking the wrong television venue for the games, selling the rights to the games to so-called "women's" channels, such as Oxygen and PAX, instead of the sports channels that women as well as men watched when they wanted to see any sport. Finally, the league mistakenly believed that women would be drawn to the sport simply because women were playing. Such a quid pro quo was also a mistake. While the women's soccer team was certainly a sign that women had advanced very far in the world of sports, it didn't mean that women necessarily felt a sisterhood with them. Nor did they hero-worship sports personalities, as men often did. Women were far less likely to buy clothing because it was marketed by Mia Hamm or Brandi Chastain than men and young boys who couldn't wait for the next Air Jordan shoes to come out. In 2004, there was discussion that the league would be re-formed, but with more of a grassroots approach than trying to mimic men's professional sports, which had the benefit of decades of marketing and organization to become multibillion-dollar industries. The association had begun a ticket drive to help it relaunch sometime in 2005, asking fans to make monetary pledges they could then turn in for tickets when the teams started playing again.[16]

The soccer league suffered in part from believing that women would follow in the footsteps of men when it came to professional, organized competitive sports. Other companies, notably Nike, have suffered from sticking with gender stereotypes that were never valid or had become invalid as women moved through a major transformation. Women were being changed by sports—and they were changing the nature of sport. It was this complex world into which Nike stepped in 2000.

Chick Cars? When Gender Matters — and When It Doesn't

Few industries have tried harder — and failed more often — to adapt their products to meet the real gender needs of women than the automotive industry. From the 1950s, when Chrysler created the pink LaFemme, until 2003 and a concept car from Volvo that featured an opening in the driver's seat headrest for a ponytail, carmakers have focused their efforts on changing the vehicles to address what they perceived to be important gender differences between men and women that may or may not have been true biological differences.

Some of the "difference"-based efforts have met with some success.

Ford Motor Co. introduced adjustable foot pedals so that its cars would more comfortable for women to drive (women in general tend to be shorter than men). Of course, the pedals were a nice option for short men as well. Ford and Honda spent thousands of hours researching how mothers used their minivans to create better versions of the family vehicles. The new versions ended up appealing to everyone in the family — including men — who could appreciate new options like dual stereo systems that allowed children to listen to different music than their parents in the front row. Hyundai, whose Santa Fe sport utility vehicle has one of the highest percentage of women owners in the industry, created programs to help women better understand car financing as well as offering a defensive driving course. In these two areas, women felt at a disadvantage to men, says Donna Kane, who until 2004 oversaw the company's women's marketing initiatives. "We wouldn't create a chick car," Kane says. "We already had cars that appealed to women. We didn't need to shout about it. Instead, we focused on the nuances that made our brand relevant to women as opposed to any big differences we perceived between women and men."[17]

But even smart "difference"-based approaches—as opposed to those that focus solely on socialized gender differences, such as color preferences or hair length—have begun to lose their impact with a new generation of women. The differences between what women want in cars and what men want may be far less important than understanding the increasing similarities between the two sexes as society moves forward in what some sociologists refer to as a post-gender, or postmodern, era. "In a postmodern era, which many Western cultures are now beginning to experience, the categories of sex and gender are beginning to collapse, and multiple categories of gender are arising," write three professors in the *Academy of Marketing Science Review* in 2003. "This transformation...will enable people to experience consumption with fewer constraints and boundaries."[18]

Toyota marketers have begun to ascribe to such theories as they watch younger generations of men and women interact. "The chasm between the sexes is getting less defined," says Ernest J. Bastien, vice president for Toyota's U.S. vehicle operations in Torrance, California. "Girls and boys spend a lot more time together, especially in sports. They are learning to like what the boys like, and the boys are learning to like what the girls like as well."[19]

With such insight, Toyota hasn't gone to great lengths to change its vehicles specifically for women, as other companies have done. "Try to pigeonhole women too much, and they will react badly," says Deborah Meyer, Toyota's director of marketing communications. "Women are as diverse as men when it comes to buying cars. Some women want power; others want safety. Some are drawn to the same features that men are, but they perceive them differently. That means you really have to listen to what your consumers are telling you."[20]

Other automotive companies have picked up on this "similarity" trend—notably in their advertising and marketing. A BMW advertisement turned the tables on gender in a 2004 holiday ad showing a man holding a set of keys above a woman's head. The tagline read "Better than mistletoe." The gender-bending ad revealed that BMW was aware that women could be just as passionate about their sports cars as the brand's traditional male audience. General Motors' Hummer division also took a gender-blurring approach to its advertising, driven by understanding that a new generation of women were as likely to be drawn to the big, brash looks of the sport utility vehicle as men were. One advertisement featured a woman navigating her Hummer through city streets with the tagline "Threaten men in a whole new way." In a 2005 campaign for its new smaller Hummer, the H3, GM appealed even more to potential women buyers. In a television spot based on Goldilocks and the three bears, it shows the three bears coming home to find the baby bear's H3 missing from the garage. Goldilocks is then shown behind the wheel of the smaller vehicle. Ads also appeared in women's magazines such as *Shape* with the headline, "Available in the petite section."[21]

Even minivan makers have conceded that what moms want in minivans may not always have to do with children or outmoded stereotypes of the harassed and harried soccer mom. Nissan redesigned the Quest minivan to look more assertive on the road, offered an engine with more power than most minivans, and added optional skylights. In its advertising, the company promoted the idea that its minivan "never forgets that mothers and fathers are lovers." Chrysler, which created the minivan segment in the mid-1980s, also shifted its advertising from solely mom-centric chores, like buckling kids into seats or storing grocery bags. In 2005, one ad featured a woman stopping to pick up her husband, whose motorcycle had died in the desert. She quickly folds the back seats into the floor, rolls the bike into the minivan's expanded cargo area, and secures it with straps, saying to her child in a rear passenger seat, "Daddy just had to have his motorcycle."

Nike's "No Finish Line" Marathon Toward Women

In the spring of 2000, high anxiety was flowing around Nike's peaceful, well-manicured campus when Mark Parker, president of the Nike brand, called together a group of executives to brainstorm new ideas he hoped might pull the company out of its sales slump. For two years, the company had tried and failed to find a strategy that would make up for Jordan's retirement.[22]

But Parker and the executive team were realizing that the company needed new ideas beyond its traditional strategies if it were to keep growing in the future. The company already had reorganized to do a better job of focusing on the future instead of the past, replacing much of its organization around specific sports with one that focused on footwear, equipment, and apparel across all sports. For the first time ever, each unit had dedicated men's, women's, and children's divisions. Under the new organization, women consumers would finally get the kind of attention that had been missing from Nike despite its numerous women's ad campaigns and support of female sports stars, such as soccer star Mia Hamm, one of only two women to have a building on the Nike campus named after her. The other was runner Joan Benoit Samuelson. After almost 30 years of creating women's clothes and shoes simply by "cutting down" men's sizes, women would get their own shoe "lasts," the molds upon which shoes are built, modeled after real women's feet. Clothing would be designed to fit real women's bodies, not the fashion-fit models that the company had long used. Instead of hiring models in size 6, the company hired real women in its headquarters town of Beaverton, Oregon, to serve as models for sizing.

But despite those changes, there still wasn't a feeling of urgency in a company that had always been driven by adrenalin. To get the creative juices flowing, Parker asked the team of long-time employees gathered in the cramped conference room next to his office to come up with some retail concepts that went beyond the company's museum-like Niketowns. Traditionally, the company had left much of its retail strategy up to its big customers, like Foot Locker and Nordstrom. Over the years, retailing had changed substantially, especially in the world of women's sports gear. The Internet and the fashion world were both making waves in sports, trends that Nike had all but missed as it continued to use its old strategies even as the world was changing.

These trends could be seen in the creation of new women's sportswear companies, such as Lucy and Athleta, which had appeared during the final years of the Internet boom. Lucy and Athleta both used the Internet as their main gateway to consumers. They also relied on clothing that was designed to fit women's bodies, from companies such as Prana and Moving Comfort. They also mimicked the fashion world's choices of colors, textures, and shapes. Scott Kerslake, a surfer and cyclist before he became a businessman and entrepreneur, founded Athleta in 2000 after hearing from his female friends that they wanted, but couldn't find, workout clothes that could hold up under the rigors of a 100-mile bike ride and still look good enough to wear to the office.[23]

When the Nike executives regrouped to test their ideas with Parker, several people in the room suggested trying a women-only retail concept to get Nike hooked into those trends. The proposed name—Nike Goddess—had been pulled from a "magalog," a catalog that also featured editorial content. The company's marketing department had created this magalog in early 2000 as yet another attempt to reach the ever-elusive women's market. The name itself paid homage to the ironic fact that Nike—before it was the name of one of the world's toughest, most macho sports brands—was the name of the Greek goddess of victory. Nike Goddess struck a chord with Parker and the other executives in the room that went far beyond the retail concept presented. "Nike Goddess was the physical personification of finally getting our act together," Parker says. "We had tried to tap the women's market before, but Goddess gave us a vehicle where we could rally all our efforts. [Goddess] also helped us realize that brand Nike could be so much more."

For years, the company had focused on male sports stars and big professional sports to drive growth, with a goal of becoming the world's biggest sports brand. But where would Nike go now that it had achieved that goal? "We don't want to be just the number one sports brand in the world," Parker says of the company's decision to rewrite its mission in 2000 as part of the changes, including Nike Goddess, that were under way at the company. "Maybe it's not a big thing at other companies, but for us it was a big deal. Our new mission: bring innovation and inspiration to every athlete, and there's an asterisk next to the word athlete that says, 'if you have a body, you are an athlete,'" he says.

Just as McDonald's and Kodak had broadened their brands by focusing on women, so too would Nike benefit from putting women at the center of a strategy that over the years has transformed many parts of the company—including the way it creates and sells products to men. The company still focuses on professional sports and the type of "Michael Jordan" marketing that made it so successful in the '90s. For example, it spent $90 million in 2003 to sign NBA star LeBron James as an endorser.

But over a period of four years, one of Nike's most important growth strategies was to take the ideas encompassed in the Nike Goddess stores and women-specific products to create a constantly evolving strategy. This strategy increasingly is driven more by what women do at the gym than about trying to tap the next great professional sports star—either male or female—who plays a traditional competitive team sport.

Much like the women's professional soccer league, Nike had often focused its efforts on women with a lens that was clouded by how it marketed its brand to men. It had signed on major women sports stars, including runners Mary Decker Slaney and Joan Benoit Samuelson, and soccer and basketball stars Mia Hamm and Sheryl Swoopes, respectively. In 2004, it signed up Serena Williams and Maria Sharapova to promote women's tennis. While women certainly appreciated the achievements of these women, they weren't like men when it came to hero-worshiping sports stars. For many women, sports were more about active personal fitness than they were about viewing the actions of others. Many women didn't see themselves in the role of sports hero, as young men often did when they watched Michael Jordan or Tiger Woods.

Yet the answer to reaching women wasn't as simple as showing the softer or "human" side of these women athletes, a tactic the company had tried with the first Nike Goddess magalog. The premier issue featured Olympic runner Marion Jones on the cover. Instead of showing her competing, there was a graceful, artistic shot of Jones' feet against grass. But it didn't seem to connect with women, said Jackie Thomas, who was director of women's marketing at the time. "Women told us it was too soft. We had swung the pendulum too far from what Nike's core image was. We thought the power exuded by Nike would be a weakness for women."

Forget Girly: Think Tough, But Feminine

As the company would realize during the creation of Nike Goddess stores and continuing with its new clothing and shoes for women, power, technology, and performance were attributes that women expected to find in Nike products. What they wanted was for those attributes to be packaged in ways that were relevant to women. Whereas Niketowns had exuded the brash, harsh, macho image that had become synonymous with the brand over the years, Nike Goddess stores were cool, clean, and comfortable. "I was used to hearing people describe the brand as brutal," says John Hoke, one of Nike's designers and the key architect for the "goddess" look of the stores, which would feature warm wood floors, blue tile, and white mannequins with muscles. "But that was simply because our initial reaction to selling the Nike brand was to turn up the volume so we could be heard above the other sports brands. With Goddess, it was all about turning the volume down. I wanted women to come in and take a breath and relax."

It was the kind of relevance Nike needed to link its brand to women's needs and wants. Men viewed sports as hard, macho, and competitive, or at least the traditional stereotypes supported such a belief. Women hadn't followed that stereotype as they moved into the sports world. Women could be as competitive and tough on the court or sports field as most men. But working out and playing sports for women also had evolved as a way to unwind, relax, and even connect with friends in comfortable competition. Therefore, Hoke sought inspiration for the stores not in sports, but where he felt women would be most comfortable: their homes. "I designed a residential space that had furnishings and clean spaces and warm colors," he says. But he adds that he was conscious of not making the stores "too girly."

"Girliness" had been a common mistake among many sports companies ever since the first women started showing up on the track and tennis court after Title IX went into effect. As more and more women moved into sports, many marketers and designers designated products for women simply by choosing softer, prettier colors. Bikes were painted pink, and backpacks came in baby blue. Even companies such as Title 9 Sports, which took its name from the very legislation that opened up sports to women, had fallen prey to the problem of "girliness," despite being an early pioneer in designing athletic apparel specifically for women's bodies. In the early 2000s, its running tanks featured flowers, and its shorts came in blues and pinks. Indeed, despite the advancement of women in sports over the years, Nike, Adidas, Ryka, and a host of other sports companies kept rolling out women's products that were driven by outdated stereotypes like the ones Hannah and her colleagues were trying to get rid of in the bio-mimicry class. As Hannah said, it was time to start creating athletic apparel that was both feminine and tough—and fashionable as well.

Those three words—feminine, tough, and fashionable—began to drive the design and function of much of the apparel and footwear that Nike created as it continued to evolve its women's initiative above and beyond the Nike Goddess stores. By feminine, Nike didn't mean soft. By tough, Nike wasn't moving back to a macho image, and fashion wasn't solely about color. Instead, feminine was more about creating products that took women's real biomechanical and biological differences into account. Tough captured the emotional, mental, and rational components of women. The clothing had to stand up to the rigors of 15-mile runs and 100-mile bike rides without falling apart. But it also had to exude an emotional and mental toughness, a toughness that was beginning to creep into women's psyches as they became more and more comfortable with their growing physical power and strength driven by running marathons and competing in triathlons. Fashion was about keeping up with the world outside of sports, where color, shapes, and styles were in constant transformation.

When it came to truly "feminizing" products to fit the biological differences between men and women, much of the sports industry didn't catch on to the idea until the mid-1990s. Nike would take until 2000 to make significant changes to its products to address major biomechanical differences in women, particularly in its important running shoe lines. In 2000, after almost 30 years of making running shoes, the company finally created the "Emily last," a mold built from a model of a real woman's foot. Nike shoe designers discovered that women's feet weren't simply smaller than men's feet. They were shaped very differently and, in some areas of the foot, were actually larger than men's. As Nike executive Hannah explained, in general, women's feet are wider through the forefoot and narrower at the heel. That meant a shoe built for a man's foot would cramp a woman's forefoot and leave her heel flopping around, making running more difficult.

The change to Nike's women's shoes was in step with where women were headed in sports and fitness. In a poll by Western WATS Market commissioned by outdoor sports retailer Recreation Equipment Inc. (REI), 36 percent of women believed that women-specific gear could enhance their athletic performance. More than one in 10 women, about 14 percent of those polled, said they believed gender-specific gear would make them participate in outdoor activities more frequently.[24]

But there was more to making products fit women than addressing their physical differences. While women were increasingly turned off by "girliness" in athletic wear, they weren't looking for the mannish clothes their mothers had been forced to wear when they started playing sports in the 1970s. Instead, women wanted their workout clothes to follow fashion trends far more closely. The reason? Women increasingly were seeing fitness as another part of the day's activities. "We were increasingly aware that the world of fitness is influenced by more than sports these days," Winslow says. "Women are influenced by what they see in entertainment and fashion. They are also influenced by the way they shop for other clothes. They want to shop from head to toe, and they want to shop for the specific activity they are doing."

That was a far different philosophy of sports or fitness from the one that had driven Nike for so long. Much of its organization and product development were built around cycles that had little to do with fashion trends. For many years, footwear designs were driven more by what designers had thought up than what consumers were pressing for. Moreover, the company's footwear designs were on different production cycles than its apparel lines. Footwear designers worked on an 18-month design cycle, while apparel worked on a 12-month cycle. That made it difficult to marry colors that were fashionable for apparel with shoes that women would wear with those workout clothes. Nike knew that making those cycles match—and making shoes and clothes in the same colors—was important to women who wanted outfits to work out in, not a random, unmatched set of clothes. The company would have to overhaul those systems to bring them more in sync with the outside world, where one year dark pinks and blacks were fashionable and the next the trends were driven by blues and browns, for example. The payoff would be big. As the company made changes to address both needs—fashion and perform-ance—its women's businesses began to take off. "We had decided that women's footwear could be a growth accelerator in 2002," Winslow says of the changes. "We expected it to grow, but what we didn't expect was that it would grow three to four times faster than global footwear, and that was off of static or declining growth for the previous five years."

If only those changes were achieved, Nike would have been more suc-cessful in adapting its brand to women consumers than ever before. But those shifts in strategy were leading Nike toward a major change in how it viewed women consumers that went beyond Nike Goddess stores and even beyond creating products designed specifically for women. Those had been steps in the right direction with women and had helped pull Nike's sales out of their slump. But the path Nike was moving toward was far big-ger than what the executives had envisioned when they approved the Nike Goddess stores. By 2004, those ideas had culminated in what Winslow says was finally "changing the game in women's fitness." Instead of continuing to focus most of its energies on traditional competitive sports, Nike was now poised to focus on how *women* perceived sports. "All the things that had happened in the past three to four years had shown us that if we put the focus on women, the company could grow," Winslow says. "That suc-cess was a real catalyst for us to begin seriously looking at defining sports through women's eyes instead of solely through men's."

In 2005, Winslow was put in charge of a new organization devoted to fitness sports that were dominated by women. Yoga, fitness dance, sport training, cardio training, running, and walking made up the new organiza-tion. Plans for marketing included the "Nike Rock Star Workout" with Jamie King, a choreographer who had worked with Madonna and Prince, and a new catalog featuring the products called Nikewomen. Nike hadn't forgotten the concept that started it all. Nike Goddess was going through its own evolution. The company renamed the stores Nikewomen to res-onate better with women around the world. It also moved ahead with plans to expand the stores in the U.S. to 12 stores by the middle of 2006 and moved ahead with a goal of opening stores throughout Europe and Asia.

It was a startling shift for Nike, which just five years ago still "cut down" men's clothes to fit women and considered yoga a tiny niche. True, the company had incorporated some female fitness trends—spinning and walking, for example—into its product lines in previous years. But by accepting that women's fitness trends were as important a profit center to the company as basketball and running—and deserved their own focused organization—Nike had come to fully realize that women were more than a niche market. Women had become a majority. More importantly, their perception of sports had become as valid to Nike as the men who had come before them.

"We had fed off the power and energy of traditional male competitive sports," Winslow says. "Now we were saying that fitness activities such as yoga and fitness dance were sports we could commit to without apology. The key is that this isn't about competition. It's not about comparing the sports of women versus men. It's about energy and athleticism. It's about being individualistic and celebrating that individuality."

Key Observations

◆ Accept that evolution and transformation are part of a successful strategy to meet women's needs. This strategy was used to evolve Nike Goddess from fewer than 10 stores in the U.S. to Nikewomen, a retail concept that will be rolled out throughout the U.S. and in Europe and Asia.

◆ Learn to understand the difference between true biological differences in women and differences that are driven by society. This strategy was used to differentiate between creating shoes that fit women's feet versus making them in "feminine" colors.

◆ Observe the difference between what society considers a sport and how women view sports—as a key part of their lives.

◆ Create products for women from the ground up instead of retooling or scaling down products that were created for men.

Nike found that in the 21st century, sports and fitness would be defined by women—whether that was practicing yoga alone or playing three-on-three basketball—not by the company or by the men who had always dominated sports. In the next chapter, Avon faces a similar transformation of its business as young women redefine the meaning of beauty.

CHAPTER 7

A New Reflection in the Mirror

AVON MAKES ITS MARK

To *create a new beauty brand for younger women, Avon focused on how women's perceptions of their beauty, their bodies, and even their sexuality had been markedly changed by their growing economic independence.*

Two years into her tenure as Avon Products Inc.'s chief executive officer, Andrea Jung was ready to pursue an idea she had nurtured since she joined the venerable beauty company in 1994 as a marketing executive: make Avon relevant to younger generations of women. As the company's first female chief executive in its 119-year history, she brought with her a far different sensibility and background about women and beauty than her male predecessors—including a teenage daughter, Lauren, who represented the exact demographic she knew Avon must reach if it would thrive for another 100 years.

So, in September 2001, Jung made an unusual hiring decision to help her pursue the idea of broadening Avon's horizons beyond its middle-class, more mature consumers. She brought in an outsider, Deborah I. Fine, a publishing executive with no experience running a cosmetics business— much like Jung, who majored in English literature at Princeton and spent most of her professional life before Avon in executive jobs at high-end department stores.

Despite being a novice at the beauty business, Fine had a sharp eye for the trends and transformations that had affected the generations of women who read the magazines, including *Glamour* and *Brides*, that she had helped direct over the years. Her insight from those 20-plus years gave Fine a unique perspective on just how different today's young women were from her generation, and definitely from her mother's generation—exactly the viewpoint Jung believed Avon needed for the project she had in mind.

Jung put Fine in charge of a group she called "Avon Teen" and gave her 100 days to create a plan to expand the Avon brand into the under-20 market.[1] But as Fine and her team explored their options with teen girls, they increasingly believed that they needed to broaden the group's mandate beyond just an age demographic if they were to do anything to help make Avon more relevant with young women.

"Limiting what we could do for teens as Avon confined what we wanted to achieve. Teens today didn't want to be talked to like teens," Fine says. "I realized as we were conducting research with teens that what we really needed to create was a new sensibility about beauty. The message that has stuck with me throughout this project is that women are now in control of their beauty as opposed to beauty being all about getting a man. So we had to explore the question: Where does beauty emanate from now?"

The more Fine considered this question, the more she came to believe that Avon had to do something far more radical than brighten its lip colors and add glitter to its blush—typical attempts in the beauty industry to tap into the teen psyche. Fine proposed to Jung that Avon create an all-new brand that would appeal to this new generation of young women who had far different ideas about what beauty is, how they expressed that beauty, and even how they used beauty as a social statement. Indeed, Fine considered the new generations of women she wanted to reach so different from past generations that she referred to the new brand as needing to "speak a different dialect" about beauty.

Fine had some of her own ideas about how she would approach these young women with a new brand. But the philosophy and ideals would come primarily from the women themselves, she says. "The common denominator among these women was that they wanted to be celebrated for their individuality, not celebrated because they represented some blonde icon," Fine says of the thousands of young women the company interviewed as it tried to understand these new ideas about beauty. "There has been this evolution where women have gained control of their lives and their finances over the past two or three generations. These young women wanted to celebrate that independence. They wanted to celebrate that they were making their mark on the world."

Far from being taken aback by Fine's radical idea, Jung had a few suggestions. First, she changed the name of Fine's team to Avon Future. Then she gave Fine just 18 months to turn her ideas into what would become, in effect, an all-new cosmetics company inside Avon. Fine took the challenge. By August 2003, the nugget of an idea—of women making their mark—had become a brand with more than 300 all-new products and a new sales team with far different goals and new ways of selling than traditional Avon ladies. The brand's name—"mark"—was derived from the insight gleaned from women about "making their mark" on the world. It was a major shift away from the soft, feminine words that often defined women's beauty brands to a stronger, more assertive sensibility. But more than anything, "mark" would reflect the changing perceptions of beauty that had been building as women gained more economic power and more freedom socially.

Such a new reflection of beauty was exactly what Avon needed to tap into the new generation of women. By the end of 2004, "mark" was on target to hit $45 million in net sales in the 18 months since it was introduced, making it the number two best-selling "youth trend" cosmetic behind MAC, now owned by Esteé Lauder Cos., according to the company. Moreover, the new brand added sales to Avon's overall revenue, instead of cannibalizing the core Avon brand. Such early success was more than even Jung or Fine had hoped for from what was an edgy idea for the staid company. "It's proven that this business unit has brought a new customer and a new representative into the company that no other business unit has ever been able to do." Avon expects the new brand to break even in 2006.[2]

Mirror, Mirror: What's the New Reflection of Beauty?

Such a celebration of women's independence and a new view of women's beauty shouldn't have been a radical idea inside Avon. As company executives were fond of saying, Avon had given women access to financial independence before they had the right to vote. But even though the company had always had a forward-looking view of women's economic rights, Avon's view of women's beauty was quite mainstream. It was increasingly reflective of an older generation's perception of beauty than the one Fine came in contact with during her focus groups.

"This is the first generation of women who were born knowing only how life looks today for women. While certainly there are pockets in cities and suburbs where women don't work, most of the young women today didn't grow up with a stay-at-home mom and only a working dad. They didn't grow up with those biases and stereotypes. Instead, they have a very different set of expectations and assumptions that define their lives far differently than even my generation, and definitely that of my mother," Fine says. "Without question, beauty for these young women was all about themselves. It wasn't about getting a man. It was about your individual style, about making yourself happy."

While Avon had known it was helping make women more financially secure and independent, it seemingly hadn't realized that such economic power would eventually have a far broader reach than the actual money it put into women's purses. Access to money and control over it was beginning to transform how women thought about their bodies, their beauty, and even their sexuality.

During the 1970s feminist revolution, Gloria Steinem was quoted as saying, "Most women are just one man away from welfare" to point out the economic inequality that kept women bound to men for financial stability. Today, the route to financial security for a growing number of women isn't marriage or a man, but a well-paying job with benefits. In the 21st century, it is simply assumed that most women will pursue jobs and careers as a way to provide for themselves. If they marry, it will be for partnership and love, not economic stability. "These young women have grown up in a revolutionary time," says New York University Professor Kathleen Gerson, who is researching the book on what she calls the "children of the gender revolution." "Thirty years ago, marriage was largely compulsory, and if you weren't able to marry that was perceived as a problem. Marriage today has become a more voluntary choice." This marked shift in marriage from economic necessity to a voluntary state—albeit still much sought-after by a majority of women and men—has had a profound impact on every part of society, as noted in earlier chapters.

But it hasn't been until the last decade that women's economic independence has begun to have a noticeable impact on the way women relate to their own beauty. "There has been a shift in America from a focus on female sexuality in the service of others—family, nation, race, men—to an emphasis on women's sexual self-determination," says Estelle B. Freedman, a Stanford University history professor and author of *No Turning Back: The History of Feminism and the Future of Women*, in the *Boston Herald* in November 2003.[3]

The transformation has been taking shape for several decades. But it seems to have reached critical mass with the youngest generations, who have been exploring the outer boundaries of what is acceptable in women's beauty, bodies, and sexuality for the past decade.

Indeed, what was shocking or unacceptable for women even 10 years ago has become more accepted by a broad swath of society. Today, a woman is considered beautiful if she has the strong athleticism of tennis stars Venus and Serena Williams or the lithe grace of Zhang Ziyi, the elfin Chinese actress from *Crouching Tiger, Hidden Dragon,* or the traditional blonde icon looks of pop stars Britney Spears and Jessica Simpson. A woman's body is considered beautiful if it is the well-rounded curves of rap star and actress Queen Latifah or the pint-sized look of Sarah Jessica Parker as "Carrie Bradshaw" in the HBO series *Sex and the City.* Moreover, the changes in beauty and body aren't simply skin-deep. In the 21st century, increasingly women's intelligence and intellect also are being considered signs of beauty beyond the surface. Also, in a noticeable shift during the past decade, more women are exploring their sexuality. The urban centers of New York and Los Angeles have invitation-only sex parties at posh nightclubs. In the living rooms of the Midwest, middle-class mothers show up to buy sex toys at Passion Parties hosted by their friends. (These parties use a direct-sales concept much like Avon ladies and Amway salespeople.) Striptease classes offered at local gyms help women learn the tricks of the strip trade for use in their own homes.

The forces behind these revolutionary shifts from the traditional norms for women to the shifting, exploratory patterns seen today are complex and complicated. Both critics and supporters of the transformations point to the pervasive, invasive media as the culprit for capitalizing on these trends, especially the new breed of women's sexuality as portrayed in the hit series *Sex and the City*. "A sexual sale pervades Western cultures, while media representations have expanded sexuality from the private bedroom into the public spaces of billboards, movies, and radio talk shows," writes Professor Freedman in *No Turning Back*.[4]

But the culprit may be something far more positive, even if its results are deemed negative: women's social and economic independence. A woman's worth historically has been measured by what she brought to a marriage, and often that was her beauty and her body, along with her family's fortunes. As Nancy Etcoff, a psychologist and author of *Survival of the Prettiest*, has noted, "good looks are a woman's most fungible asset, exchangeable for social position, money and even love. But dependent on a body that ages, it is an asset that a woman uses or loses."[5] In the past, if a woman fell outside the prevailing norms set down by society—by expressing her sexuality in "abnormal" ways, for instance—she often faced poverty, banishment, or even confinement. Fear of reprisal—in particular, economic reprisal—was a major force in keeping women from stepping outside the norms, especially the beauty norms, set down by society.

Breaking away often meant giving up the opportunity for economic stability and support brought about by marriage. But that is no longer the case. Today, women's bodies and their beauty aren't their only and most important commodities. Women no longer need the economic support of men or the financial stability of marriage to survive and thrive. Such financial freedom leaves women free to define what is beautiful, sexy, and acceptable to them. No doubt critics will argue for decades over whether these transformations are any healthier than past stereotypes of women, and proponents will continue to push the edges of acceptability. Stereotypes and unattainable ideals of beauty still remain, as evidenced by the slew of television shows about women (and a growing number of men) who undergo plastic surgery to attain elusive ideals of beauty instead of accepting the beauty they already have. Yet today women have far more choices when it comes to determining what is beautiful. Young women are pushing the boundaries of how they portray their beauty, intelligence, confidence, and sexuality. They don't choose between the two traditional stereotypes of women—the Madonna or the whore, as they have been broadly defined. Instead, they are deciding that beauty can be a mixture of many attributes, including intelligence, confidence, and a healthy dose of sexuality.

Whatever the criticisms and whatever the fits and starts associated with this unexpected effect of economic power—the transformation in how women see their beauty, bodies, and sexuality—it isn't about to go away. "The real freedom women have now is that they set their own paths, and society isn't going to tell them what they should look like, or how many hours they spend in the office, or how many hours they spend at home with their children. We have this freedom to follow our own paths," says Shelley Lazarus, chief executive officer of the global advertising agency Ogilvy & Mather.[6] In 2004, the agency garnered rave reviews for a series of Dove commercials it created for the U.K. market featuring real women who were large, small, fat, tall, wrinkled, and rosy-cheeked. In 2005, it rolled out a new marketing program for Dove in the U.S. under the tagline "Campaign for real beauty." It featured women in various stereotypical roles, including a woman dressed as a Las Vegas showgirl, discarding the accessories of those roles to reveal their real beauty.

Indeed, in just one generation, it seems, there has been a noticeable shift in the way women think about their beauty and their bodies, especially when it comes to size and sexuality. A January 2003 article in the *New York Times* summed up the shift with the headline "Young and Chubby: What's Heavy About That?" As writer Ginia Bellafante explained, the young women she met with at a coffee shop near her home in Brooklyn were far more comfortable with their bodies, no matter their size, and far more willing to show them off in sexy skin-revealing fashions than her generation—just one up from the young women she interviewed. Bellafante notes that the girls, many showing off sizable bellies above their low-rider jeans, appeared at ease with themselves and their size compared to herself and women in their mid-30s, who still believed they should look like the rail-thin models they saw in fashion magazines.[7]

This shift is due to a combination of factors. First, there is this generation's sense of independence and empowerment. But there's also the sheer reality that women are getting bigger. By the turn of the 21st century, the average woman wore a size 12 and weighed 155 pounds, compared to size 8 and 143 pounds in 1960. Fifty percent of U.S. women ages 15 and over wear a size 14 or larger. Some of the increase can be attributed to the obesity epidemic that has been building for more than 20 years. The number of overweight young people ages 12 to 19 has tripled in the past two decades, according to the Surgeon General's office, which brought the issue of obesity to the public discourse in its 2000 report on national health trends.

Women, particularly women under 30, are also larger and taller for reasons beyond the obesity epidemic. One reason is the notable increase in physical activity by young women at earlier ages and over longer spans of time. In the past 30 years, since the passage of the Title IX legislation, millions of women have taken up sports and fitness (discussed in Chapter 6, "Finding the Goddess: Nike's Marathon to Reach Women"). That has helped lead to some healthy increases in height and weight. But more importantly, those trends in fitness have expanded the boundaries of what is acceptable in a woman's body. As Colette Dowling writes in her book about women and physical strength, *The Frailty Myth: Women Approaching Physical Equality*, bodies like the one soccer player Brandi Chastain showed off on the cover of *Newsweek* after winning the World Cup soccer championship in 1999 would have been inconceivable to women in her generation. "Even if one could have imagined such muscle on a woman, it would have been thought freakish."[8]

The increases in the size of women—and the growing acceptance that bigger can be beautiful—are also being driven by the growing number of immigrants from Latin America, where beauty applies equally to the likes of the curvaceous Jennifer Lopez as to the slender Penelope Cruz. In the entertainment world, particularly in music, female singers such as Beyonce Knowles and Pink have helped break down the long-held beliefs that curvier women didn't want to attract attention, let alone flaunt their sexuality. Avon also caught on to this trend for the parent brand by signing up Mexican actress Salma Hayek to represent the brand in 2004.

Indeed, the curvy looks of these women have sparked change in some of the most traditional industries—at least traditional when it comes to what is acceptable in women's bodies—most notably, the clothing industry. Conventional wisdom has always held that women don't mind seeing models and mannequins that are significantly thinner than average women. Women were—supposedly—inspired by those unattainable images they saw walking the catwalks or in the pages of popular magazines. But in 2004, such conventional wisdom began to take a nosedive. For example, mannequin makers decided to break their molds based on models that wore a size 6 tall and manufacture mannequins in more voluptuous sizes with 38-inch hips and well-rounded derrieres. Stores that featured the new mannequins—some with sexy lingerie slipping over their curves—saw their sales increase dramatically.[9]

Torrid Takes on Tradition

In 1999, Betsy McLaughlin, chief executive officer of one of the country's trendiest teen retailers, Hot Topic, began taking note of a growing number of requests from the customer comment cards she read every week without fail. Amidst the requests for more Green Day posters and Goth-inspired fashions, Hot Topic's female customers were noting that the retailer's clothing didn't come in their sizes. At first, the notes from girls—and the requests for black vinyl pants in size 15 and fishnet stockings in extra-large—were just a trickle. But they soon turned into a torrent. "It was sheer numbers that led us to these consumers," says Patricia Van Cleave, president of Torrid—the plus-size store Hot Topic created in 2001 to meet these consumers' needs. "These were young women who simply hadn't had a chance to shop for fashions like the ones their slimmer friends could so easily find."[10]

Torrid's rapid growth—it planned to add 45 stores to its existing 76 locations by the end of 2005—marked a dramatic change in both young women's attitudes about their bodies and the fashion world's willingness to listen and respond to those new attitudes.

For decades, teen girls in search of clothes above a size 14 had been forced to choose from fashions that ranged from conservative to downright frumpy. Most mainstream retailers turned a blind eye to the growing numbers of plus-size women—in general, size 14 and above. Specialty retailers, such as Lane Bryant, had long catered to the market, but many skewed toward conservative fashions more suitable for the office environment of the '80s, not the new, more liberal, and sexy fashions that had become popular in the '90s. Lane Bryant did expand its lingerie lines with trendier items, such as push-up bras and extra-large thong underwear, in the 1990s, yet its traditional reputation for conservative looks may have kept the younger generation away. "Lane Bryant does a great job for their consumers," Van Cleave says. "But there was this young woman who wanted the fashions she saw her friends wearing. She wanted to be just as attractive as any other teen girl."

For the most part, mainstream retailers, such as The Gap and Limited Stores, with its popular brands like Victoria's Secret, catered to size 12 and under. By the late1990s, even as women were getting larger, the problem actually began to get worse for plus-size teens. They found it nearly impossible to find fashions in their size at trendy retailers, such as Abercrombie & Fitch. While some teen retailers simply assumed that larger girls wouldn't be interested in wearing the revealing looks they offered, other retailers made conscious decisions not to add bigger sizes to their stores' stocks, says Dan Hess, a former Macy's buyer and founder of the retail analyst firm Merchant Forecast. "They believed that catering to plus-size teens would drive thinner customers away," he says. "We've known for 10 or 15 years that women sized 10 and up make up 60 percent of the market. But there is this stigma attached to that market."[11]

Sticking to that stigma, however, was actually working against retailers, if they had cared to take notice. In 2001, NPD Fashionworld, a retail analyst firm in Port Washington, New York, estimated that plus-size women size 14 and up spent $17.1 billion on clothing that year. But the research firm predicted that sales could be more than two and a half times that amount, about $44 billion, if they were to more accurately reflect that women size 12 and up made up 50 percent of the market.[12] What had once been a small niche had turned into a majority market—albeit underserved.

If other retailers refused to take action, Hot Topic's chief executive McLaughlin—a plus-size woman herself—did not. She decided to test whether catering to these young women would result in real sales. In 2000, Hot Topic put a limited selection of plus sizes in its stores. The first item—the black vinyl pants in size 15—was a top seller in both the stores and on the company's Web store just weeks after they appeared.[13] The success indicated that there was definitely pent-up demand. But Van Cleave says there was more to customer requests than just asking for bigger sizes at Hot Topic's existing stores. These young women deserved a place of their own, she says, where they felt comfortable trying on clothes—especially clothes that might be the first fitted items they had ever bought. "There are two kinds of personalities we see in plus-size girls," she says. "One is the young woman who grudgingly comes into the store. Maybe she's dressed in her dad's T-shirts and jeans because they hide all the contours. She doesn't have self-esteem, and she needs a place that will give her that. The other personality is angry and tired of not finding what she wants at other stores. She wants to show off her body no matter what her size is."

Before the company could move forward with creating "a store of their own," to steal from Virginia Woolf's *A Room of One's Own* writings on financial independence, Torrid executives including Van Cleave had to make certain they could find the right products to fill the shelves—not an easy task in a fashion world where most clothing is built from size 4 or 6 patterns. "To build fashions for bigger women takes more than adding 2 inches to the overall pattern," explains Hess, the retail consultant. "Not everything gets bigger as you gain weight, so you need fashion designers and manufacturers who understand that."

There were manufacturers that worked solely for the plus-size market, but Van Cleave says Torrid needed the cutting-edge fashion that the girls saw everywhere else, or the concept simply wouldn't succeed. The Torrid team instead turned to Hot Topic's clothing manufacturers. They agreed, because of their relationship with the parent brand, to begin making the fashions in bigger sizes. "Hot Topic had to teach its vendors to redesign their clothes," Hess says. "No one was really willing to believe in the plus-size teen market, especially not this idea that they want sexy fashions. Hot Topic was really swimming upstream with the idea." Encouraged by the strong sales online and in stores, and the fashions its manufacturers were creating in plus sizes, the company decided that there was enough demand and inventory to go ahead with the plan to build the stores Van Cleave had envisioned with hot fashions and a warm atmosphere.

By April 2001, just two years after McLaughlin began receiving the first requests for bigger sizes, Torrid opened a prototype store in the Brea Mall in Los Angeles. It featured red laminated glass and hammered metal silhouettes in keeping with Hot Topic's "Goth-inspired" décor. Inside, the store was decorated to look like an old New Orleans hotel with dark gray paint on the walls and touches of silver and red. The cash register area had a huge canopy over it to simulate a bedroom, and the shoe area featured couches in red "pleather." In the back, the fitting rooms were designed to be spacious, with big mirrors and warm lighting. Lingerie was kept in the fitting room area so the girls could easily choose larger or smaller sizes without having to get dressed again.[14] The Brea store proved successful, and by 2002, Torrid had expanded to 20 stores and then close to 50 by 2003.

Van Cleave says that even though they hit the mark with many of the elements in Torrid's stores, they still had things to learn from consumers as they expanded the concept. "We had to take a step back from the dark look of the stores," she says. "Many of these young women simply didn't identify with those

Gothic stores, and we wanted them to feel welcome. That was the whole point of Torrid." That insight led to a revamp of many of the existing stores and a new, lighter look for new stores, Van Cleave says. Even the logo was changed from the dark Gothic look it had in 2001 to softer pink script. Van Cleave says they've also expanded Torrid's sizing both up and down. "We added size 12 and size 28," she says. "Twelve isn't a plus size, but we realized that, like all women, these women are bigger in some parts and smaller in others." While there have been requests from consumers to make Torrid's fashions in even smaller sizes, Van Cleave is less inclined to follow those consumers. "The other sizes have the whole world to choose from."

Torrid's success has become very important to Hot Topic, whose fortunes had been somewhat battered by 2004. In 2002, it was named one of *Fortune*'s fastest-growing retailers, but in 2004, the company's sales stumbled as its focus on the punk look began to run its course. The company began to make corrections in 2004, but analysts were still wary, although not about the Torrid division. Retail analyst Lauren Cooks Levitan of SG Cowen says she believes that "Torrid could be even bigger than the Hot Topic concept."[15]

Van Cleave counts success in other ways—primarily from what she sees in the stores and the consumer comments coming in from the stores and online, which she, like McLaughlin, still reads every week. The comments are much like the postings on Torrid.com's discussion boards. "Normally, shopping in trendy shops makes me feel a little out of place since I don't exactly fit into a size 0," one girl wrote on the site in December 2004.[16] "At least I can browse around Torrid and not feel like everyone is gawking at me like they did Julia Roberts in *Pretty Woman*. The chicks at Torrid do an awesome job of making everyone feel at home."

If women are pushing the boundaries of body size and shape, they also are pushing the outer limits on women's sexuality as they break free from long-held stereotypes about what's acceptable and what's not when it comes to sex and women. "Women are increasingly rejecting the double standard, which presumes that women aren't sexual or, at least, shouldn't express it openly," says Professor Gerson of New York University. "Yet while women are more likely to see themselves as sexual beings, that doesn't necessarily mean that they are less responsible. It means instead that as they have gained control over their reproductive lives, they have sought control over their sexuality as well."

This shift in the way women—and indeed society as a whole—view women's sexuality has been building for decades. Two events just five years apart show how far younger generations have pushed the boundaries of acceptability. In 1999, soccer player Brandi Chastain shocked many when she tore off her jersey—revealing a full-coverage black sports bra—after landing the goal that would make the U.S. women's soccer team the World Cup champions. Chastain's picture—sans jersey—was plastered on the covers of newsweeklies and in newspapers with commentary on what her bra-baring actions signified.

By 2004, Chastain's sports-bra baring was demure when compared to the poses struck by several female members of the 2004 U.S. Olympic team in the pages of *Playboy*. They also were featured on the cover of "lad" magazine *FHM* wearing revealing lingerie and swimsuits. But their body-baring actions prompted no searing headlines, no cover stories in the newsweeklies, and no fanfare over their racy actions. In fact, there was so little reaction—either positive or negative—that the *New York Times* wrote about the nonreaction in a front-page story. Dominique Dawes, athlete and president-elect of the Women's Sports Foundation, told the *Times* that the athletes had earned the right to choose where and how they appeared in the media.[17]

Women's broader expression of their sexuality also is giving rise to a brisk market in everything from sex toys to women using the Internet as a way to "hook up." The slang term can mean something as benign as grabbing a drink with a friend to having sex (without the confines of a relationship). It also became the name of a new product from Avon's "mark." "The gender shift in sexuality has been measurable with online personals," says Rufus Griscom, co-founder of Nerve.com, a soft-porn Web site that also offers a personals section where Nerve members can meet.[18] "The Internet is the ideal flirting habitat. It's not about matchmaking so much as it is about 'hooking up,' and it's just as likely that it will be a woman looking for that as it is a man," Griscom says. He estimated that 60 percent of the "flirters" on Nerve.com's personals in 2003 were women looking, quite simply, for sex.

While statistics vary on the impact of women consumers in business-es that cater to sexual exploration, research does show that women have become influential consumers—and even business owners—in industries once considered not only unacceptable for women, but also unwanted by women. The Internet has been a driving force behind the increase in sales of sex toys, videos, and other goods. Instead of having to shop at the often-sleazy adult stores or porn shops frequented by men, women can buy products from the comfort of their own homes. Comscore Media Metrix estimated that 42 percent of all visitors to adult sites in January 2004 were women. Adam & Eve, a catalog company that sells sexual toys and aids, estimates that 10 years ago its consumers were virtually all male. In 2003, the company estimated that women accounted for 30 percent of the com-pany's catalog sales and 40 percent of Internet sales.[19] Passion Parties, where sex toys are sold much the same way as Tupperware, is a growing $20 million business with 3,200 saleswomen nationwide that has found itself under attack in communities such as Burleson, Texas.[20]

It's not just sex behind closed doors or through the Internet that women are looking for, either. Parties hosted by organizations such as Cake.com, One Leg Up, and Flirt NYC attract thousands of women in such urban areas as New York City. At the parties, women are in charge of the scene, as opposed to past generations of sexual exploration, such as swing-ing in the '70s, when men were often the ones in control.[21] The organizers, many of them women, describe the parties as the next realistic step in fem-inism. "The philosophy is that women need their own place to explore sex-uality. The women in the room direct whatever happens," Melinda Gallagher, founder of Cake.com, told the *New York Times*. Cake's Web site Cakenyc.com says it is "an entertainment company dedicated to providing education and information about female sexual culture. Cake online is a resource for exploring female sexuality, pleasure, health, and politics."

Click from the innocuous start page into the site, and the viewer sees pages of products to buy, editorials to read, and photos to browse.[22] Cake plans to evolve beyond parties, with plans for a book and much more. As one of its founders, Emily Kramer, described to *Vanity Fair* in September 2002, "They dream of one day seeing the Cake brand on books, films, perhaps a magazine; a flagship club in New York and more around the world; 'love hotels' on the Japanese model with 'Ian Schrager-like' touches. They've been meeting with 'executive producers' about bringing 'sexy and informative entertainment geared toward women' to television and film. 'Isn't that how you change culture?'"[23] Such sexual exploration isn't likely to slack off as younger generations of women continue to strike down the rigid definitions of what is acceptable and what's not for women—especially young women raised in the age of the Internet.

Avon Makes Its Mark

Against such a backdrop of empowered sexuality and expanding norms of beauty and body, Avon's traditional middle-of-the road view of beauty had grown far out of sync with a new generation of consumers drawn to the dramatic or sexy beauty ideals of brands like Mac, Hard Candy, and Pout. But just as McDonald's continued to see women primarily as moms, Avon had continued to see its consumers through the traditional roles and beauty stereotypes that had served it so well for most of its history.

From its very beginnings, Avon was fashioned as a beauty brand for the masses, women of the middle class who were rarely drawn to or driven by the outer fringes of fashion or beauty. It wasn't that Avon didn't keep up with beauty trends. It moved more conservatively than its competitors as it formulated products that would suit its mainstream consumers and keep prices affordable for a broad swath of women. For decades, such a middle-class sensibility served the company well in the U.S. and most definitely abroad. Avon took its middle-class view of women from the U.S. to Canada and Europe in the mid-century and to Russia and China in the late 1990s, where it would begin to reap some of its biggest sales and profits. By the mid-1990s, however, that middle-class sensibility had begun to hurt Avon's sales and brand image, especially in its core U.S. market. By 1999, the company's overseas units were shoring up sinking sales in the U.S. While the U.S. economy boomed through the latter half of the 1990s, Avon's sales crept up an average of 5 percent a year and slowed to just 1.5 percent in 1999.[24] The median age of Avon's consumers was in the mid-to-late 30s, and its sales representatives were even older. The disconnect between the company's traditional attitudes about beauty and the changing landscape of women was obvious at the company's annual convention in Las Vegas. Jung, dressed in fashionable pointed high heels and a striking red ball gown, seemed to represent the future and a new generation while the speakers pointed to the past. Suzanne Somers, who had been a television star before many in Generation Y were even born, was on the program to give the keynote speech, and Richard Simmons was on the docket to give the ladies a lesson in aerobics.[25]

Many women under 30, and even some over 40, considered Avon a brand for their mothers or grandmothers. These women had been raised on the beauty and fashion trends set by an ever-increasing and ever-pervasive media, including MTV on cable and *TeenVogue* on newsstands. "They have very different assumptions about what it means to be a woman and what it means to be beautiful," Fine says. But even when Avon tried new ideas to attract the younger generation's attention—for example, launching a psychedelic color line inspired by the U.K. girl band Atomic Kitten, or signing up fashion-forward spokeswomen such as tennis superstars Venus and Serena Williams—the efforts often were hidden from younger consumers by the staid symbol of the Avon lady.

What had once been the company's most important calling card had become one of the biggest turn-offs to the fastest-growing demographic in the beauty industry. Avon's top 30 markets have 300 million women ages 16 to 24 with annual spending power of $250 billion.[26] In the U.S., 17 million women between the ages of 16 and 24 spend $75 billion a year on beauty and fashion.[27] But they weren't spending that money on Avon products sold by Avon ladies. They were shopping for new brands, often with sexual overtones—one of Pout's nail colors was called "Lick My Cherry"—in cosmetics superstores, such as Sephora, or buying affordable but funky cosmetics at Target.

At Avon, those trends went mostly unnoticed by the male executives who had run the company for decades, until Jung began bringing the trends to their attention. "We looked at the market through one set of glasses," former chief executive officer James E. Preston told *BusinessWeek* in 2000. "[Andrea] had a fresh take on what Avon could be."[28] That fresh take was embodied by Jung herself, who was often seen wearing three-inch spike heels from trendy shoe designer Jimmy Choo, designer suits, and a signature double-strand pearl choker—a far cry from the plain-Jane, unglamorous attitude of the company she had been put in charge of.

Almost from the moment she moved into the chief executive role, Jung began casting about for ways to overhaul Avon's image. Despite changes over the years, Avon was still defined by its well-known tagline that had been shelved in the 1970s: "Ding Dong: Avon Calling." Jung over-hauled the company's marketing, including launching the new tagline, "Let's talk," and fired the company's ad agency. But Jung went beyond her marketing roots to change the company. She put millions of dollars into research and development to come up with new products that could com-pete with department store brands that were moving further into "nutraceuticals," cosmetics combined with medicines and vitamins to change skin from the inside out, not just cover up blemishes and add color, as traditional cosmetics had done. She consolidated regional brands and rolled out more global brands that cleaned up the company's distribution system. By 2004, Avon's sales had increased 45 percent in the five years she has overseen the company, hitting more than $7 billion in 2004.[29]

By 2001, early success from her new strategies would give Jung the leverage and revenues she needed to make significant changes at Avon. By the time Fine came up with the idea for the new brand, Jung was more than ready to overhaul Avon's image with young women. But Fine's ideas were a big gamble for a company that had not changed its core strategy for more than a hundred years. The big question for many at the company was just how much the new brand would cannibalize Avon. But first, Fine had to find ways to turn her consumer insights into real products and a real brand.

Fine already had her brand name: "mark."[30] But she needed a visual way to express the independence and strength that was so evident in the young women who attended the focus groups. She took to scribbling the word "mark" on scraps of paper in her own bold handwriting. It seemed to match the sense of control and power these women so adamantly proclaimed was important to them. In addition to "mark" playing off the "making their mark" attitudes of these women, there also was something alluring about using a man's name, Fine says. It gave the brand a "gender-neutral" attitude that seemed to play well with women tired of overly feminized beauty products that too often focused on soft pastel colors. The team played up the stronger image by using stark black-and-white packaging for the products, which negated the need to prescribe a specific color to the brand.

Along with individuality and independence, another philosophy—dubbed "social beauty" by the team—was culled from the focus groups. It would be instrumental in setting "mark" far apart from Avon and from its competition. This philosophy also helped the Avon Future team further define product and sales strategy for the brand.

Historically, Avon ladies met one-on-one with their customers. While Avon ladies often became friends with their consumers, the young women in "mark's" focus groups talked about hanging out with groups of their friends, sharing secrets, gossiping, and exchanging ideas about cosmetics. There was little desire to have someone tell them what beautiful was or what products were trendy and must-haves. It was a very different idea of sharing beauty secrets than the ones adopted by many cosmetics companies, which often used the ubiquitous white-coated women at their counters to dispense advice. It was even different from the approach taken by Avon with its Beauty Advisors, a special group of representatives created with Jung's support.[31] Instead, these young women shared their ideas, picked up what they liked, and discarded what they didn't. They didn't necessarily need approval for how they looked; what they wanted was the sharing—not unlike what Kodak had tapped into with its EasyShare cameras and printer docks. "This concept of sharing has always existed. It's when six women get together to get ready for a wedding or 12 girls dressing for the prom or girls going for drinks," Fine says. But there was something quite different about how these young women shared tips and products without passing judgment, she says. Moreover, while Fine admits that the idea of individual beauty and independence had been in style "out in the world culturally for 10 or 15 years, Avon was one of the first companies to harness the idea for a brand identity."

The "social beauty" philosophy quickly became the touchstone for how "mark" created its new products and even refashioned Avon's direct-selling model to fit the younger generation. For Fine and her team, the philosophy of "mark" had to be made three-dimensional in products and a newly trained sales staff. The brand would definitely fail if the company took existing Avon products and branded them "mark," because most women would be able to see through the marketing hype. "This philosophy had to resonate in the actual products," Fine says.

Creating the "Hook-Up"

Armed with this philosophy of social beauty, Fine and her team set out to design an unusual set of cosmetics, including the "Hook-Up." It quickly became Avon's most successful product and an item touted by the magazines that young women look to for beauty ideas. The Hook-Up makes use of a unique connector that gives a consumer the option of mixing and matching several different beauty products, depending on what look she wants that day, not what the cosmetic company has prescribed for her. "Say you want to have mascara and a concealer when you are at work," Fine says. "But when you go out for the evening, you want lip gloss and something else." Other versions of the Hook-Up included stackable lip and cheek colors that open and close like books. The colors can be used anywhere on the face, so a woman doesn't have to carry specific colors for eyes, lips, and cheeks. Fine admits that other companies have introduced similar products, but many of them are fixed, meaning that consumers can't switch lipsticks for mascara. "You're stuck with what they want you to have, not what you want," she says. "With the Hook-Up you are literally making your own beauty when you create your version of it," Fine says. "This is where we get into the cultural phenomenon, the philosophy, that we heard from women. Women relating to women; women multitasking; women wanting portable, adaptable products—those are all part of this philosophy of 'social beauty.'"

The team went a step further to capture the attention of young women. By using the generation's slang to name the product, the brand showed that it understood these women's changing attitudes about sexuality that have spread deep into mainstream America. There were certainly people inside the company who considered the product's name somewhat risqué, Fine says. It went back to the idea of "speaking a different dialect" to these young women. "We needed to create products with names that told young women that they didn't need to look any further. The products all had to do that within 20 seconds. They have to say to the woman, 'We understand you,'" Fine says. The team also took one final step to solidify Fine's belief that the philosophy of "social beauty" had to pervade the entire brand—even and especially through its sales force. Fine knew that "mark" couldn't be sold through the traditional Avon Ladies. It would get lost just as other efforts to reach young women had in the past. The Avon Future team decided to recruit a wholly new sales force that looked, acted, shopped, and behaved just like their target market. But to create this new direct-selling model for the 21st century, Fine asked for help from inside Avon—just as she had when creating the products. "We knew that Avon had one of the best sales models, so we didn't need to create it from scratch. We needed to modify some of the parts so that it resonated with a new consumer and a new woman who would be selling the products." Fine adds: "In many places, we used the best practices of Avon and adapted them for 'mark.' In other places, we had to create something new from scratch so that it would speak the language we need to reach this customer. I don't think 'mark' would exist or would have become what it is today if we didn't have the opportunity to both incubate new ideas outside of Avon, but also have the freedom to listen and learn and glean insight from the 100-plus years of Avon practices."

As "mark" began preparing for its launch in August 2003, the team tapped into the company's U.S. sales force to find the first "mark" women. "No one realized that there are 17 million Avon 'daughters' out there," Fine says. "There were millions of girls who had grown up around Avon. They had packed their mother's Avon boxes and stuffed Avon bags with products for Christmas." The team began talking to these young women about selling "mark" just as their mothers had sold Avon, but with some major differences. Gone was the "Avon lady" who met personally with each customer. Instead, "mark" put more emphasis on parties and gatherings of girls by producing a sales kit it called the "party selling kit." It included many more products and ideas for hosting parties, including a recipe for "mark" punch. "It was about being part of a community; you can learn, explore, share, and chat," Fine says. While the saleswomen for "mark" take orders during the parties, much of the ordering is done online. This is a major shift away from Avon representatives, who still take most of their orders in person and who balked early on at having customers use the Internet. "We had to be relevant to women's lives today. This is a 24/7 world. You might want to order at 1 a.m. after you get home from a party. Or if you're a mom, ordering when the kids are taking a nap," Fine says.

Finally, "mark" pitched itself to potential saleswomen in a far different way from how Avon has added to its workforce over the years. Click through Avon's representative section on Avon.com, and you see a number of "day in the life" articles about how women have used Avon to overcome many of life's struggles. There are discussions of single moms raising families on their Avon earnings or using Avon sales to help pay the family's bills. While the stories are heartwarming, they evoke more traditional stereotypes about women.

Click over to "mark's" Web site, www.meetmark.com, and the difference is obvious. The messages are more modern, with discussions of making money to go to college or using it to buy a dream car. The focus is far more on individual empowerment. Selling "mark" is a stepping-stone to something greater—to higher education or a career. It isn't necessarily an end in itself—as Avon's representatives are often cast. Instead, "mark" is about getting ahead and achieving—all while having a bit of fun along the way. "The empowerment idea in 'mark' is absolutely huge," Fine says. Unlike Avon ladies, whose main goal has been financial empowerment through selling cosmetics, "mark" representatives can use their sales experience to help plan for their future careers by taking a 12-part online training course and applying for college credit through the University of Phoenix. So far, the company says more than 100,000 women have been to the college training site. There are now about 20,000 "mark" representatives, with top sellers hitting $10,000 in annual sales.

"Avon was born giving women financial independence. We gave it to them before women had the right to vote," Fine says, reciting the oft-told homily. "Now 'mark' is the next generation of that, and we are again giving a new generation of women access to even greater financial independence before we have a female president. One day that will sound as archaic as saying there was a time when women didn't have the right to vote."

Key Observations

◆ Instead of focusing on age—a traditional demographic used by companies—Avon focused on how younger women perceived their beauty differently from older generations. This strategy drove the creation of a new brand instead of a "teen" version of Avon.

◆ Use consumer insights to drive product design, not just marketing strategies. This strategy was used to create "hook-ups" that spoke to young women's desires to create an individualistic beauty.

◆ Combine the talents of outsiders with the expertise of the parent company's research and development.

◆ Avon redesigned its direct-sales model to meet the needs of a new generation of women, including offering college credit along with sales revenue for "mark" representatives.

Instead of overhauling the company's main brand to meet the needs of a younger generation—and risk alienating its existing customers—Avon created an all-new brand that tapped into the changing views women had about beauty. In the next chapter, the same trends that forced Avon to create "mark" create the right environment for a new toy company to do the unimaginable—topple Barbie from her pedestal.

CHAPTER 8

Toppling Barbie

BRATZ PREDICTS THE FUTURE

B*y creating a toy brand that reflected the real world in which young girls were growing up—while keeping the roles of play and fantasy very much alive—MGA Entertainment Inc. struck a chord with new generations of girls ready for a post-Barbie future.*

In 2001, it was virtually unthinkable that Barbie could be knocked off her pedestal as the world's best-selling doll and favorite "girl" brand.

Mattel Inc.'s powerhouse Barbie franchise had survived numerous attacks by critics who maintained that her overtly sexual body and blonde good looks placed unrealistic expectations on the girls who played with her. She had fended off the few attempts at marketing more realistic dolls, and even some knock-offs by strong competitors. She had even remained a consistent best seller and profit center for Mattel as new outlets for play, like the Internet and video games, grew in popularity with young girls.

But Barbie's more than four-decade grip on girls was about to be threatened by upstart toy company MGA Entertainment Inc., whose founder saw several chinks in Barbie's armor.

The privately held company was best known for licensing Mighty Morphin' Power Rangers and selling handheld electronic games. It was about to introduce a set of dolls it called Bratz in June 2001 to be ready for the year's holiday season. The dolls—with names such as Yasmin, Jade, and Sasha, which matched their ethnic features—were in sharp contrast to Barbie's white, Anglo-Saxon looks. Yasmin's Middle Eastern looks and her name took cues from the daughter of MGA's founder, Isaac Larian, an Iranian immigrant.[1] Her best friend, an African-American, inspired Sasha's looks. Bratz dolls also were more realistically shaped than Barbie dolls. Bratz were curvier and shorter than Barbie. If Barbie were a real woman, she would stand 6 foot 2 and most likely would be unable to stand because of her tiny waist and large bust. Her measurements were, until a slight makeover on a few Barbie models in 1997, 39–18–33.[2] By contrast, if Bratz were real girls, they would stand about 5 foot 6 and sport bodies that looked more like entertainers Beyonce Knowles and Jennifer Lopez than the Amazon stance of Barbie.[3]

But the differences didn't stop with the dolls' looks. With Barbie, there had always been a specific recipe for how she was clothed and what career choices were open to her. Through the years, as women pushed further into the world of work and men, Barbie was there with accessories, such as a doctor's stethoscope, an astronaut's space suit (introduced in 1965, 18 years before an American woman went into space), and even a NASCAR driver's outfit. But Bratz displayed none of the "role modeling" that had been such a major component of how girls had played with Barbie for decades. Bratz didn't have careers per se, or at least their clothes didn't reflect that. Instead, the dolls' clothing and accessories were knockoffs of the fashions young girls saw—and wanted—in the real world. The clothing options included belly-baring, body-hugging t-shirts, low-rise jeans, and clunky platform shoes that were de rigueur on the videos featured on cable channels such as MTV and BET. It was up to the girls to decide how they would play with their Bratz dolls. The girls decided what they wanted their dolls to be when they grew up or if they just wanted to hang out and try on clothes. There was no rule book on what was appropriate for these young girls, no role model of what they should be or shouldn't be.

However, one thing was less realistic than Barbie: Bratz facial features. While their skin tones and hair colors were far more in keeping with America's changing demographics than Barbie, Bratz faces were far more *unrealistic* than Barbie's small, sharp features. Bratz came with comically big, pouty lips and huge doe-shaped eyes that took up most of their faces—more like a cartoon than a real person. The unusual combination of realism and fantasy was a carefully planned dichotomy by MGA.

"We wanted to create dolls that would appeal to everyone. We didn't want to give girls just one idea of what was beautiful or what we thought they should do in life," Larian says. "Not everybody is blonde and perfect, and we wanted dolls that expressed that. We wanted girls to be okay with expressing themselves and being different."[4]

The combination of realism mixed with fantasy and fashion struck a chord with young girls during the 2001 holiday season. By the time all the Christmas shopping was over, Bratz had racked up $100 million in sales for the year, according to company reports. While miniscule compared to the $2 billion in global sales Barbie would bring in, those sales figures were just the beginning of a Bratz revolution. By November 2002, sales results for the first six months of the year revealed that Bratz had done what no other new doll had been able to: knock Barbie out of her first-place position, according to NPD, a research firm that tracks toy sales. For the first time in most people's memory, Barbie was no longer number one with girls. Bratz—with their funky fashions, clunky shoes, and comic-book features—had climbed to the top of the pedestal.[5]

During the next four years, Bratz proved that it was more than a one-hit wonder despite aggressive moves by Mattel to make over Barbie's looks. Mattel also filed lawsuits against Carter Bryant, the originator of the "Bratz" concept, and against a former Mattel executive who left the company to become head of sales and marketing at MGA. (The court dismissed the latter suit with prejudice in early 2005.) By the end of 2004, Bratz had held on to the number one fashion doll spot for three years—both in the U.S. and increasingly abroad in countries such as the U.K.—by employing many of the strategies that put them there in the first place. Primary among them was staying current with the fast-changing desires of girls by watching them at play and reading their letters that showed up by the hundreds at the company's headquarters north of Los Angeles. By the time the holiday season for 2004 came to a close, the Bratz brand, which had expanded to include hundreds of licensed products, such as bikes and computers, had racked up more than $3 billion in sales (including licensed products)—making the funny-looking dolls one of the most successful new toy brands in the industry's history.[6]

Looking into the Future

Bratz's success is in many ways a natural outcome of the social and economic changes that have transformed women and girls over the past five decades. It seems inevitable that a generation of young girls—brought up in a world where women were gaining economic and social power and changing society forever—would gravitate toward a radically different doll from the one their mothers, and even sisters, had played with.

"This is the first generation of young women to have no collective memory of the struggles their predecessors have endured in securing the rights they now take for granted—the pill, abortion, and equality in the workplace, among others," wrote Rebecca Gardyn in *American Demographics* in 2001. "Confident and commanding respect, they are taking with them into the marketplace a vastly different view of their 'place' in society. Some 35 million strong, a group almost as large as their Boomer foremothers, they are poised to alter every industry they touch."[7]

Indeed, Bratz were far more in keeping with that different view than Barbie, despite her best efforts to keep up with the fast-changing roles of women in her 40 years as the number one doll. Barbie did advance as women advanced. She had a doctor's outfit, she went into space, and she wore glasses, even though Mattel's made-up backstory for her was that she was born Barbie Millicent Rogers and was a teen model from Willows, Wisconsin. But she was still blonde and blue-eyed when a majority of girls in the U.S. and the world were not. She still followed stereotypes of women, not necessarily setting them or ignoring them, as in the case of Bratz and their distinct lack of "career" choices.

Where Barbie represented the past, Bratz represents at least one view of the present and quite possibly some insight into the future of where women and girls are headed. It is a future where young girls don't need their dolls to show them the career choices they have open to them. They already know they can choose any career and pursue it. It's a future where the rules about the size and shape of women's bodies, and how women express their sexuality, are far broader and more open. It's a world where purple and black—Bratz's primary colors—are as feminine as Barbie pink.

No doubt Bratz dolls still maintain girls' fantasy images, with their pouty lips, curvy bodies, and sexy fashions. Certainly, women still have more room to grow and expand their power, both economically and socially. But Bratz tapped into the same underlying trends that Nike and Avon followed as they overhauled their brands and products for new generations of women and girls. Bratz are brash and bold, sexy and sophisticated. In short, they can be anything they want to be, much like Avon's new generation of young women, who wanted nothing more than to "make their own mark" on the world.

"It's interesting that they call these dolls 'Bratz.' It undermines the notion that young girls are just sugar and spice," says professor of sociology Kathleen Gerson at New York University. "It conveys the message that girls aren't just sweet little things. In this way, it may help expand the range of possible identities beyond the image of Barbie. When many girls have grown up in a post-feminist world where rigid distinctions about gender are on the wane, perhaps we are beginning to see more than one ideal conveyed by dolls."[8]

Certainly, during the past 50 years women have shown that many of the ideas once considered inviolate about gender—especially about the abilities of the female gender—don't hold water. Five decades ago, many people believed women couldn't run marathons; they couldn't run companies; they couldn't fight in combat; they couldn't do math or science. (This last belief continues to pervade some parts of academia, given the early 2005 furor over Harvard president Larry Summers' comments that women may not have the same innate abilities in math and science as men.) Fifty years ago, the conversation about women was still more about what women "couldn't" do. In the 21st century, the conversation increasingly is about everything women *can* do.

As outlined throughout this book, women on the whole have come a long way in the past 50 years. Much of this change has come in the form of increased economic power and financial freedom. Women also had experienced a great deal of social and psychological change. Even as women gained access to more money and power, their sense of self and self-worth have been transformed. That has given rise to a whole new attitude toward what is appropriate and acceptable for women. This includes the careers they can pursue to what is beautiful and sexy to what type of reflection they want mirrored back to them in the dolls they play with, the media they watch or read, or even the photographs they see of women on product packaging. No doubt, some of those images are tough to take for earlier generations of women, who fought not to be so highly sexualized. But the expectation by some feminists that the younger generations of women would throw off the desire to be sexy and pretty has been dashed. "Unlike their '70s feminist ancestors, who believed that 'acting like a girl' was asking to be treated as such, most of today's young women do not feel any disjoint between being a feminist (or identifying with feminine ideals) and being feminine," Gardyn writes in her *American Demographics* article.

But still there is much to commend in the new images of women—images that helped spur the invention of dolls like Bratz. These images offer a far broader, more interesting, and ultimately more real view of women than the one presented by Barbie for so long.

Barbie reflected the world of much of the 20th century. She was a product of her environment and her history, just as the girls who played with her were shaped by the world in which they lived. Try as she might by changing her clothes and careers to reflect women's move into the corner office or the space program, Barbie was still reflective of a world that was fast becoming history.

Indeed, even in 1959—the year Barbie was introduced to American girls—the world was on the verge of major social upheaval. Women were beginning to even more vocally question their roles in society. The first rumblings of yet another feminist movement, which built on those in the 19th century and early part of the 20th century, were being heard on college campuses. Other social changes were affecting the world of women as well. Some would help give rise to the multiethnic look of Bratz more than 40 years later. The civil rights movement and the increase of immigrants from Asia and Latin America would begin to lay the foundation for an America that looked and felt far different from the world of the 1950s that spawned Barbie's looks. In the ensuing 50 years, the majority of women would go to work. They would grow more confident and capable. Some would upset the rigid mores of American society by choosing to stay single and have children alone. Others would marry and divorce and marry again. Most women would say they were better off than their mothers and grandmothers as they made their own money, bought their own homes, saved for their own retirement, and created more equal partnerships with the men in their lives.

But Barbie, with her white middle-class sensibilities, stood the test of time against those changes until she came up against a force that she couldn't withstand—a generation of girls transformed by the social and economic changes of the past 50 years. As generation after generation of women defined and redefined women's roles in the workplace and the home, they were teaching their daughters—either consciously or unconsciously—that the stereotypes personified in Barbie were no longer valid in a world where women were questioning everything about their lives.

The concept of playing with dolls through predetermined roles—be they career woman or stay-at-home mom—had ceased to be a big draw to many girls, especially young girls ages 8 to 12, once a sweet spot for Barbie. Certainly, Barbie was and is just a plastic toy. But she was often more than that for young girls. She became whoever they wanted to be. It can be easy to overstate the impact of dolls, such as Barbie and Bratz, on girls and the women they will become. But the imagery that little girls have played back to them through toys—and increasingly for present and future generations on television, film, and the Internet—do have an impact beyond the playroom. "Imagery is by no means a purely superficial phenomenon, but is rather the means through which we articulate and define the social order and nature," writes Sharon MacDonald, a literary scholar.[9]

By the late 1990s, Barbie had ceased to reflect the modern social order. Nor was she the type of role model to which young girls were gravitating. This new generation of girls had been raised in a world that played back to them very different ideas about what a woman was or could be from the images presented to their foremothers. Just as Torrid and Avon had found, girls' images of their bodies and beauty were far different from their mothers and grandmothers. Their ideas about what roles they would play in life also weren't as constrained as the women who came before them, just as McDonald's and The Home Depot had discovered. In a survey by the

National Opinion Research Center, only 9 percent of girls and young women ages 13 to 20 agreed with the statement "A woman's place is in the home." By contrast, 68 percent of women over 70 agreed with the statement "It is much better for everyone involved if the man is the achiever outside the home and the woman takes care of the home and family."[10] While not surprising, these statistics reveal the significant changes that have occurred in the 46 years since Barbie was introduced.

MGA Entertainment certainly wasn't the first company to tap into what had become obvious shifts in women and society. In fact, a number of companies—particularly in the film and television industries—had been reflecting the shifting roles of women for more than 20 years and had laid the groundwork for a new way of play and a new way of looking at women. They played back a broader, deeper, and ultimately more realistic view of women that would help shape a new generation of girls and their images of women—and force more industries like toys and comic books to pay attention.

Some film and women's studies historians date the shift back to Sigourney Weaver's breakout role as a tough, gun-wielding alien fighter in the 1979 film *Alien*. But for many girls of an even younger generation, the images of independent female characters came from watching Saturday morning cartoons. By the early 1990s, a whole new set of girl characters were everywhere on Saturday morning. They included the comically round-faced Powerpuff girls, intrepid Dora the Explorer, Kim Possible with her belly-baring T-shirts, and even the bratty Angelica on *Rugrats*. These girl characters were quite different from the female characters earlier generations had watched on Saturday mornings. By and large, cartoons in the 1970s and early 1980s featured traditional female stereotypes. For example, *Scooby Doo* had two roles for young girls to relate to and mimic in play. They could be pretty like Daphne or unattractive and smart like Velma—although both of them fought crime along with the guys. By the mid-1990s, cartoon girl characters were becoming as varied as the real girls who watched them. "A young woman growing up now can project herself into a variety of roles—one of the Powerpuff Girls, or a smart kid who isn't a nerd, like Ginger," said Robert Thompson, Ph.D. and head of the Center for the Study of Popular Television at Syracuse University in New York, in an article in *Child*. "It dilutes the power of any one stereotype. Now we have a whole pantheon of smart, adventurous girls."[11]

The same has been true—in fits and starts, admittedly—on the big screen and on other days of the week besides Saturday on television. In 1997, a television show debuted that changed the way many people looked at the role of young women on or off the small screen. *Buffy the Vampire Slayer* featured Sarah Michelle Gellar in the title role as a brainy, pretty girl who happened to slay vampires in her spare time. The series' creator and main writer, Joss Whedon, was the son and grandson of television screenwriters. Notably and somewhat ironically, Whedon's grandfather wrote for the *The Donna Reed Show* and *Leave It to Beaver*, and his father wrote for *Alice*, the 1970s series about a tough-talking waitress.[12]

The Buffy character was a reflection of young teenage girls despite her vampire-slaying nature. She was so different that she soon became the topic of conversation in women's studies programs, and students began writing essays on the transformation of women characters on television. What made her different from past tough females was the mixture of the serious and the funny, the sexy and the strong, the feminine and the masculine that hadn't been seen that often in mainstream pop culture. "[Buffy exposes] stereotypes and coded symbols that shore up a rigid war-influenced gender system in an attempt to chart new meanings for womanliness and manliness," writes Frances Early, a history professor at Mt. Saint Vincent University.[13]

Buffy helped give rise to a cadre of stronger, albeit still sexy, female characters on television shows. While critics still complain about the overly sexualized roles that women are given on television and in films, today's young girls are as likely to see a woman playing a hard-charging lawyer or a smart, capable doctor on a television series as they are to see a woman in a subservient or sexist role—although those stereotypes still persist. During the 2004–2005 television season, the most popular show on television was *Desperate Housewives*, which featured every traditional stereotype or icon of women, including the neighborhood hottie, the overachieving mother who had left her high-powered job to raise her children, and the single mom looking for a date with her hunky neighbor.

Girls also were seeing far more strong, empowered women elsewhere in pop culture. On the big screen, the "female action hero" genre had become highly lucrative for film studios by the early 2000s. The studios were discovering that young women, along with young men, were as likely to watch a film about sword-wielding heroines as they were an emotionally charged chick flick. In 2003, women showed up as the main characters in a number of action movies, including sequels to *Lara Croft: Tomb Raider* and *Charlie's Angels*. In 2004, Halle Berry appeared in *Catwoman*, and Jennifer Garner, who played a CIA agent on the hit television show *Alias*, appeared in the title role in *Elektra*. The executive director of *Catwoman* told the *Wall Street Journal*, "Today's action heroines are more in sync with the sensibilities of Gen Y. It gives more choices to an audience that is less sexist. You can now hit [all demographic audience targets] with a female action hero."[14] Of course, equality among genders meant that critics and audiences alike panned several of these movies, despite their tougher, stronger images of women. One duo of films that did receive both critical and audience acclaim was the two-part series *Kill Bill*, Quentin Tarantino's homage to spaghetti Westerns and Chinese kung fu films. It featured a primarily female cast of characters who were as vicious, cunning, and violent as any male cast could have been. In the film, Uma Thurman plays a wronged hit woman who seeks revenge on her former assassin-colleagues and the man who killed her fiancé and her unborn child and left her for dead. The film took in $31 million the first weekend it opened, and women accounted for 40 percent of ticket sales, according to Rick Sands, chief operating officer of Miramax Films.[15]

Similarly, the horror film industry also has been transformed by the infusion of young women as both consumers and lead actresses headlining big-budget horror films. "You would think they would be the last audience to be excited about a scary thriller or a horror movie," Sony Pictures Entertainment's head of marketing Geoffrey Ammer told the *Los Angeles Times* in November 2003. "But they are the first audience." By 2003, some film companies began offering screenings to all-female audiences to gauge their interest. Five years ago, such a practice would have been laughable, but Sony's remake of the horror flick *The Texas Chainsaw Massacre* opened with a 50 percent female audience, mirroring other big horror movies like *The Ring* and *Jeepers Creepers*.[16]

Girls and young women also have invaded the male-dominated world of comic books. This has forced companies in the industry to overhaul their offerings to attract a growing number of girls who bear little resemblance to past generations of young women, who rarely showed up at horror movies or cracked open the pages of a Superman comic. By 2002, young girls were driving U.S. sales of "shojo manga," or girls' comic books imported from Japan. Sales grew from about $50 million in 2002 to $110 million in 2003.[17] Those sales made the books, with their distinctive bright colors and characters with huge, almond-shaped eyes—not dissimilar to the looks of the Bratz dolls—the fastest-growing segment of the publishing industry, according to *USA Today*. Their popularity forced U.S. comic book publishers to create new lines of manga cartoons that appeal specifically to girls. Moreover, young women who read early "shojo manga" cartoons, such as *Sailor Moon*, which appeared in the U.S in the mid-1990s, are helping fuel an explosion in sales of graphic novels—more involved, better-written, art-house comic books sold at big booksellers such as Barnes & Noble.[18] DC Comics, known for its Superman and Batman superheroes, publishes the hardcover graphic novel series *The Sandman* by Neil Gaiman, which has a big following among young women. Driven by that popularity, the tenth installment in the series, *The Sandman: Endless Night*, published in 2003, had a first printing of 100,000, the biggest for any DC Comics or its Vertigo imprint, which publishes Sandman.[19]

Unlike the traditional comic books, "shojo manga" and graphic novels feature more than the superheroes and villains that so appealed to boys. Instead, they are a fascinating mixture of traditional boy-girl relationships laced with girl power—all part of the gender somersaulting that virtually every generation of women is going through.

Many of the story lines, especially in "shojo manga," feature a young girl who is transported to a fantasy world where she battles evil spirits and demons. "Shojo manga are popular because they tap into the social obstacles and challenges that girls face: feeling excluded by cliques, having crushes on boys, and often wrestling with issues of their own sexuality," says Eve Zimmerman, who teaches a course on "Gender and Popular Culture" at Wellesley. "But they also are popular because they present a glossy image of a different kind of existence where everyone dresses up fashionably and looks cute."[20]

Given such an onslaught of diverse, compelling, and sometimes disturbing images of women, coupled with all the real-world changes affecting them, it was just a matter of time before the toy industry began to feel the effects of the past 50 years of change that had transformed women. But where other potential competitors to Barbie had seen only her negative side, Bratz creators saw the positive in play and fantasy that had made Barbie so popular for so many years. Indeed, Bratz followed the theme of many companies described in this book by melding the old with the new. Other companies had tried to create more realistic dolls to coun-teract Barbie's sexy influence, but they often ignored the fact that little girls still wanted a fantasy world in which their dolls were pretty. Barbie com-petitors often focused their efforts on breaking down the traditional stereotypes of body and beauty without asking the very girls who would play with these toys what they wanted from a new doll. Even Mattel, which has a solid reputation for its intense focus groups with children, had missed the core truth that MGA would use to create Bratz. "Barbie gave the message that in order to be good and successful as a woman, you had to be a lawyer, a nurse, a president," Larian says. "Today's generation of girls just doesn't see the world that way. These girls have no limits to their ambi-tions, so we don't tell her what those ambitions will be."

Listening to Girls, Not Their Moms

Bratz successfully tapped into this new generation of ambitious, no-boundaries girls—and toppled an icon—by creating a new kind of fashion doll that would take a far different approach to young girls than most of the toy industry, including Barbie.[21] Larian's team of fashion designers and toy makers, many of whom came from Mattel and other toy companies, began by listening to their young consumers in unusual ways. They then used what they learned to react quickly to the changing interests and atti-tudes of young girls, a consumer group that was changing, it seemed, by the day.

Larian appears an unlikely candidate to have shaken up the world of girls' toys. For most of its history, MGA had focused heavily on boys' elec-tronic games and products through licensing properties such as the Mighty Morphin' Power Rangers. The company's original name was Micro Games of America, which Larian changed to MGA Entertainment when he began promoting Bratz. Larian's personal background, as an Iranian immigrant, also didn't lend itself to upsetting the traditional norms. But Larian was more entrepreneur than anything, he says, always on the lookout for new ideas and products for the company. By the late 1990s, he had begun to see an opportunity where others would have shied away— Mattel's monopoly on girls with Barbie. "The monopolist nature is often to stop being innovative," he says. "They had a 90 to 95 percent share of the girls' market, and that wasn't really good for consumers, and it wasn't really good for the toy industry, including their toy business."

Larian believed there was room in the market for another fashion doll—one that would appeal to girls whose tastes skewed away from Barbie. But it had to be more than a Barbie knockoff or another attempt to woo girls with a more "realistic" doll—an insight he says he gained from watching and listening to his own daughter and her friends. Larian says he learned from his daughter that only "little girls of 3 or 4 or 5 still played with Barbie," he says. "The younger girls looked at her as a mommy figure. But most little girls didn't want to play that game after a certain age. They wanted dolls that looked like them or like the teenage girls they loved to emulate." What Larian heard from his daughter and her friends tracked with what the rest of the industry had been recognizing for several years. Children were growing up faster earlier and were looking for toys that were more in keeping with that sophistication. The industry even had a term for the trend, "kagoy," which is short for "kids are getting older younger."[22]

Larian's insistence on focusing on what girls wanted in their dolls was a far different approach than what would-be competitors to Barbie had tried when introducing their realistic-looking dolls. In 1991, entrepreneur Cathy Meredig created a doll called "Happy to Be Me" that had more realistic measurements than Barbie. Although the dolls were far less sexy-looking, little attention was paid to how the girls really played with dolls or even what they thought of Barbie's looks. The focus was primarily on what adults thought of Barbie, not what girls thought of Barbie.

Even Mattel took that "parent-approved" approach when it began designing new products for girls in the early 2000s. A group of designers, model makers, and other employees working in a program called Project Platypus created a new toy for girls called "Ello" in 2001–2002. The toy, which included unusually shaped, but still interlocking, pieces in bright primary and pastel colors, was meant to inspire girls to build and make things—but on their own terms and with materials they would like, according to the group's leader, Ivy Ross.[23] The project's members did look at how girls played and how they constructed things—noting the differences between girls and boys. But there was little discussion of how different *girls of today* are from the *girls of yesterday*. Instead, one of the highlights of the product was that it was "a rarity: a toy that appeals as much to parents as children."[24]

Larian, however, wasn't looking for a toy that appealed to parents. He was driven instead to come up with a doll that would appeal to his daughter and her friends. Older girls were looking for a doll that was more like themselves than a fantasy role model. He believed it was a core truth the company could build a brand on.

What he didn't have was the actual doll. Throughout 2000, he told his people to find him a fashion doll that was different. But nothing really captured his attention until a new designer he had never met before and who had never created a doll, Carter Bryant, walked into his offices.[25] Bryant's sketches featured dolls of varying ethnicities with cartoonish facial features. They had the pouty lips and big doe eyes reminiscent of the "manga" cartoons from Japan. The clothes they were wearing looked just like the clothes Larian saw his daughter and her friends wearing—the low-rise jeans and midriff-baring T-shirts made popular by music stars such as Britney Spears.

Their varied ethnicity hit a chord with Larian. Their fashion-forward looks appealed to his daughter. Both liked the fact that they didn't offer a single ideal of what was beautiful. With their over-the-top cartoon looks, it was up to the girls playing with the dolls to create their own ideas of what was beautiful and fashionable. "The cartoonish look of them was important. They were fantasy, not reality. They didn't necessarily look like real people, but they did represent diversity," Larian says. "We set out to have dolls that weren't realistic, who were more cartoons than mimics of real life. These dolls are more about fantasy and playacting with fashion and trends than they are about 'I want to look like that' when I grow up."

Using Bryant's sketches as a springboard, MGA's team of young employees created the Bratz dolls. Larian knew from his informal research with his daughter that the dolls had to be more than physically different from Barbie. How the girls played with Bratz would be just as important to making the dolls a long-term success as their unusual ethnic looks would be to capturing the attention of young girls in the store aisle.

If Barbie had evolved into girls playing "mom" with her over the decades, Bratz would have to tap into the world of play that attracted older girls. After a series of informal focus groups with children, as well as bi-weekly dinners with Larian's daughter, nieces, nephews, and their friends, the team decided the dolls had to be on the cutting edge of fashion and pop culture, the biggest areas of interest for the 7-to-12-year-old set, often called the "tween" market in the toy industry. Capturing that "tween" market was crucial given how economically powerful the demographic has become. Harris Interactive, a marketing research firm, estimated in 2003 that the 30 million "tweens" in the U.S. had $19.7 billion worth of spending power.[26]

By the time Bratz were ready for launch in 2001, the dolls were sporting the same fashions that girls would see in the stores as well as on their favorite actresses and singers. "What we were looking for primarily were designers who weren't conditioned to think about toys for girls in a traditional way," Larian says. He also pushed them to think beyond the fashions and put the same quality fabrics and finishings they would put into human clothes in the dolls' clothes. They also took care in the types of accessories they offered to girls. Instead of a house that mimicks middle-class life, Bratz have a three-story condo designed by architect Richard Landry, who has designed homes for Eddie Murphy and Rod Stewart. The condo was more like what girls saw on shows like MTV's *Cribs*.

Combining those two forces—the consumer insight gleaned from interactions with his daughter, her friends, and other young members of his extended family and the fashion sense of his designers—was enough to put Bratz in contention for the title of number one fashion doll. But despite the early impressive sales numbers, Larian knew he needed to keep pushing the envelope with Bratz or he could end up being outmaneuvered by Mattel. By 2002, Mattel was ready with several "Bratz fighters." During Christmas that year, it launched My Scene Barbie, a doll featuring more fashionable clothing options. Then in 2003, it rolled out Flavas, a group of dolls with ethnic looks and more urban street fashions that looked similar to Bratz. Then in 2004, it rolled out Barbie Fashion Fever, featuring more fashion forward looks for Barbie herself. Mattel also signed a deal to create dolls based on the winners of *American Idol*, the highly successful television show. Mattel also had begun taking cues from MGA and other companies that were doing a far better job of listening to their consumers in different ways. By 2004, Mattel had begun using what it called "in-home intercepts" to gain a better understanding of how girls were interacting with the brand. Mattel's senior vice president of girls' marketing and design, Tim Kilpin, told an audience at the Licensing Letter Symposium in 2004 that it would always conduct focus groups and quantitative research. "But we're finding that when you get out and watch consumers interact with your product and your competitors' products in their own environment, you get much richer insights."[27]

What About the Boys . . . and Computers?

Given Mattel's assault, Larian had to keep moving if he wanted to keep Bratz top of mind with the "tween" girls who were so important to the brand's success. For inspiration, Larian would turn again and again to his consumers. By 2002 it wasn't just his daughter and her friends who served as his research team. Letters and e-mails from girls around the world had begun to flood into MGA's headquarters, suggesting ideas for new products. Like Hot Topic's Betsy McLaughlin, Larian began taking many of the letters home over the weekend in a bright purple folder. Many of the letters asked for the introduction of boys to the Bratz lineup.

It was an interesting insight given that sales of Ken, Barbie's male sidekick, had sputtered for years. Mattel would end up discontinuing Ken in 2004. But girls weren't asking for boyfriends or husbands for Bratz, Larian says of the stacks of letters he received. Instead, the comments were more in keeping with a significant change that had occurred among the genders for at least one generation, if not more. But many toy makers hadn't picked up on it. The girls wanted boys as part of their Bratz circle of friends, Larian says. It wasn't about the type of "role modeling" that little girls of earlier generations had often taken part in. Barbie and Ken were rarely just friends. He was often cast as the boyfriend or husband in play scenarios that mimicked the world of adults, not the real world of children. Instead, these girls said they had boys as friends in their group and would like to have the same for their Bratz dolls, Larian says. So in 2003, MGA added four boys to the mix—Dylan, Eitan, Koby, and Cameron—complete with fashion-forward looks and ethnic features to complement the Bratz girls.

The inclusion of boys in the lineup sparked criticism from parents, who expressed concern that the company was pushing adult ideas on young girls and boys. Larian countered the criticism by pointing out that the company launched the dolls only after young girls expressed an interest in having boys added to the lineup. "As adults, we put our adult paradigms on the dolls; we see them from an adult perspective," he says. "That's been a problem in the toy industry that we aren't really aware of what is going on with our consumers. What do we as adults really know about the world of young children?" But by listening to his "kitchen-sink" focus group, as he calls his daughter and her friends, and reading the comments from girls around the world, Larian argued that adding boys was simply a reflection of the world of children of the 21st century. "They don't look at this in a sexual way. My daughter has friends who are boys, who are part of her social crowd," he added. "The world has changed, and these kids do have relationships between genders that have nothing to do with sex."

This wasn't the first time Larian had had to defend Bratz. Early on, critics and parents complained that the dolls were too sexualized, although they applauded the Bratz ethnic looks. Parents, especially mothers, complained that the quality of play also wasn't very high given that most of what these dolls were about was dressing up in cool fashions. Some academics, however, say the Bratz dolls are no more harmful than any other cartoons and possibly offer a better depiction of women than Barbie. "They are actually a much healthier depiction of girls than Barbie. No girl will take seriously that this is a body image she ought to be striving for," said Dr. Claudia Paradise, a psychoanalyst who works with children.[28] Barbie herself had come under fire for her sexy looks. In fact, her figure was based on an adult toy called Bild Lilli that Mattel's founder Ruth Handler found in Germany.

Larian has countered much of the criticism by pointing out that the company responds to what young girls say they want in dolls. "Ask them what they think. They think the dolls are fashionable and let them express themselves," he says. Larian says listening to his young consumers has helped him discard preconceived stereotypical ideas about what girls want or how they want to play. "We're learning to break down a lot of barriers and misconceptions about girls, what they should be or shouldn't be, what they will buy or won't buy," he says.

By listening and then acting on what his consumers want, Larian has been able to move quickly to pick up on trends that he otherwise would not have seen—like creating boy Bratz. Indeed, he admits that when he has had an idea for Bratz—and has pursued it—it has sometimes been less successful than the ideas from girls' letters and e-mails. MGA came up with the idea for Bratz Tokyo-a-Go-Go, which featured a roller-skating rink and fashions mimicking those Larian had seen on teenage girls in Tokyo's hip Shibuya shopping neighborhood during a trip to Japan. The Tokyo-inspired products sold well, but they weren't the blockbusters that MGA had expected, Larian says. "In hindsight we realized that kids in America didn't have much of an idea where Tokyo was or why Bratz would be there," he says. The company helped solve some of the problem by adding information about Tokyo to the packaging. "It made it more educational," Larian says.

Staying in touch with its primary consumers also helped MGA move beyond dolls and into areas that are now considered a must-have for survival in the toy industry: movies, television shows, and products like bikes and computers that take the brand far beyond the toy aisle. Such a broad range of items has moved Bratz beyond the dolls and into a lifestyle brand complete with furniture and accessories for girls' rooms. MGA isn't alone in pursuing a "lifestyle" brand approach for the dolls. At least as far back as 1990, Mattel was selling bed sheets and human-size clothes imprinted with Barbie's logo as a way to extend the doll's franchise. Ironically, the company moved into new products in direct response to focus groups that showed "girls still liked the doll, but were somewhat sensitive to playing dress-up or even advertising the fact that they still played with Barbies," as Pauline Yoshihashi wrote in a *Wall Street Journal* article in 1990.[29]

More than a decade later, MGA found itself having to persuade retailers that expanding a doll brand beyond dolls made sense. Larian already had had to persuade some retailers that Bratz—with their new view of girls and society—was something that would sell when he first began pitching the Bratz concept to retailers in 2000. Larian says he had to overcome some of the preconceived ideas retailers still had about girls, demographics, and even race. "Some of them said that girls wouldn't buy black and white dolls that were packaged together," he remembers. Bratz are sold together as a set, instead of the way Barbie often is, as a stand-alone doll. Other retailers, particularly electronics retailers, have suggested that girls wouldn't buy products such as computers, boom boxes, or karaoke machines because girls aren't into technology, Larian says. "We had the toughest time getting our Bratz laptop into retailers, simply because they didn't think girls would buy it or that girls would even shop in their stores," he says. Finally, electronics retailer Best Buy decided to give the Bratz-inspired laptop some shelf space. "They are flying off the shelf now," Larian says. "We have taken the tactic that if consumers like it, then that's what is important. We can't be driven by what the retailer thinks. They are just the middlemen, and if consumers start asking for our brands, they will have no choice but to carry it."

There's no doubt that girls are asking for Bratz dolls or, for that matter, Bratz anything. In the four years since they were introduced, their sales have grown almost exponentially. From 2001 to 2003, Bratz sales surged from an estimated $100 million to more than $1 billion in retail sales, according to the privately held company's statistics. In 2004, MGA estimated that its sales and sales of its licensed products such as computers, video games, bikes, and sleeping bags would top $3 billion. By contrast, Mattel's sales and profits continued to slide, although the Barbie makeovers and new products had begun to turn around the icon in the first quarter of 2005.

But as Larian and his team have learned from watching what happened to Barbie and Mattel, girls can be fickle consumers who move to the next trend as quickly as they picked up the last one. His designers continue to pick up ideas for new clothing lines, including more than likely more modest fashions going forward as the fashion industry and its consumers drive toward a "modest" look over the skin-baring fashions of recent years. Larian keeps reading his consumer e-mails and taking letters home to read in the purple folder and looking for the next idea that will take Bratz to the next level.

Key Observations

◆ Don't allow personal history or preconceived ideas of women—in this case, young girls—to overshadow insight from consumers.

◆ Read, listen, and respond to correspondence from consumers—not their parents. MGA used this strategy to create a line of boy Bratz.

◆ Consider the consumers' whole world, not just the time when they are using the product. This strategy was used to expand Bratz beyond dolls and clothes.

◆ Move with consumer trends, not industry timelines. MGA creates new clothing lines for its dolls every three to six months, not just once a year.

MGA Entertainment built a multibillion-dollar children's brand in just three years by listening to girls who had grown up in a far different world than their grandmothers, mothers, and, indeed, even their older sisters. As Bratz illustrates, the social and economic trends set in motion more than 50 years ago have created ripples and consequences—sometimes unintended—that are just beginning to be understood by companies that are fast realizing that women are their most important, yet sometimes most elusive, consumers.

The next and final chapter features a series of questions and core concepts culled from experiences of the companies featured in the preceding chapters. They offer insight into how other companies can navigate through the ripples from those trends that will continue to affect business for the foreseeable future.

CHAPTER 9

How to Put the Power of the Purse to Work in Your Company

M cDonald's and The Home Depot. Procter & Gamble and Kodak. Avon and AXA Financial. Nike and Torrid. Bratz and DeBeers. On the surface, these companies have little in common that would bring them together in one book. They operate in very different industries, selling vastly disparate products and services. Some, like AXA, sell services directly to consumers. McDonald's relies on franchisees to sell burgers and fries. Kodak is dependent on thousands of retailers with their own brands to consider. Avon must depend on thousands of independent sales representatives to put its brand in the hands of consumers. Bratz and Torrid are less than six years old. Kodak and Avon have been around for more than 100 years. Moreover, they may have very little in common with your specific business. What could a doll company teach a marketer of tires? What do diamonds have to do with convenience stores? What does selling hamburgers have to do with selling software?

The core idea that draws all these companies together, and ultimately to your company, is the drive to do a better, more holistic, more realistic, long-term job of reaching and responding to the needs and wants of the world's most powerful consumers.

These companies have acknowledged that succeeding with women consumers is no longer a nice-to-have accomplishment that makes management feel as if it is doing a good thing for a minority market. It's no longer about putting women in advertising or even making products that fit women better. Instead, the constant drive to adapt to women is a must-have for a profitable future.

To achieve this somewhat-elusive goal, these companies have worked for years to adapt their businesses to women consumers instead of forcing women to adapt to their products, services, or retailing practices, as was so often the case in the past. In the process of adaptation, they all have followed very different strategies, using a wide variety of tactics to arrive at a process that works for their company in their specific industry.

Kodak went back to its past to meet the needs of its present and future customers. Avon, by contrast, looked into the future to find a new generation of consumers. McDonald's looked beyond motherhood, while Procter & Gamble embraced traditional ideas that came from women's long-held roles as wives and mothers. The Home Depot focused on the equal partnership between men and women, while DeBeers explored what single women wanted from a brand that had been all about the love of a man for a woman.

Such disparity in the process of these companies reveals that there is no one perfect way to reach women. There are no easy patterns to follow, no tried-and-true strategies, no magic bullets to reach a market that, in the U.S. alone, is made up of more than 112 million people and that stretches across several generations—each of which has been transformed by the changes fought for by the preceding generation.

But a few core concepts are common to these companies. Common questions have aided them as they have pursued the strategies that have added billions of dollars in sales to their coffers, breathed new life into dying brands, and helped create all-new products.

First among the concepts: The social and economic shifts of the past half-century have shifted the balance of power to women as consumers—making them not just an important minority, but the majority market. This has significantly transformed the way these companies think about women as consumers. Instead of thinking of women as a separate group narrowly defined by their gender, these companies instead have put women at the center of their overall business strategies—not only to create better products and services for women, but as a way to do a better job for all consumers. This shift—from minority to majority—cannot be overstated. The trends that have driven women into the forefront of the global consumer economy aren't about to stop and reverse. If you don't think women are having or will have any effect on your industry, the next 50 years are likely to prove you wrong, just as the past 50 years of change have taught lessons to the home improvement, sports, and technology industries, to name a few.

As noted throughout the book, young women are graduating at much higher rates than men from colleges and business schools in professions that are far more in keeping with where the world is headed. Men once dominated in well-paying jobs, such as manufacturing, that required little higher education. But those types of jobs are no longer the high-paying professions they once were. Women, who are now more likely to graduate from high school, college, and graduate school than their male counterparts, increasingly dominate in the professions that are driving the future. As Peter Francese, founder of *American Demographics*, wrote in the magazine in 2003, "High-growth fields such as health care, education and professional services often require a college degree and employ mostly women. Low-growth and highly cyclical blue-collar industries—manufacturing, transportation, construction, etc.—seldom require an education beyond high school and employ mostly men. These trends are mirrored by the June 2003 U.S. unemployment rate, which was 6.1 percent for adult men and 5.2 percent for adult women."[1]

Add women's vast power as consumers to their increasing power as producers, and the next 50 years are likely to see even more change beyond the shift of power in consumption. Women will change the nature of work as well. "There are only eight women CEOs of Fortune 500 companies, but right below them, usually operating below the radar, is a big talent pool of women who are running multibillion-dollar divisions," Ilene H. Lang, president of Catalyst, a New York research group, says in the *Wall Street Journal's* "Women to Watch" Report in November 2004. Those women came of age when it was still virtually unheard of for a woman to run a company or run for president. They were still minorities in business schools and graduate math and science classes—traditionally areas dominated by men.

According to statistics compiled by the chief economist of the Federal Reserve Bank of Dallas and an economics writer with the bank, in the 1970–71 academic year, only 3.6 percent of master's degrees in business were awarded to women. Only 0.8 percent of bachelor's degrees in engineering were given to women. Only 7.6 percent of doctorates in mathematics were awarded to women that year.[2]

Yet from that small, minority base, those women and millions of others have helped give rise to the consumer majority that is forcing change at companies such as The Home Depot, McDonald's, and Nike. So consider what the impact of the graduating class of 2001–02 will be 30 years from now. In that academic year, women's share of master's degrees in business was 41.1 percent, 18.9 percent of bachelor's degrees in engineering went to women, and 29 percent of doctorates in mathematics were awarded to women.

Certainly, not all women are benefiting from these shifts in the global economy and global workforce. But there are far more signs today that instead of living in a world in which women are perennially cast as the losers, women are now being cast as winners with the power to make even greater changes than their foremothers. It's impossible to know how the women of the graduating classes of the 21st century will change the world. But change the world they will. If those transformations follow even the most conservative trajectory based on the remarkable changes of the past 50 years, every business and industry must be prepared for even greater change in the next 50 years. "We have gone through a social and a psychological revolution with women during the past five decades," says Professor Kathleen Gerson of New York University. "But we have yet to have the institutional revolution. We don't yet have business policies that are changing the way business operates even as women have changed. But the coming generation will be acutely aware that their social and business structures don't support this."

Certainly there is room for growth in the number of women in upper management and in achieving pay parity between genders. There is more work to be done in creating workplaces that are flexible and accommodating to the way women and men work.

But many companies, including the ones featured in this book, are taking the first big steps to change by really listening to the women who make up their most important target audience. That's the second core concept that ties these companies together. They have listened to women both inside and, even more importantly, outside their companies and then used that insight to drive change in their products and organizations. By listening to real women in a variety of ways, these companies have come to understand how the past 50 years of social and economic change have truly transformed this important majority. By listening instead of assuming, they have uncovered a key lesson that many have used successfully to tap into today's women. Even as women have been transformed by their new roles, they don't shun all their traditional roles. Instead, the blending of the old with the new has been a key differentiator in beating the competition for many companies described in this book, among them McDonald's, Procter & Gamble, and Kodak.

The final core concept is that these companies have learned to stay in constant transformation. A majority of these companies have learned the tough lesson of standing still while women have moved on. To make certain such stasis doesn't happen again, they have instilled a sense that constant change and evolution are the nature of doing business today if they plan to keep up with women, if not stay ahead of them.

It is never easy to see how broad philosophical concepts can be turned into real, actionable strategies that will result in tangible products that draw more consumers and add profits to the bottom line. It is one thing to read a case study of how McDonald's created a Premium Salads line that helped return the company to profitability or how Nike overhauled its organization to focus on women's fitness. It is quite another to understand how to make such a transformation happen inside your company.

While my main purpose as a journalist is more to enlighten readers than to teach or preach, as I interviewed executives I began to keep a list of questions that seemed universal to these very disparate companies. Some were more specific to individual companies; others were broader and involved several companies. These questions define some of the toughest stumbling blocks that these companies had to overcome before they could move forward successfully with their strategies:

1.   **Do you have stereotypical views of women consumers that haven't changed in more than a year?** Often we think of traditional stereotypes of women as the bad ones from the 1950s. All

women are drawn to pink and pastels. They are all wives and mothers. Other bad stereotypes hang on from the 1980s and 1990s. All women are harried, harassed, and in search of time-saving tools. But even the perceptions or stereotypes that we consider more insightful or truthful can hold us back from really understanding where women are today and where they are headed. Consider the stereotypes that Nike, The Home Depot, and Procter & Gamble had to break down to discover their new ways of thinking about women. In 2000, Nike launched its "magalog," which focused on the softer side of athletes. It did so because it heard from women consumers that they weren't drawn to the harsher, more aggressive stance the company took with its male athletes. Fast-forward to 2002. The company was quickly realizing that a softer, gentler Nike wasn't necessarily working for women who had grown up playing competitive sports. They didn't have the same perceptions of themselves or Nike as older consumers did. While they didn't worship sports stars like many men did, they still wanted women to be portrayed as powerful and assertive. The Home Depot would have failed if it had stuck to the once-true but quickly aging stereotype that women influenced home improvement projects but didn't actually do them. Understanding how quickly women had shifted in just a few years helped The Home Depot move beyond a stereotype that for many still rang true. Ironically, P&G moved past the '90s traditional stereotype of women wanting only time-saving tools and focused on an older "traditional" stereotype—that maintaining a clean home was an important part of a women's role—but with some modern twists to create the Swiffer.

2. **Do you still think of women as a minority?** It's easy to get stuck in "minority think." Both male and female executives I interviewed said they had to fight such thinking—even when it felt like the right thing to do. Even when they had really let the numbers—$7 trillion in spending in the U.S. alone and more than 112 million people—sink in, it was hard to let go of the long-held perception that women are minorities who need to be

treated with kid gloves. Even women consumers often requested special attention be paid to them because they had been so neglected in the past. Such thinking often sparked the creation of special groups. Indeed, in some instances in this book—Women and Company and AXA Financial, notably—companies have used such organizations to push forward change. In some cases, special marketing groups can work to bring about change or transformation in an industry where women still are the minority consumers. But holding on to such "minority think" can be damaging. For women, it narrows our perception of our power in society—a power that is greater now than it has ever been. For companies, "minority think" can too narrowly focus what a company wants to achieve instead of broadening the company's focus. For example, Kodak and McDonald's both could have created special marketing organizations devoted to women, using many of the same ideas incorporated to create EasyShare and Premium Salads. But both would have ended up being less successful, because they would have narrowly described those products as "women-only" items as opposed to what they did do: design products with women in mind that they then marketed broadly to all consumers.

3. **Do you think your product could never—ever—appeal to women?** I'm certain there many companies out there that think their products could never appeal to women or be affected by women. But if the male impotence drug market could find success by appealing to women, it's hard to imagine any industry that couldn't benefit from understanding how women feel about the industry, its companies, and products.

4. **Are you afraid to be the first in your industry to focus on women?** Kodak's leadership certainly was concerned about breaking away from the competitive pack. What if women weren't drawn to the EasyShare brand? What if it was labeled "too feminine"? But by paying attention to what women really wanted in a digital camera, while never giving up on the technological benefits that would keep men and technologically-savvy

women interested, Kodak was able to move far beyond the consumers the digital camera industry had so narrowly focused on. Kodak's approach, much like The Home Depot's, was to be more "inclusive" than "exclusive." Both companies redefined and broadened their target audiences instead of narrowing and constraining who would buy their products. Both have been followed by their competitors instead of being shunned by consumers.

5.   **Do you think if you focus on women that you will turn off male consumers?** For all the companies in this book, a focus on female consumers has had a far more positive effect on all their consumers than a negative effect on men. Procter & Gamble discovered that by focusing on women's issues about housework, it could also draw more men to the Swiffer—a surprise for one of the several companies in this book that hadn't seen men as their core target. For The Home Depot, a focus on women has made its stores easier to shop for both genders and has given it insight into the changing relationships between men and women, which has helped it break away from competitors.

6.   **Do you still think one ad campaign or marketing message will work for all women?** The shift in thinking of women as majority consumers means a holistic, company-wide approach as opposed to strategies often taken in the past, in which marketing made up messages to sell products that hadn't been designed with women in mind. DeBeers didn't just create an ad campaign to cast diamonds as the new power jewel for newly assertive women who weren't going to wait for a man to buy them a ring. It also designed rings that were expressly for the right hand and then coupled them with an ad campaign that understood how women felt about their old and new roles in the world. By contrast, Nike had done a remarkably good job of creating beautiful, inspiring advertising for women, but it had done little to change its products to meet the specific biological differences of women. It wasn't until 2000 that Nike built a running shoe made from a last molded to the shape of a woman's foot. It continued to size

clothing based on fashion model bodies as opposed to women's real athletic bodies until the early 2000s. By then it had created a number of ad campaigns that inspired young women, including one well-regarded campaign, "If you let me play," that spoke to the positive impact of sports on women. But the ads often fell flat when women went in to try on clothes and shoes that didn't seem to fit a real woman's body.

7.   **When was the last time you talked to a real woman consumer?** Each of these companies has worked overtime to find ways to really listen to its consumers. But two companies stand out for the attention they paid to their customers and their adeptness at driving the insights back into the brands—no matter how counterintuitive the ideas may have seemed. Hot Topic's chief executive officer, Betsy McLaughlin, had always been a huge fan of reading customer e-mails and comment cards. It was the one sure way to keep on top of new and emerging brands and cultural icons, like Spongebob Squarepants, before they became too mainstream to appeal to Hot Topic's core consumers. These consumers were always on the lookout for the next big thing before it became the next big thing. By reading consumer mail closely, McLaughlin picked up on a trend that was far bigger and long-lasting than the next hot rock band: plus-size sexy and fashionable clothing for young women. MGA Entertainment, creator of Bratz, also has used e-mail comments and customer mail as a way to pick up on ideas that will keep its dolls ahead of the curve with its quickly changing girl consumers. This kind of listening goes far beyond the traditional focus groups and consumer feedback of the past, where already-created products were given a once-over by consumers. Instead, this listening makes consumers partners in the creation of ideas and products—a tactic that fits well with women who are hungry for their ideas to be heard after years of settling for products that didn't fit their needs.

8.   **Do you think your company or brand needs a complete overhaul to appeal to women consumers?** It can seem like a big, risky

investment to overhaul your brand to appeal to women. But as Nike, Kodak, and The Home Depot found, it wasn't a matter of tearing down the brand and building it up to be a "women's brand." Instead, the key strategy was finding the relevance of those brands to women consumers. Nike found that women still expected performance and high technology from the company, but they wanted it in products that fit women's bodies better. The Home Depot remained the trusted source for home improvement advice and products and even retained much of its stores' look and feel because it realized that women responded to the brand's authenticity.

9.   **How aware are you of the social and economic changes affecting the women who buy your products?** As each of these companies demonstrates, it is not enough to know that women are the majority consumers with lots of money to spend. Knowing those basic facts is just the first step in understanding the many economic and social changes that are still transforming women. Avon certainly already knew that women were the most important consumers of its products. That had been true for all of its 119 years. What it hadn't realized was how different the perceptions of beauty were between generations of women. Indeed, these companies have found that there are sometimes greater differences between generations of women than there are differences between men and women, especially in younger generations. For example, Bratz has had to withstand criticism from mothers—who grew up playing with Barbie—who don't like the looks of the dolls or their lack of "role model" career clothing. Car companies such as Toyota are increasingly finding that men and women of younger generations are likely to be drawn to the same features and options in vehicles because they have grown up spending far more time together in relationships that, until 20 years ago, weren't necessarily mainstream. Instead of focusing on what had been considered the core "wants" of women consumers—quality, reliability, and safety—more car companies have found that power, speed, and sexy designs are as important to young women as they are to men.

10.   **Do you ever wish the whole idea of "gender" would just go away?** In the more than 15 years I have written about marketing and consumer trends, there have been times when gender seemed to be taking a backseat in certain industries and with certain products. The financial industry during the early 1990s seemed determined to view women simply like the men they were joining when investing in the stock market. Even the fashion and cosmetics industries have occasionally played with the idea of unisex products, including clothes sized for both genders and perfumes, such as CK One, that could be shared by both sexes. Indeed, many products do transcend gender. Take the iPod, which doesn't seem to skew one way or the other, with a design that seems to appeal equally to men and women. But gender continues to play a lead role in how we define ourselves. But whereas gender was once defined strictly by the traditional roles that men and women had played throughout much of history, increasingly individuals are in control of how their gender is expressed. In one day, a woman may move from being a mother, a wife, a chief executive, and a fixer of plumbing. A man may be a father, a husband, a homemaker, and the fixer of meals. For both sexes, all those roles are important to their lives, important to defining who they are. But unlike in the past—and this is particularly true for women—no one role strictly defines them. No one role is more important than another. Instead, the power of the purse—economic power and financial freedom—has given women the freedom to be all those roles. Now it's up to you to determine how your brand, product, or service will be relevant to this broader, more inclusive view of gender.

Endnotes

Chapter 1

1. McDonald's company reports; "Red Light Flashes for McDonald's," CNN, December 17, 2002.

2. McDonald's corporate reports.

3. Interview conducted December 14, 2004 with Kay Napier.

4. Census 2003, females age 16 and over.

5. "101 Facts on the Status of Working Women," *Business and Professional Women's Foundation*, October 2004.

6. Ibid.

7. Constance Sorrentino, "International comparisons of labor force participation, 1960-81," *Monthly Labor Review*, February 1983.

8. James Morrow, "A Place for One," *American Demographics*, November 2003.

9. Census 2000; the statistics are somewhat skewed because the census begins counting marriages at age 15 when most people aren't married.

10. Peg Tyre and Daniel McGinn, "She Works. He Doesn't," *Newsweek*, May 12, 2003.

11. Louis Uchitelle, "Gaining Ground on the Wage Front," *The New York Times*, December 31, 2004.

12. Denise Venable, "The Wage Gap Myth," National Center for Policy Analysis, No. 392, April 12, 2002.

13. Peter Francese, "Top Trends for 2003," *American Demographics*, December 2002/January 2003.

14. Peter Francese, "Ahead of the Next Wave," *American Demographics*, September 2003.

15. Isobel Coleman, "The Payoff in Women's Rights," *Foreign Affairs*, May/June 2004.

16. Martha Barletta, *Marketing to Women: How to Reach and Increase Your Share of the World's Largest Market Share Segment* (Chicago: Dearborn Trade Publishing, 2003), pg. vii.

17. Interview conducted December 2, 2004 with Wendy Cook.

18. Interview conducted January 24, 2005 with Randi Minetor.

19. Shirley Leung and Suzanne Vranica, "Happy Meals Are No Longer Bringing Smiles at McDonald's," *The Wall Street Journal*, January 31, 2003.

20. Nanci Hellmich, "Average Weight Up 25 Pounds Since 1960," *USA Today*, October 28, 2004.

21. Aaron Barr, "Sonic, Out to Court Females, Mixes Salads into Advertising," *Adweek*, October 4, 2004.

22. Elaine Lipson, "Food, Farming...and Feminism?", *Ms. Magazine*, Summer 2004.

23. Interview conducted December 2, 2004 with Carol Koepke.

24. Neil Buckley, "Since James Cantalupo was appointed chief executive officer eight months ago, the fast-food chain has begun to improve its 30,000 restaurants," *Financial Times*, August 29, 2003.

25. "No. 1 and Trying Harder," *Restaurants & Institutions*, June 15, 2003.

26. McDonald's corporate reports.

27. Viewing of *Super-Size Me* documentary by Fara Warner, December 2004.

28. Interview conducted December 3, 2004 with Kim Todd.

29. Interview conducted December 3, 2004 with Cathy Kapica.

30. Interview conducted November 5, 2004 with Kelly Mooney.

31. Michael Arndt, "McDonald's: Fries with That Salad?", *Business Week*, July 5, 2004.

32. Melanie Warner, "You Want Any Fruit with That Big Mac?", *The New York Times*, February 20, 2005.

33. Martin Fackler, "Will Ratatouille Bring Japanese to McDonald's?", *The Wall Street Journal*, August 14, 2003.

Chapter 2

1. Fara Warner, "Yes, Women Spend (and Saw and Sand)," *The New York Times*, February 29, 2004.

2. Home Depot corporate reports.

3. Kate Betts, "Doing Their Nails with a Hammer," *The New York Times*, October 27, 2002.

4. Brian Grow, "Gender Watch: Who Wears the Wallet in the Family?," *BusinessWeek*, August 16, 2004.

5. Interview conducted January 26, 2004 with John Costello, and e-mail correspondence on February 23, 2005.

6. Company reports.

7. Estelle B. Freedman, *No Turning Back: The History of Feminism and the Future of Women* (New York: Ballantine Books, 2002), pg. 22.

8. Interview conducted January 24, 2005 with Stephanie Coontz.

9. Nancy Baker Wise and Christy Wise, *A Mouthful of Rivets: Women at Work in World War II* (San Francisco: Jossey-Bass Inc., 1994).

10. Michelle Conlin, "Unmarried America," *BusinessWeek*, October 20, 2003.

11. "Women, Employment of," *Microsoft Encarta Online Encyclopedia 2004*.

12. Mireya Navarro, "For Younger Latinos, a Shift to Smaller Families," *The New York Times*, December 5, 2004.

13. Ellis Cose, "The Black Gender Gap," *Newsweek*, March 3, 2003.

14. John Leland, "He's Retired, She's Working, They're Not Happy," *The New York Times*, March 23, 2004.

15. Interview conducted January 24, 2005 with Phyllis Moen.

16. Hilary Groutage, "Relief society women should belong," *The Salt Lake Tribune*, September 26, 2004.

17. Peg Tyre and Daniel McGinn, "She Works, He Doesn't: The Latest Twist in Jobs & Family," *Newsweek*, May 12, 2003.

18. Interview conducted January 24, 2005, with Kathleen Gerson.

19. John Simons, "Taking on Viagra," *Fortune*, June 9, 2003.

20. Ibid.

21. Dana Knight, "Cialis campaign to go full speed in Super Bowl," *The Indianapolis Star*, January 26, 2004.

22. Rich Thomaselli, "Levitra battles to regain share," *Advertising Age*, October 11, 2004.

23. Scott Hensley and Suzanne Vranica, "FDA Tells Pfizer to Pull Viagra Ads About the 'Wild Thing,'" *The Wall Street Journal*, November 16, 2004.

24. Interview conducted November 4, 2004 with Dr. Neeli Bendapudi.

25. Interview conducted February 12, 2005 with Maddy Dychtwald.

26. Interview conducted January 27, 2004 with Ellen Dracos.

27. Dean Foust, "Home Depot Still Hasn't Nailed Lowe's," *BusinessWeek*, November 20, 2003; company reports.

28. Bruce Upbin, "Merchant Princes. There's a new big-box in town," *Forbes*, January 20, 2003.

29. Interview conducted January 26, 2004 with Jason Feldman.

30. Fara Warner, "Yes, Women Spend (and Saw and Sand)," *The New York Times*, February 29, 2004.

31. Ibid.

Chapter 3

1. All statistics on Swiffer unit-sales numbers provided by the company.

2. Interview conducted January 28, 2005 by Peg McNichol with Melissa Johnson of Procter & Gamble communications staff.

3. Kara Swisher, "Testing Out the Spawn of Swiffer—Its Success Spurs a Wave of Throwaway Cleaners," *The Wall Street Journal*, September 23, 2004; Cliff Peale, "P&G Scrubs Stodgy Image," *The Cincinnati Enquirer*, November 21, 2004.

4. Interview conducted March 2, 2005 with Linda Kaplan Thaler.

5. Interview conducted November 8, 2004 with Kristine Decker.

6. Interview conducted January 18, 2005 with Maddy Dychtwald.

7. Interview conducted January 24, 2005 with Phyllis Moen.

8. Interview conducted October 26, 2004 with Mary Quigley.

9. Sue Shellenbarger, "The Secrets of Sequencing: How Moms Can Set the Stage for a Return to Work," *The Wall Street Journal*, July 24, 2003.

10. Linda Berg-Cross, Anne-Marie Scholz, JoAnne Long, Ewa Grzescyk, and Anjali Roy, "Single Professional Women: A Global Phenomenon, Challenges and Opportunities," *The Journal of International Women's Studies*, Vol. 5, No. 5, June 2004.

11. Elizabeth Enright, "A House Divided," *AARP, The Magazine*, July/August 2004.

12. Alexandra Star, "Desperately Seeking Single Women Voters," *BusinessWeek*, June 21, 2004.

13. Kemba J. Dunham, "Stay at Home Dads Fight Stigma," *The Wall Street Journal*, August 26, 2003.

14. Sue Shellenbarger, "The Juggling Act," *The Wall Street Journal*, June 6, 2004.

15. Keith Hammonds, "Balance Is Bunk," *Fast Company*, October 2004.

16. The Family Caregiver Alliance and National Center on Caregiving, www.caregiver.org, "The State of the States in Family Caregiver Support: A 50-State Study," November 2004.

17. Marcia Stepanek, "Using the Net for Brainstorming: Smart companies are exploiting cyberspace to spark innovation," *BusinessWeek*, December 13, 1999.

18. Ibid.

19. Connie Nelson, "Housework lovers come out of the broom closet," *Fort Wayne Journal Gazette*, April 30, 2002.

20. Nancy Einhart, "Clean Sweep of the Market: How P&G's Swiffer inspired a nation of neat freaks," *Business 2.0*, March 1, 2003.

21. Jack Neff, "P&G to keep budget level as it aims to build sales: New CEO Lafley puts marketing priority on 10 major global brands," *Advertising Age*, August 7, 2000.

Chapter 4

1. www.adiamondisforever.com.

2. Laura Kipnis, "The State of Unions: Should This Marriage Be Saved?," *The New York Times*, January 25, 2004.

3. Tavia Simmons and Martin O'Connell, "Married-Couple and Unmarried Partner Households: 2000, Census 2000 Special Reports," February 2003, U.S. Department of Commerce.

4. Rose M. Kreider and Jason M. Fields, "Number, Timing, and Duration of Marriages and Divorces," Fall 1996, Current Population Reports, pg. 70–80, U.S. Census Bureau, Washington, D.C., February, 2002.

5. From 1945 to 2004, DeBeers was unable to do business in the U.S. because of price-fixing accusations. The U.S. Department of Justice brought a suit against the company in 1994 that remained unsettled until DeBeers on July 13, 2004 pleaded guilty to charges of conspiring fix prices and was sentenced in a federal court in Columbus, Ohio, to pay a $10 million fine, according to a press release issued by the Department of Justice.

6. Interview conducted October 29, 2004 with Claudia Rose.

7. Blythe Yee, "Ads Remind Women They Have Two Hands," *The Wall Street Journal*, August 14, 2003.

8. Interview conducted October 19, 2004 with Susan M. Cooper.

9. Interview conducted October 27, 2004 with David Bennett.

10. Interview conducted September 19, 2004 with Fred Cuellar.

11. Notably, the creative team on the campaign also included Linda Kaplan Thaler, who would go on to found her own agency and create "counterintuitive" advertising for Procter & Gamble's Swiffer brand.

12. Diamond Trading Co. statistics.

13. Anuradha Raghunathan, "Banks Put Priorities on Women's Needs; As Clients' Wealth Grows, So Do Options in Investment Advice," *The Dallas Morning News*, November 23, 2003.

14. Michael Sisk, "Target: Women. Are Your Investment and Insurance Programs Adding More Female Clients?", *Bank Investment Consultant*, October, 2004.

15. Ibid.

16. Interview conducted November 8, 2004 with Vanessa Freytag.

17. Amy Martinez, "Today's Women and Money: Firms Work to Meet Different Needs," *The Palm Beach Post*, April 6, 2001.

18. "Female-Headed Households May Earn Less," *The Wall Street Journal*, January 13, 2004, by wire reports.

19. National Committee on Pay Equity, "The Wage Gap Over Time: In Real Dollars, Women See a Continuing Gap," based on U.S. Census bureau figures updated in August 2004.

20. Robert Julavits, "Higher Profile at Citigroup's Women & Co.," *American Banker*, November 6, 2003.

21. Amy Joyce, "Easing Women's Financial Concerns: Lisa Caputo's Firm Keeps Focus on Long-Term Needs," *The Washington Post*, September 30, 2002.

22. Interview conducted October 20, 2004 with Dianne Smyth.

23. Peter Hull, "Sexes Invest Differently; Men Put More in; Women Hold on Longer," *Daily Press*, November 16, 2003.

24. Katharine Q. Seelye, "Softening the Clinking Sound of Money," *The New York Times*, February 28, 2005.

25. Interview conducted October 18, 2004 with Pam Little.

26. "America's Online Pursuits: The Changing Picture of Who's Online and What They Do," *Pew Internet & American Life Project*, December 22, 2003.

Chapter 5

1. Interview conducted January 28, 2005 with Pierre Schaeffer; Saul Hansell, "Kodak Updates Its Brownie to Compete in a Digital Age," *The New York Times*, December 27, 2004.

2. Unmesh Kher, "Getting Kodak to Focus: The Film Giant Was in Digital Denial for Years. But Now It Has Cool Cameras, Lower Costs and a Real Strategy. Too Late?," *Time*, February 14, 2005.

3. Company reports; February 2, 2005 press release.

4. "America's Online Pursuits: The Changing Picture of Who's Online and What They Do," *Pew Internet & American Life Project*, December 22, 2003.

5. "Women Surpass Men as E-Shoppers During the Holidays," *Pew Internet & American Life Project*, January 1, 2002.

6. May Wong, "Women spent more money on technology than men in 2003," *Associated Press*, January 16, 2004.

7. The 360 Youth College Explorer Study, "College Women Close Technology Gap," *PRNewswire*, March 4, 2004.

8. "How Americans Are Using Instant Messaging," *Pew Internet & American Life Project*, September 1, 2004.

9. "The State of Blogging," *Pew Internet & American Life Project* (data memo), January 2005.

10. Ben Berkowitz, "Women Over 40 Biggest Online Gamers," *Reuters*, February 10, 2004.

11. Colin Gibbs, "Girls Got Game," *RCR Wireless News*, February 7, 2005.

12. Jose Antonio Vargas, "Gender Marketing: Girls are gamers too, guys. Females are largely ignored by video and PC game makers," *The Washington Post*, August 12, 2004.

13. Pamela Klaffke, "Pink Games: Studies show girls want in on video-game action—but game makers can't quite figure out what they like," *The Edmonton Journal*, April 5, 2002.

14. Jose Antonio Vargas, "Gender Marketing: Girls are gamers too, guys. Females are largely ignored by video and PC game makers," *The Washington Post*, August 12, 2004.

15. Michel Marriott, "Fighting Women Enter the Arena, No Holds Barred," *The New York Times*, May 15, 2003.

16. Ibid.

17. Vince Vittore, "Game On: Carriers Play Hide and Seek with Gaming Strategy," *Telephony*, April 5, 2004.

18. Steve Smith, "Playing Well with Others (Follow the Money)," *eContent*, November 1, 2004.

19. Kimberly Palmer, "Tech Companies Try Wooing Women with Girlie Marketing," *The Wall Street Journal*, August 26, 2003.

20. www.olympus.com, "Olympus Named Title Sponsor of Fashion Week," corporate press release, November 17, 2003.

21. Kimberly Palmer, "Tech Companies Try Wooing Women with Girlie Marketing," *The Wall Street Journal*, August 26, 2003.

22. Saul Hansell, "Kodak Updates Its Brownie Image to Compete in a Digital Age," *The New York Times*, December 27, 2004.

23. E-mail discussion conducted March 15, 2005 with Jordan Warren.

24. Interview conducted February 3, 2005 with Michael Borosky.

25. Laura Heller, "Doing to Demographics What's Never Been Done Before," *DSN Retailing Today*, September 6, 2004; Beth Snyder Bulik, "Electronics Retailers Woo Women: Best Buy, others refine design and marketing," *Advertising Age*, November 15, 2004.

Chapter 6

1. Fara Warner, "Nike's Women's Movement," *Fast Company*, August 2002.

2. Fara Warner, "Feminine Mystique," www.fastcompany.com, August 2002.

3. Interview conducted February 22, 2005 with Darcy Winslow and Joani Komlos.

4. Colette Dowling, *The Frailty Myth: Women Approaching Physical Equality* (New York: Random House, 2000), pg. xviii–xix.

5. Sally Jenkins, "Evening the Playing Field for Women," *The Washington Post*, June 25, 2002.

6. Outdoor Industry Association, State of the Industry Report, 2004.

7. Ron Dicker, "After a Few Pioneering Steps, Women's Running Took Off," *The New York Times*, November 3, 2004.

8. Isabel Gonzalez, "The New Wave: The Girls of Summer," *Time*, August 12, 2002.

9. "Planning for 2004? Stay Informed and Get Ahead of the Trends with the Fifth Edition of the Participation Study," Outdoor Industry Association press release, September 17, 2003.

10. Fara Warner, "Dressing Women to Sweat, Fashionably," *The New York Times*, July 6, 2003.

11. Dowling, pg. 62–63.

12. "MacArthur sails into record books," www.bbc.uk, February 8, 2005.

13. Shannon Ryan, "For WUSA, business as usual. Will the public buy women's soccer? Lynn Morgan is betting yes.", *The Philadelphia Inquirer*, June 18, 2002; Diane Pucin, "Time to Move Beyond Their Cause's Effects: Title IX put women in the game, but pro leagues will need a lot more than that to succeed, say experts.", *The Los Angeles Times*, September 19, 2003.

14. Ibid.

15. Mark Starr, "Don't Dis the Soccer Daddies," *Newsweek*, October 6, 2003.

16. Associated Press, "Good Seats Available in WUSA Ticket Drive," February 16, 2004.

17. Interview conducted October 15, 2004 with Donna Kane.

18. Lee McGinnis, Seungwoo Chun, and Julia McQuillan, "A Review of Gendered Consumption in Sport and Leisure," *Academy of Marketing Science Review*, Volume 2003, No. 5.

19. Fara Warner, "Detroit Discovers That Women Like Power Too," *The New York Times*, August 10, 2003; interview conducted in August 2003 with Ernest Bastien.

20. Interview conducted November 1, 2004 with Deborah Meyer.

21. Suzanne Vranica, "Hummer Pitches New H3 to Women," *The Wall Street Journal*, April 22, 2005.

22. Interviews conducted in April 2002 with Nike executives John Hoke and Mark Parker; some quotes and information appeared in the *Fast Company* article "Nike's Women's Movement" in August 2002.

23. Fara Warner, "Dressing Women to Sweat, Fashionably," *The New York Times*, July 6, 2003.

24. All About Women Consumers: 2005 Edition, New York: EPM Communications, Inc., 2005, Sports and Fitness section, pg. 212.

Chapter 7

1. Interview conducted October 28, 2004 with Deborah I. Fine. Fine left Avon Products Inc. in February 2005 to oversee the rollout of Pink, a new lingerie store concept from Limited Brands Inc. for the 16-to-24-year-old demographic.

2. Interview conducted April 7, 2005 with Avon communications executive Vic Bode.

3. Stephanie Schorow, "Women on Top: Hub Sex Boutique's Success Hurts So Good," *The Boston Herald*, November 8, 2003.

4. Estelle B. Freedman, *No Turning Back: The History of Feminism and the Future of Women* (New York: Ballantine Books, 2002), pg. 245–254.

5. "Pots of Promise," *The Economist*, May 24, 2003.

6. Interview conducted October 20, 2004 with Shelley Lazarus.

7. Ginia Bellafante, "Young and Chubby: What's Heavy About That?", *The New York Times*, January 26, 2003.

8. Colette Dowling, *The Frailty Myth: Women Approaching Physical Equality* (New York: Random House, 2000), pg. 43–44.

9. Mireya Navarro, "Store Mannequins Can Now Breathe Out," *The New York Times*, November 14, 2004.

10. Interview conducted January 25, 2005 with Patricia Van Cleave.

11. Interview conducted November 19, 2004 with Dan Hess.

12. Alynda Wheat, "Plus-Sized Prospects: A Few Niche Retailers Are Primed to Make a Bundle Selling Clothes in Large Sizes," *Fortune*, April 14, 2003.

13. Leslie Earnest (*Los Angeles Times*), "Young women snap up fashions in plus sizes," *Milwaukee Journal-Sentinel*, May 6, 2001.

14. Marianne Wilson, "Hot Topic opens new Torrid concept for young women," *Chain Store Age Executive*, July 1, 2001; store visit by Fara Warner, December 9, 2004, Great Lakes Crossing.

15. Jennifer Pendleton, "Hot Topic: Betsy McLaughlin, CEO," *Advertising Age*, November 17, 2003.

16. www.torrid.com, Web site posting, December 2004.

17. Joe Drape, "Olympians Strike a Pose, and Avoid Setting off a Fuss," *The New York Times*, August 12, 2004.

18. Interview conducted October 14, 2003 with Rufus Griscom.

19. Mireya Navarro, "Women Tailor Sex Industry to Their Eyes," *The New York Times*, February 20, 2004.

20. Skip Hollandsworth, "Good Vibrations," *Texas Monthly*, October 2004.

21. Warren St. John, "Parties Where an ID Is the Least of What You Show," *The New York Times*, January 11, 2004.

22. www.cakenyc.com.

23. Nancy Jo Sales, "Girls, Uninterrupted," *Vanity Fair*, September 2002.

24. Nanette Byrnes, "Avon: The New Calling," *BusinessWeek*, September 18, 2000.

25. Ibid.

26. Company statistics.

27. Dody Tsiantar, "Avon's Makeover: The beauty giant comes calling with a fresh face, a brand called Mark, made for teens to buy and sell," *Time*, November 10, 2003.

28. Nanette Byrnes, "Avon: The New Calling," *BusinessWeek*, September 18, 2000.

29. Ramin Setoodeh, "Calling Avon's Lady: Andrea Jung," *Newsweek*, December 27, 2004.

30. Note to readers: To maintain the trademark of Avon's new brand, I use a lowercase "m" throughout this book when referencing the brand "mark."

31. Nanette Byrnes, "Avon: The New Calling," *BusinessWeek*, September 18, 2000.

Chapter 8

1. Barbie took her name from the daughter of Mattel's founder, Ruth Handler. Her daughter's name was Barbara, and Ken was named after Handler's son.

2. Katie Fraser, "The Woman Who Gave Us the Barbie Doll," *Daily Express*, April 30, 2002.

3. Tanya Gold, "The Queen Is Dead," *The Guardian*, October 6, 2004.

4. Interview conducted January 25, 2005 with Isaac Larian.

5. Lisa Bannon, "Fashion Coup? New Doll Grabs Some of Barbie's Limelight," *The Wall Street Journal*, November 29, 2002.

6. Ibid; interview with Larian.

7. Rebecca Gardyn, "Granddaughters of Feminism," *American Demographics*, April 1, 2001.

8. Interview conducted January 24, 2005 with Kathleen Gerson.

9. Frances H. Early, "Staking Her Claim: Buffy the Vampire Slayer as Transgressive Woman Warrior," *Journal of Popular Culture*, January 1, 2001, quoting from Sharon MacDonald's work "Drawing the Lines— Gender, Peace and War: An Introduction." *Images of Women in Peace & War: Cross Cultural and Historical Perspectives*. Eds. Sharon MacDonald, Pat Holden, and Shirley Ardener. Madison: University of Wisconsin Press, 1987.

10. Rebecca Gardyn, "Granddaughters of Feminism," *American Demographics*, April 1, 2001.

11. Eric Schmuckler, "The New Kid Heroes: Inside TV's Girl Power Explosion," *Child*, April 2004.

12. Frances Early, "Staking Her Claim: Buffy the Vampire Slayer as Transgressive Woman Warrior," *Journal of Popular Culture*, January 1, 2001.

13. Ibid.

14. John Lippman, "The Next Action Hero," *The Wall Street Journal*, July 11, 2003.

15. John Leland, "I Am Woman. Now Prepare to Die," *The New York Times*, October 19, 2003.

16. Lorenza Munoz, "The Female Fear Factor: Young Women Are Flocking to, and Revolutionizing, Horror Films," *The Los Angeles Times*, November 8, 2003.

17. George Gene Gustines, "Girl Power Fuels Manga Boom in the U.S.," *The New York Times*, December 28, 2004.

18. Nancy Johnson, "Girl Talk: Graphic Novels' Fantasy Relationships and Action a Hit with Young Women," *South Bend Tribune*, September 16, 2003.

19. Dana Jennings, "At a House of Comics, a Writer's Champion," *The New York Times*, September 15, 2003.

20. Andrew D. Arnold, "Drawing in the Gals: The Explosion of Japanese Comics for Girls," *Time*, February 9, 2004.

21. David Rowan, "Valley of the Dolls: Bratz," *The Times (of London) Magazine*, December 4, 2004.

22. Constance L. Hayes, "More Gloom on the Island of Lost Toy Makers," *The New York Times*, February 23, 2005.

23. Chuck Salter, "Ivy Ross Is Not Playing Around," *Fast Company*, November 1, 2002.

24. Ibid.

25. Bryant had been a designer with Mattel. At the time he showed Larian his sketches in September 2002, he was planning on leaving Mattel if he could find someone interested in developing his idea, according to MGA. He has maintained that the sketches he showed Larian were done when he wasn't in the employ of Mattel, according

to MGA. Mattel would later sue Bryant for allegedly breaching his employment contract with Mattel, a lawsuit that was still ongoing in mid-2005.

26. Joanne Ostrow, "Why big 'tween' spenders have retailers and TV execs peddling sexed-up products to exploit the new hot-pink power," *The Denver Post*, November 23, 2003.

27. "Mattel's Kilpin: Research insights drive new Barbie marketing plan," *Youth Markets Alert*, November 1, 2004.

28. Ruth La Ferla, "Underdressed and Hot: Dolls Moms Don't Love," *The New York Times*, October 26, 2003.

29. Pauline Yoshihashi, "Mattel Shapes a New Future for Barbie," *The Wall Street Journal*, February 12, 1990.

Chapter 9

1.   Peter Francese, "Ahead of the Next Wave," *American Demographics*, September 2003.

2.   W. Michael Cox and Richard Alm, "Scientists are Made, Not Born," *The New York Times*, February 28, 2005.

Selected
Bibliography

Martha Barletta, *Marketing to Women: How to Understand, Reach, and Increase Your Share of the World's Largest Market Segment,* (Chicago: Dearborn Trade Publishing) 2003.

Stephanie Coontz, *Marriage, A History: From Obedience to Intimacy, or How Love Conquered Marriage,* (New York: Vintage Press) 2005.

Colette Dowling, *The Frailty Myth: Women Approaching Physical Equality,* (New York: Random House) 2000.

Anna Fels, *Necessary Dreams,* (New York: Pantheon Books) 2004.

Lisa Finn, Ed., *All About Women Consumers,* 2005 Edition, (New York: EPM Communications, Inc.) 2005.

Estelle B. Freedman, *No Turning Back: The History of Feminism and the Future of Women,* (New York: Ballantine Books) 2002.

Lisa Johnson and Andrea Learned, *Don't Think Pink: What Really Makes Women Buy—and How to Increase Your Share of This Crucial Market,* (New York: AMACOM) 2004.

Robin Morgan, ed., *Sisterhood Is Forever: The Women's Anthology for a New Millennium*, (New York: Washington Square Press) 2003.

Faith Popcorn and Lys Marigold, *EVEolution: The Eight Truths of Marketing to Women*, (New York: Hyperion) 2000.

Mary Lou Quinlan, *Just Ask a Woman. Cracking the Code of What Women Want and How They Buy*, (New Jersey: John Wiley & Sons) 2003.

Lionel Tiger, *The Decline of Males*, (New York: Golden Books) 1999.

Nancy Baker Wise and Christy Wise, *A Mouthful of Rivets: Women at Work in World War II*, (San Francisco: Jossey-Bass Inc.) 1994.

Acknowledgments

This book is the product of the hard work of dozens of people. Without them, I would never have put pen to paper or my fingers to the computer keyboard. First, thanks to my editors, Paula Sinnott and Russ Hall, who stood behind me through reviews and revisions and gave me the support and guidance to make this the best book it could be. To my agent, Anna Ghosh, who recognized something of value in a hastily written four-page document of a young, untested author. To Christian Williams, my mother, who transcribed dozens of hours of interviews, who listened as I read every rewrite of every chapter, and who talked to me through every heartache and happiness on this book. To Ed Petru for reading the entire book and loving it. To Micheline Maynard, whose steady advice on the craft and art of book writing made the difficult times easier to understand and live through. To Amy Rubin and Susan Shiner Simison, who read early drafts and told me where I had gone right and where I had gone wrong. To my research assistants, Peg McNichol and Erin Zaleski, who discovered many nuggets of wisdom that are found throughout this book. Most importantly, my heartfelt thanks and love to Frank Zsirai for his unwavering support, even when I wanted to give up, and for listening to every "epiphany" I had about the book—even if it was 3 a.m.

This book would have been impossible without the gracious help of the dozens of executives I interviewed. For their time and insight, I am grateful, but there are many people at the companies whose names and work would go unnoticed if I didn't mention them here. My thanks to all the executive assistants and public relations executives who listened as I pleaded for an interview, read through my executive summaries, and finally found time on the schedules of busy executives. Thanks especially to Danya Proud of McDonald's; Eric Oberman and Mandy Holton at The Home Depot; Melissa Johnson and Marie-Laure Salvado at Procter & Gamble; Brendi Rawlin at WomensWallStreet.com; JoAnn Tizzano at AXA Financial; Amy Nobile, who represents Eleven and first put me in touch with Kodak; Joani Komlos at Nike; Jennifer Wolinetz at Avon; and Nancy Koppang at MGA Entertainment Inc.

Beyond the day-to-day writing of this book, thanks to people who may never know how much they have given to the process. To Gina Imperato, Alison Overholt, and Cheryl Dahle, who were there when all this started. To Mary Louise Luczowski for sharing our "coffee office" and making me go to lunch even if I thought I should be writing. To George Anders, William Taylor, and Alan Webber for sharing the opportunity to work at Fast Company and publishing the first Nike story. To Stan Wakefield for reading that article and seeing a book in its contents. To Mark Stein and Trish Hall of the *New York Times* for publishing parts of these stories in one of the world's greatest newspapers.

Finally, my apologies to the hundreds of companies I missed and executives I didn't interview who do a phenomenal job of reaching women. I know that some readers will argue with my choice of companies and do exactly what I often do when I read a book on marketing to women. I talk to myself, saying "Well, what about this company?" and "I never had that experience there; why would she pick that company?" But don't just talk to yourself or wonder why your company didn't come across my radar. Click the contact button on www.thepowerofthepurse.com. I'd love to hear from you.

Index